STOP
TALKING
ABOUT
WELLBEING

A
PRAGMATIC
APPROACH
TO
TEACHER
WORKLOAD

KAT HOWARD

First published 2020

by John Catt Educational Ltd,
15 Riduna Park, Station Road,
Melton, Woodbridge IP12 1QT
Tel: +44 (0) 1394 389850
Fax: +44 (0) 1394 386893
Email: enquiries@johncatt.com
Website: www.johncatt.com

ISBN: 978 912906 48 2

Set and designed by John Catt Educational Limited

Contents

Foreword

This book needed to be written. It needed to be written in order to provide a counterpoint to the casual disregard for work-life boundaries in much of the sector and the poisonous atmosphere in a minority of our schools. With extensive experience in business and now a senior leader, Kat, the creator of the highly successful LitDrive, is in a unique position to provide hard-hitting insights into what needs to be addressed. She outlines in stark detail some of the things going on in schools that are contributing to a retention crisis; even when there is no bullying or overt unpleasantness, there is a flabby attitude to getting to grips with the core of the problem.

There are, as Kat points out, a number of strands to the 'wellbeing agenda'. The obligation to restore the balance and boundaries needs to come from all parties: on the one hand, we need leaders who focus on the 'human' in their roles – recognising that people are human beings first, and professionals second – and who, as a consequence, make sure that they consider the workload implications of every aspect of school life. And on the other hand, it is important that teachers are able to say when there isn't enough time to do everything to a high standard and to have sensible conversations with leaders about what might be cut. If we shy away from this, then we are never going to get to a space where we have the time, let alone the energy, to take care of ourselves properly.

Too many procedures and systems in schools are in place because they are in place. No one has asked that fundamental question, 'Why?' Why exactly are we doing this? Why are we in a situation where if it moves, we mark it? Why do we have verbal feedback stamps? Assessment and data drops every six weeks? Just why? If each of these is examined in turn, through the lens of evidence and in terms of the amount of difference they are making to pupils' learning, then we quickly see that their effect is minimal. But the fact is that in many schools these conversations are not being had. And until we do, the retention crisis will simmer on. It will not be fixed with a lip-service, box-ticking culture of wellbeing – yoga and meditation when staff are working all hours to meet unreasonable demands.

While wellbeing has correctly been identified as 'something to be tackled' by the sector, it has too often been translated into the quick fix and the cheap remedy. The problems are systemic and will not be sorted by sticking plasters. Kat urges leaders to stop talking about wellbeing: no more aromatherapy sessions, after-school yoga classes or biscuits on a Friday. No more payday cakes, sports socials, meditation that no one can fit in because, ironically, they cannot see past the marking pile or even get the time to leave their classroom for long enough to participate.

Instead, we need to be tapping into the human desire to do meaningful work, to have our opinions heard and to feel that we are making a difference within a system that does not demand every fibre of our being. And the problem is that if we don't go back to the root causes of overwork and lack of support then we are on a hiding to nothing.

Rather than putting in place the superfluous activities designed to address the problem, we need to look systematically at those parts of the system that are getting in the way of good mental and physical health, of the deep satisfaction of a job well done. And this is what Kat tackles with forensic precision: from marking and feedback, to assessment, to flexible working, she makes the case that it is here that the real shift happens. This is deep work and it doesn't happen overnight. It is a fundamental shift in culture.

The good news is that there are many schools that are doing this well. It means that we can learn from the likes of Jeremy Hannay at the Three Bridges school in Ealing, where professional trust and professional growth mean that professional practice can really fly; we can learn from the likes of Sam Strickland at The Duston School, where systems and structures are stripped back to allow colleagues to do their best work.

There is hope for improving conditions, but only if we take a long hard look at some of the dysfunctional practices, get shot of any that aren't making a difference to pupil's learning and lean in to a better, more fulfilling professional life. We all have a responsibility to open up this conversation, because we need well-balanced and well-supported professionals working with our pupils.

Mary Myatt
25 November 2019

Acknowledgements
The most important page of them all

This book had many false starts, near-misses and stumbling blocks (writing pun intended) before it came to fruition. Every time I doubted my capabilities, muttered incoherently at the laptop, sat up until midnight tapping away words that I was not quite sure about, my partner Ben always reassured me that what I was doing was brilliant. As the only non-teacher of an entire teaching family, he is the oddity responsible for my sanity – and he's pretty good at making a decent gin. And so, thank you Ben for always telling me to be quiet when I started to witter about whether I had a book in me, and instructing politely but firmly that I just had to get on and finish the damn thing.

Claire Hill has become a firm friend over the last two years and without her, I would be absent of a much-needed sounding board. With the honesty and nudges that she provided, along with what is such a monumental amount of knowledge that I can only ever aspire to possess, she has been the decisive voice necessary when difficult decisions have had to be made. I will repay her one day, perhaps with more than a mutual love (and bankruptcy) for Estée Lauder.

I would not still be in teaching or in a position to write this book without Martyn Reah. From encouraging me to speak at his Pedagoo event in 2016 (at a time that I was deeply unhappy professionally) to offering unrelenting support every time I toyed with what to do next, Martyn was a part of the foundations on which this book was built. He is a true agent of change for the profession. I cannot wait to see where he takes the #teacher5aday community next.

Litdrive was never a lone effort by any stretch, and it took the help, advice and collegiate approach of many, many English teachers to take it from strength to strength. Thanks to the support of #TeamEnglish, and English teachers worldwide, Litdrive has become such a wonderful place. It has an incredible team that work tirelessly behind the scenes, and they are the most compassionate, effervescent bunch of people I have ever had the honour of meeting. The friendships that I have made will be for life: conversations, shared moments and the endless, endless proofreading! This group of people has helped me more than they will ever know, so thank you to every single one of you.

The original draft of this book was a bit of a mash-up, and I struggled with the hefty task of bringing clarity to my thoughts and ideas, as is always the way! Jill Berry is one of the most inspirational voices that I have followed throughout my career. One of the first people I followed on Twitter, Jill's tenacious positivity and support has been invaluable to the entire process and she told me in the kindest of ways when things just didn't make sense. All credit for rational logic goes to Jill, and the rambling is down to me. You're welcome.

The almost-final thank-you goes to the incredible teachers that I have trained, worked alongside or connected with over the years; thank you for challenging me, inspiring me, or helping me become (to quote Carly Waterman) 'respectably objective'. If we all thought the same about the same things, it would be a very dull profession indeed.

Last of all, thank you to Noah, Ted and little Max. I am and will always be so proud and overwhelmed to be your Mummy.

And not forgetting the chapter opening icons, thanks go to Freepik, Icongeek26 and prettycons from www.flaticon.com

A reading route

'Time isn't the main thing. It is the only thing.' – **Miles Davis**

Inspired by Oliver Caviglioli, I wanted to be able to make a recommendation of routes that readers could use as a journey map through the book, dependent upon where you are in your teaching career. These suggestions make for great starting points if you plan to dip in and out and may help you to find your own point of clarity. I am mindful that at our most busy, or mentally unrested, consuming an entire book can be incredibly daunting. If this applies to you, just pick a starting point and go from there.

Trainee/ NQT/RQT	Classroom teacher: 5+ years and enjoying the ride	Leading a team	Senior leader	I want to quit
My why	My why	My why	My why	My why
The nature of the beast	Being human	Hunting and gathering	Being human	Crisis indicators
Being human	Hunting and gathering	Conversation and connection	People before procedures	Objective rebellion
Imposter syndrome	Objective rebellion	Being human	The nature of the beast	Finding your fit
Objective rebellion	The nature of the beast	People before procedures	Finding your fit	Being human
A manifesto for workload	A manifesto for workload	A manifesto for workload	A manifesto for workload	A manifesto for workload

Preface

Why do we need to stop talking about wellbeing?

'If you steal another person's time you are as big a thief as one who steals another person's money ... Do you steal from yourself?'
— Arne Sigurd Rognan Nielsen

People are trying to prey upon your mental health like it's something to be conquered.

You see, the media, the advertisement industry and independent consultancies have discovered the goldmine that is wellbeing. Why is it so? Because when intertwined with the possibility that you are already suffering from even a moderate amount of stress, it becomes all too easy for someone to sell you something to resolve a matter like wellbeing that is practically impossible to measure.

You will try (and fail) to eat seven vegetables a day, or clamber out of bed four days out of seven at 5.30 a.m. to attempt (and fail) that yoga YouTube tutorial, skipping over the beginner's one and straight to the eight-minute power-yoga, expert level, because that's going to help you get relaxed quicker. You will get an early night, listening to white noise – only to sit curled around your phone until an ungodly hour, comparing yourself in measurements of weight, height, age, success (in monetary terms or otherwise), achievements, or all other metrics of what you perceive to be the success or happiness of others. You will see happiness, contentment, doing well at 'it' (whatever 'it' may be) as an endpoint, rather than the journey that you are on. You will never reach the end of your journey. There is no end. But you will never stop to consider how effective these routines are, or even why they may not be working. You will simply focus on the fact that you are failing at them.

As a teacher, you are even more susceptible. Long hours? Check. Workload that feels both unwieldy and never-ending? Check. Guilt-ridden occupation? Check. Pressures of external agencies? Check. At its most basic, lack of fresh air? Check. Daylight? Check. Poor diet? The emergency chocolate drawer.

The public sector is under the largest strain, with horror stories of schools with photocopying restrictions at best, and teachers suffering from chronic, recurrent mental health problems at worst. As a result of work, one in five of you reading will suffer panic attacks, almost half will have issues concentrating (remember the last week of term, when the words coming out of your mouth just won't stay in the right order?) and over half will have difficulty sleeping on a regular basis.[1] If you're reading this in January, you are all too aware that you are entering the most difficult point of the academic year, with the chances of you reading this in natural daylight slim to none. If you are reading this in the summer holidays, you will be lying on a sunbed, thoughts of results day nestled in the back of your mind. Work follows you around like a silent companion, because you care about the work. But does it care about you?

Wellbeing has become like happiness: something that we talk about; a distant concept that no one actually masters in reality. A feature on television adverts or a pay-as-you-go fitness plan, accomplished by strangers and unrecognisable to any of us as reasonable or achievable within our lives as teachers. Something to be worked at. Wellbeing is hard to attain, because it is not an outcome, but part of the process. Wellbeing is a by-product of the solid grounding of several successful strategies on a teaching,

1.   www.bit.ly/2D8kKzO

leading and whole-school level. It's the end result, but not the product. Your wellbeing is not a state in isolation that you can collect from the supermarket on the way home in the form of a protein shake, or something that will slot neatly into an hour of a Saturday morning in the shape of a sloth to 10k programme, which will then set you up nicely for the remaining 167 hours of your week. More to the point, if you do not have time in the workplace to feel fulfilled, or that you are meeting regular milestones that you feel are worthy of self-recognition, fitting in a run on a Saturday morning after an exhausting week is the last thing on your mind.

Considering recent responses to workload is very revealing, and an apt place to start our exploration. Under Nicky Morgan's reign as Education Secretary in 2015, 44,000 teachers completed the workload challenge, sharing the root causes of their workload and exactly where their 50–70 hours a week were being spent. Three review groups were set up, with a plethora of recommendations resulting from their respective reports. The recommendations for teachers on the planning guide? Plan collaboratively, and use guides and textbooks to save on prep time. What was lacking was the way that these would be implemented, the resources created to enable teachers to do so, and the training on how collaborative planning would be embedded into a school directive.

Ofsted has attempted to provide support through the infamous myth busters campaign in 2016,[2] which outlined eleven key principles for schools to understand perhaps not so much what Ofsted did want to see during an inspection, but that they wanted schools to stop investing energy into the wrong sort of busyness through excessive evidencing. Unfortunately, some of it fell unnoticed or disregarded: posters stuck in staff rooms gathered dust, as the processes continued to be the same, and policies remained unaltered in schools. Misinterpretation of key information from the campaign was lost as senior leadership teams encouraged staff to create arbitrary evidence folders 'to make it easier to see progress'. Seating

2. www.bit.ly/2EbWjTn

plans continued to be colour coded, pupil premium students' books marked first, verbal feedback stamps at the ready. Date stamping of marking to prove when it had been done. Minutes and minutes of time dedicated to tasks which carried absolutely no evidence of impact, because it was deemed to be effective.

The myth busters campaign was not revolutionary, brand-new information; Ofsted released a similar document in 2005 with the slightly less media-worthy title, 'Clarification for schools', which, again, made a profound attempt to break down the barriers and misconceptions that our regulators were asking for excessive evidencing or extravagant reams of data. Whilst Ofsted make an easy target for us all to poke a pitchfork at, the nuts and bolts of workload run fundamentally deeper than simply drawing the hasty conclusion that we are being dragged to account by one solitary external agency. Admittedly, the historic relationship between Ofsted and schools means that Ofsted struggles to be viewed as anything more than a measuring stick, as opposed to the support mechanism that they have provided as an organisation for many years.

Finally, November 2018 sees the publication of the interim findings of Amanda Spielman's research into teacher wellbeing during summer of that year.[3] The survey's reach was not equal to that of union surveys of the same nature (84% of NASUWT's membership body completed a questionnaire), but the research was finally drawing two important elements together: wellbeing, and workload. We are at last having conversations about how our workload is, of course, intrinsically linked to our wellbeing. The report also made the acknowledgement that this wasn't just about the reduction of workload, but that there were genuine concerns revealed from the HSE report that teaching was one of the top three occupations in the UK where individuals suffered from severe depression and stress.[4] Action was required nationally because not

---

3. www.bit.ly/33ifjZm
4. Health and Safety Executive Work related stress depression or anxiety statistics in Great Britain, 2018, accessed at www.bit.ly/37ADvtt on 20th May 2019.

only was the work too much for teachers, but it was enough to make them leave – because, quite rationally, they were making a decision between their health and their job.

However, the gap between policy change and the reality of teacher narrative around mental health could not paint a starker image. As I write this in National Mental Health Awareness week, Education Support report that they have had their highest number of calls from educational staff this month. Their helpline report informs that 57% of their calls are from educational staff that have been in the profession for five years or less.[5] Why might that be? The evidence provides a multitude of anecdotal responses: wrong school, challenging working conditions, poor leadership, unsupportive systems, no provisory networks, and a failure to support people on a human level. Teaching is a broken system at its very worst; and at best, a series of poorly constructed franchise outlets, all trying to do the same thing differently, for their own context, but not necessarily in the most effective way. How can we inform and empower ourselves to lessen the damage?

I have felt the weight of a hefty and unwieldy workload at various points throughout my career. I will often write in this book with reference to English as my topic of choice; I know that teachers of other subjects share a variation of this workload. A classroom teacher teaches 22 hours a week; that leaves, on paper, 10½ hours for: internal emails, marking and feedback generation, parent contact, data input, planning, resourcing, meetings, duties, standardisation, moderation, continuing professional development and everything in between. When it's stated as so much time, even with the ream of tasks, why is it that teachers are reporting such a monumentally overworked schedule in proportion to that 32½-hour ideal, with some working in excess of 60 hours a week regularly, without question, all year round?

Schools have the best of intentions: no one, at any layer of a school system – and I stand by this statement with utter conviction

---

5.   www.bit.ly/2scL35r

– no one is setting out to do a poor job. Unfortunately, 'educational systems seem to rush to implementation with little understanding of what new standards imply for the work of teachers and students and the resources needed to support that work, including appropriate means of assessment and evaluation'.[6] I will start with the caveat that everything I explore or outline in this book needs time and structure to do so successfully; if we are to create a model in schools that will last to support even me to retirement then we must set out as we mean to go on: through the avoidance of a 'plastered cracks' approach.

'Teacher stress is the collective responsibility of teachers, principals, training programs, and superintendents, and educators ignore it at their own peril. Much can be done at the personal, interpersonal, and organizational levels.'[7] But for some, this feels like a last-chance saloon, as teachers leave before their careers have truly begun. Teaching is a type of consumption: if well executed in schools in a way that aligns with purpose – to make staff feel as though they have found their place – it can feel like an exquisitely cooked meal: satisfying and fulfilling. At its worst? It leaves a bitter taste.

We need to talk about wellbeing in a concrete fashion, and not in the form of a cake on a Friday, or the promise of a sports club that we are too exhausted to attend. Foundations are certainly not built on sugar and fatigue, and when you are speaking to a collective who train, sacrifice and give as much as the teaching profession do – regularly and repeatedly – it just isn't good enough. At its very core, the mental health of teachers is deteriorating because when we lose a sense of moral purpose or feel as though our moral purpose can no longer be fulfilled, the reasons that we came into teaching in the first place lose substance.

What if the professional bodies and associated agencies within education and unions accompanied teachers in looking at the

---

6. Prilleltensky, I., Neff, M. and Bessell, A. (2016) 'Teacher stress: what it is, why it's important, how it can be alleviated', Theory Into Practice 55 (2) pp. 104–111.
7. Ibid.

fundamental methods that would make people feel more valued, less tired, more productive, less despairing, more successful in accomplishing their personal and professional goals, less worthless – and it didn't really cost anything, or very little? Wouldn't that be an interesting thing to act upon? What if we started examining wellbeing not as something to tick off, but as an ingrained part of school life, through our evidence-informed practice and approach – with a consideration of people at the heart?

How do we start to examine workload in a way that moves beyond the current landscape? How do we find a semblance of purpose?

A wander through

Using an evidence-informed approach underpinned by research, case studies and interviews with experts of the profession, each chapter of this book explores an aspect of a teacher's professional workload, and works to provide practical strategies that you will be able to apply to help you assert control over your working day, week, month, academic year – career, even. The exploration of each particular aspect of teaching aims to shine a light on the nature of teaching itself and characteristic traits of this profession that perhaps have been overlooked, or not placed under sufficient scrutiny, so that we may understand them better. At the end of each chapter, I encourage you, through a series of reflections, to compile your own manageable, pressure-free intentions, allowing you to start to make small changes that will work towards a great impact overall. My proposal is that currently, we fail to notice that teaching as a craft has a monumental impact upon the logistical aspect of our role – the workload – and as a result, it also has an equal influence over our sense of purpose, our moral imperative. Your wellbeing is, on the whole, linked to your ability to teach so that you experience a sense of purpose and meaning. It really is that simple.

In the first chapter, I start with my own narrative, because it is vital to me that you in turn reflect upon your own narrative, and not only what led you to want to teach, but also the challenges along the way that have threatened that desire. The value of good mental health is something that I have only been acutely aware of since becoming a mother and a teacher because of the reflective nature of the role; and it is a strength that we can utilise if we revisit this core that drove and motivated us to teach in the first place.

Chapter two develops this notion further by exploring the individual characteristics of teaching that perhaps feel a sense of disconnect. Through a thorough examination of the traits of teaching that set it apart as a profession – such as extended breaks, fast-paced working and the peaks and troughs of the academic year, in addition to our unique approach to recruitment or the use of time in schools – this section provides ways for us to anticipate trigger points over the year, finding satisfaction in a sustainable way, and maintaining professional development that gives you a sense of fulfilment within your role.

Chapter three considers the implications of imposter syndrome – a condition that acts as a side effect of the self-critical aspect of teaching – with a dissection of the syndrome itself so that we can understand how to ensure we use it to our advantage when working in our schools.

Chapter four moves towards the topic of feedback, marking and assessment – an area that, along with planning, 53% of teachers reported was a key driver of burdensome workload. We start by looking at the most recent recommendations around both formative and summative assessment, particularly within English as an example of where marking takes a large proportion of teacher working time. Our motivations and driving factors with regards to marking have a range of influences, some not linked to the outcomes of students, and this is where re-evaluation is possible. We will then look at various methodologies that have been developed to reduce teacher workload – not as a compromise, but that actually improve the quality of assessment as a result.

The fifth chapter will consider effective resourcing, looking at successful examples of departments and school communities that have created systems to approach resourcing in a way that supports staff and students, in addition to those teaching communities further afield that act as support mechanisms to the teaching profession. We will examine the connection between resourcing and workload, and how we can work as a conglomerate to connect with one another from what can feel like the isolation of a classroom. The medium with which we teach the rich tapestry of our subject can be burdensome when coupled with time constraints, and this section offers a multitude of workarounds for purposeful resourcing in classrooms.

Chapter six considers how we communicate in schools. This is often overlooked because it can feel likes a minor feature of day-to-day duties, but it is fundamental to building successful relationships in schools that are both symbiotic and supportive.

Relationships are the focus of chapter seven: considering the impact that negative or unsupportive relationships can have within the educational workplace and between the various agencies with which we work: colleagues, students, and parents. It is then possible for us to examine ways that frontline teachers and management can improve and adapt their working culture, informed by the practices in other professions that may have more substantial knowledge of effective leadership than perhaps the training systems within teaching currently provide. Using my experience of management within the financial sector, and drawing upon the experiences of key school leaders, I explore how sometimes, as a result of excessive workload, personable qualities can get thrown by the wayside – and, more importantly, what can be done to remedy that.

Chapter eight explores the concept of objective rebellion, in consideration of the way in which we can be agents of change, through working with staff and senior leaders towards more solution-driven discussions around small change to impact larger policy. Through a series of working examples, this chapter provides a template of how objective rebels are some of our most essential voices within a staff body, and how we can utilise them further.

This moves us to chapter nine, which aims to aid teachers with the salient task of finding a workplace that's right for them. Taking a journey through the different ways in what attracts us to schools, this chapter provides ways in which teachers and schools can create symmetry in purpose, a key aspect that was highlighted in the *Summary and recommendations: teacher well-being research report* of 2019.[8] If we are to excel in the workplace, we need to ensure that it is the right workplace for us.

As this moves us towards school systems and processes, chapter ten will look at the evolution of more people-friendly schools. Reviewing a series of examples (from both outside and within teaching) of how we can re-centre our approach to human resourcing, this section will explore what many different organisations and schools have done to develop their approach using a 'life first, work after' attitude to employment, and how this mindset could essentially develop teaching as an enviable profession, rather than an unfavourable one.

We will consider the significance of crisis points in chapter eleven, sharing important teacher narratives on a subject that we cannot shy away from: that teaching is having a detrimental impact upon the mental health of teachers. This chapter will give time and thought to how we can support ourselves and others to manage what is a profession that carries great emotional labour for us as individuals.

The final chapter reviews readings that speculate on the future landscape of teaching, and wellbeing's place within that. Looking at campaigns and systems that have been developed to assist with wellbeing in a meaningful and strategic way, I propose a manifesto for workload in order to start conversations around what we can do at a local and national level to ensure that teachers are able to continue to carry out roles in school. This chapter also provides a range of narratives from a wealth of schools getting it right in a multitude of ways. This should give even the most despairing of teachers some semblance of hope that there are schools out there that care deeply for their staff. I close with my manifesto for wellbeing, outlining the pragmatic ways in which we can keep teachers in schools until they actually want to leave or retire (rather than reluctantly leaving because they do not have the energy to be in our schools anymore).

8.   www.bit.ly/2RYAZqa

Drawing upon research, my own perspective and the experience and ideas of experts in their field, this book is not an answer, but a proposal that we look at wellbeing in the same way that we want to approach provision for children in schools: the best bet for the many. As I will mention countless times during this book, context is key, collaboration is king and there are no silver bullets. It's about making informed choices about your practice that will ultimately help you to feel like you're not chasing your tail, as such. I draw many English based examples (as this is my forte) but have called upon respected teachers and leaders to debate the place of wellbeing within schools. Redressing wellbeing really could be as straightforward as shifting the way in which we look at it and opening up conversations so that we can drive change from the bottom up.

This book aims to stop senior leadership, middle management and you talking about wellbeing. No more aromatherapy INSETs, after-school yoga classes or biscuits on a Friday. No more payday cakes, sports socials, meditation that no one can fit in because, ironically, they cannot see past the marking pile or even get the time to leave their classroom for long enough to participate. Instead, let's get down to business and apply research and evidence to improve the standards of teaching for teachers and pupils, because that is what is going to improve teacher wellbeing. A sense of resolution and a sense of fulfilment are what teachers crave, not their sixth chocolate bar of the week – well, perhaps that too, but it certainly isn't going to remedy the impact that their workload is having on their lives. If we are going to make a concrete effort to reduce workload and improve the conditions of our schools for teachers, we are wasting time in chasing the tokenistic. Instead, let us return to our purpose and reason. To begin our examination of wellbeing, and to explain the importance of keeping our why, I want to share my own sense of purpose – and how it has sometimes been threatened.

My why
What is teaching to me?

'We don't have a teacher shortage; we have a shortage of teachers willing to work in our schools.'
— @PedroANoguera #ILConf19

'Proper teaching is recognized with ease. You can know it without fail because it awakens within you that sensation which tells you this is something you have always known.'
— Frank Herbert, *Dune*

This won't be a narrative which tells you about that one teacher who inspired me, who pushed me to try when I was on the brink of giving up. But at some point, teaching was something that attracted me because of its sense of purpose, of doing something that might help other people.

I left school feeling completely disengaged, having walked out of one A level exam because I felt incapable and inadequate. Even now, I feel a little angry at the gaps that I have in my education. I needed future me to give 16-year-old me a good shake, point out how incredibly privileged I was to come from a family who would financially support my education, and to tell me to get on with it. In time, I wanted to teach because I wanted someone to believe in the students that didn't believe in themselves; but at that early point, teaching looked like absolute torture.

Making money for money's sake

Working in the financial sector, I managed a large number of people, mostly remotely, and with a shared and linear vision to convey and direct. Stress levels were talked about in small talk on the back of a long meeting, but were in no way comparable to the ebbs and flows of teaching. The lines of success were clear cut, measurable and explicitly demonstrable to others, and I knew what was brilliant, and what was not. I was fantastic at my job. I knew this because I was explicitly thanked, regularly winning national awards within the organisation, particularly around the recruitment and retention of staff. (The company worked incredibly hard at acquiring and keeping excellent people because it cost in excess of £10,000 to recruit and train them.) However, eventually, I felt little reward in the role. I enjoyed managing people and projects, but the lack of moral purpose in creating a profit for a bank meant I felt incredibly unfulfilled. This was a time where financial regulation was lacking to say the least, and conversations at senior management level encouraged practice that just didn't sit comfortably with me. We were thriving as a result of people's debt. I would drive to work and count the hours until I was home again. Purpose was never an aspect of my professional working life prior to teaching; projects were managed, completed, and then you moved on to the next task. No one lingered on the evaluative stage: we moved through initiatives so fast that it wasn't necessary. The monotony and lack of accomplishment started to make me pretty jaded. I wondered if that was all there was to the working world: getting up, going to work, going home, getting up again. It was the conflict between the predictability of my current existence and the unpredictability if I chose an alternative, walked away from what I had been told was a 'good' job with 'good' prospects. I didn't want good; I wanted *purposeful*.

A friend of mine had left for Cyprus a month earlier and rang me to tell me how incredible it was to live on the beach all day and work in a bar at night. She needed a new UK phone and suggested I fly out instead of posting it. I put my house on the market, handed in my notice, and left the following month without a second thought; the job didn't mean anything to me.

Perfect is not an option

After a year, I decided to return to the UK and embark upon a degree in English literature, the only subject I had ever adored. I found literature a way to understand why fulfilment was so valuable, exploring the theory of the self in autobiographies from Hilary Mantel to Dave Eggers. Lecturers introduced me to writers as old friends, describing them in such a way that I felt they spoke to me from the page, and enabled me to see ideas in ways I had not seen before. I marvelled at the magic of language, at being able to connect people with your ideas in such a beautiful way.

Being accepted to complete a PGCE at the University of Warwick was a monumental day for me, and becoming a teacher is the professional achievement that I am most proud of. However, of course, it came with its supercharged dosage of feeling incapable, and a learning curve with such incline as I'd never experienced before. I hadn't known what it was like not to instantly succeed at something on a professional level, and that process is essential to learning. Teacher training was one of the hardest years of my life. I was a lone parent, and we had a miniscule amount of money each week for food, petrol and treats. I would swing between love and guilt as I dropped off my three-year-old son every morning, waiting outside for his nursery to open with anxiety that I would be late for the sometimes hour-long journey to university, and then my placement schools. He was always the last one to be collected, and I lacked the energy to invest in both him and the course that year as I struggled to work out exactly what teaching wanted of me. What made it all the more painful was that I loved it so much.

The course forced me to evaluate my sense of self, taking me through a series of reflection studies, which felt like a surreal state of vulnerability that we don't tend to experience in a professional capacity. I wanted to be confident and capable, and the entire process made me feel anything but. So eager to be good, but not really knowing what good was, I read everything – and as Mary Myatt shares, 'The paradox of mastery is that the more we know and understand something, the more we realise how little we know.'[1] The volume of knowledge that I was trying to take in in such a short space of time just emphasised to me how inadequate I was. My mentor at my first placement told me that he couldn't tick the 'outstanding' box because I 'wouldn't have anywhere to work towards' and I was absolutely devastated. What do you mean, I haven't grasped teaching in three months flat? I have nailed everything I have ever put my mind to! But perfectionism wasn't an option; following eight years of teaching, I now realise that time is essential to cultivate the ability to teach, and at the time, it pained me. I had succeeded at everything I had ever set out to do, and this profession stood in the way of my track record. My second placement was tougher still, as I tussled with fitting into a team at a school that didn't fit me. But I found camaraderie and comfort in the drama department, a diverse group of people that got me through a challenging few months – thanks, Kacey and Amber, for holding my hand in the first school where a student called me a less-than-favourable word for the female genitalia. Much appreciated.

Teaching was an entirely different career to any other. Once I had completed my training, the spaces of time where I felt like I fit were few and far between. Somewhat anticlimactic, although I was afraid to admit that at the time. I was pulled between gratitude at being able to do what I loved every day and a sense of embarrassment that I found it incredibly challenging. More so, I didn't understand how I could simultaneously love and dread the ventures of each new day. There were so many aspects of the day-to-day that had a real sense of disconnect.

My life was on show; I couldn't operate in the same way in this career. If I was having a bad day on a personal level, I needed colleagues to lean on instead of locking myself in an office. Children would play upon weakness – as children sometimes will – asking

---

1.   Mary Myatt, 'Useful and Beautiful', April 2019, accessed at www.bit.ly/33lMbk3

personal questions, or shouting obscenities to see what would happen, how would the new teacher react? In my training year, a boy casually offered me career advice that I could try being 'less of a bitch'. He meant it with the deepest sincerity. In nine short, intense months, I had to assert myself and set out my intent. I hadn't really worked out my purpose yet, the reason why I felt compelled to teach, and I wish I had started by doing so. To work that out whilst under the scrutiny of a system such as teaching was incredibly difficult. Teaching is a five-hour solo performance: you have to know the title of your play, your values, your ethos, and what you will present as your teaching self. Teaching is a labour-intensive process, and I grew to realise how instrumental a strong team was so that I could deliver such a performance, day in, day out.

Conflict and consequence

I have found, during my time teaching, that if you are going to crumble, the breaking point does not come all at once, but in chips and a smattering of cracks. When you reach a point of crisis, one of the most despairing moments is the realisation that it is simple to look back at the contributions that led you to that point. To shift the metaphor somewhat, it's a poor depiction, the talk of alarm bells, as they do not feature as booming gongs of eureka moments, but soft chimes, barely noticeable and yet present enough to be taken notice of. We just choose not to do so.

For me, a large number of those chimes were trigger factors caused by a series of circumstantial things that were not within my control.

The first splash or hint of concern I had was working with at least one colleague in a position of management – in almost every school that I have ever worked at – that did not support my development, celebrate my achievements or, in my opinion, operate or manage people in a benevolent way. To be candid, I have experienced this flippant, neglectful method of management in various forms, ranging from passive-aggression to projecting insecurity; paranoia over conversations that took place without them and running (yes, running) from another building to break up a chat between myself and another teacher after seeing us nattering about the latest episode of *The Handmaid's Tale* through the window, assuming that we would be discussing something that could bring them into disrepute. At its least offensive, a lack of professionalism can make staff feel constrained, play upon an already simmering imposter syndrome, or make people feel excessively monitored with an absence of motive that they are then left to construct for themselves, pondering over why they are not good enough. Systemically, this is also abundant in schools, beyond the individual management style: learning walks where feedback was only received if improvement was required, never when fit for praise; multi-coloured streams of bold, bullet-pointed emails that are sent before my milkman arrived of a morning; lunchtime meetings; same-day deadlines; and receiving lesson observation feedback and being told that it was being graded a 'good' but wasn't really a 'good', and that they were doing me a favour by giving me an opportunity to improve. These small gestures all began to lead me to question my ability as a professional. It became somewhat meta: was I an effective teacher? Or was I just here because someone had done me a favour, or overlooked my flaws?

I started a new role, a promotion, and found it difficult to fit into the dynamics of the department and school. Workload had been sold to me as remedied at interview, a concern that didn't exist at this school, this school that would value me and support my CPD, with its forward-thinking, outward-facing approach and record-breaking achievement levels. I had been told that the school didn't send reports, and finished early one day a week – but it transpired that actually, parents' evening was five hours long and meetings ran on for hours at a time, with little regard for leniency. Completing a lesson observation? There was a 16-page booklet to complete, with a time column to ensure that every minute was accounted for. Each grading was segmented into three sections, so you discussed 'low good' as a grading. This was often used as a way of making a member of staff feel mediocre, without having a huge impact on the overall teaching standard for the school – clever, right?

Surveillance and silence

Removing a student from your lesson? There was a carbon copy sheet for you to write a full statement, should there be any discrepancy between your story and theirs. Marking policy was once a fortnight, and a data folder to be presented to any member of SLT during learning walks, which took place every half term. I felt more supervised in my capability as a teacher than ever before, and I felt tense as a result. In an ironic attempt to construct a coping strategy, I started to try to regain control of my anxiety and got into work for 7 a.m., so that I could then start to prepare for the aspects of my day that were within my control, and marking at any given opportunity so I could attempt to combat the feeling of not doing enough, leaving at 7 p.m. in the hope that the hours would alleviate my unease. It didn't work, and by summer I was pretty burnt out.

Just like Iesha Small in her own narrative in *The Unexpected Leader*, the choices that I was making were as a result of external pressures, and it became a perpetual cycle of double guesswork. The school was unsupportive and unfulfilling to work for, and this led to a constant feeling of underperformance amongst staff which then, in a self-fulfilling prophecy, led to failure. My own insecurities influenced the advice I gave to staff, and how and when I shared information, bombarding department staff with emails as I constantly tweaked and refined assessment or communicated information. This often led to management amending my emails and thus me feeling as though I was being undermined. Alternatively, my work was amended repeatedly, or I was instructed to redo it as it didn't meet the requirements and perhaps this would work better, or this, or this? It was exhausting, and crippling for my self-confidence. There became a level of dual responsibility to my professional fulfilment: the system's ability to develop me in a responsible manner, but also my ability to challenge the system on the occasion that it didn't fulfil its role. I was given the task of creating a key stage 3 handbook. I laboured over it for hours and gave it to my line manager, who promptly 'marked' it and left it in my pigeon hole, covered in annotations and corrections or questions like 'Do we do this?' or 'I don't understand.' Without the support of a dialogue around how to improve my work, I would keep on producing more and more content, taking the approach that if I just covered everything, some of it would be worth keeping. The handbook never saw the light of day, as I was informed that 'we're not running with a handbook anymore,' the week before the summer holiday. I despaired at the hours I had wasted working on it, and was told that 'lots of things don't get used, because they're just not very good'.

I felt bullied. Having represented union members in a previous role before teaching, I knew the classic features of what bullying looked like. I think we all do. The issue was that workplace bullying was and continues to be such a difficult delicacy to handle, because it is such a matter of perception and interpretation. The term itself makes the victim seem weak, or cowardly. Questions start to arise, both internal and from others, around your sense of judgement: is this bullying? Did I just take those words the wrong way? It becomes a case of what has been said versus how you have interpreted it. With the best of intentions, I knew, in this case, my words did not carry weight here. And when policies are so stringent and prudent to highlight error in the first place, they become an ideal document to hide behind for bullies. The atmosphere was toxic, and distrusting of staff, and I felt as though I didn't fit – predominantly, because I didn't feel that a punitive approach grows people.

Over the summer break, I convinced myself that it would be different. I took responsibility for the way I felt, dismissing my anxiety and insomnia in term time to the shift of a new job, the introduction of a commute and the pressure I put on myself regularly to excel.

I spent all summer manically overcompensating for my feelings of inferiority by working the entirety of the six weeks off, tweeting proudly about the array of resources I had made (and would probably never use). By this point, I was acutely aware that I wasn't the problem, but my environment was. A collection of us started to discuss our uncertainty and anxiety and realised that there were elements of the style of management that could have had an impact here. The systems at play did not accommodate for wellbeing; the speed-dating-type after-school events were there (and enforced: you must attend and DO NOT just talk to your department colleagues – mingle, for Christ's sake!), yoga classes, the social team rallying round in briefing every Monday morning to radio silence. We didn't need a social life; we needed support in our professional lives to muster up the energy reserves for a social life. It is difficult to convey just how tiring the dissatisfaction of feeling as though you are doing a poor job really is.

The second chime in my professional career was a personal life event that brought my crescendo approach to working to a halt. I suffered from a missed miscarriage.

In the weeks before my miscarriage, I struggled with the physical symptoms of pregnancy. When I shared the news of my pregnancy, my head of department looked at me aghast and asked if it was planned. Shocked and not really knowing what to say, other than the truth, I said yes. Not even my immediate family had asked such a question. Watching her whisper to the assistant head through the head's morning address, I anticipated an unsympathetic shift a little further from the already uncompassionate treatment that I was used to. I will never be certain what that conversation contained, of course, but your instincts are usually right. I stand by that conviction.

I will try to find the balance for this. For the most part, I'll admit, I want to skirt over it, as perhaps it isn't pertinent to the story. But for many, many women that I have spoken to, and for my unborn child, I feel that I need to find the letters and form them into words, somehow. It is relevant, because it embodies our place as humans before operatives.

The day of our scan, the sonographer was silent, and the room was dark, so no one could see my face of realisation, the fact that I already knew but that my partner did not. This was my second child; I knew the screen should be turned towards us by now, and she should be indulging us in making jokes about the baby waving, or how it would be on the stage with that level of energy. Maybe something about its career as a footballer. But the screen wasn't turned in our direction, and I never saw my child.

I asked my partner to call work to let them know, and usually stoic, his voice cracked as he let our receptionist know, sobbing openly as he attempted to explain what had happened with words that had yet to even be spoken between us. 'The baby's died, our baby is dead.'

The days that followed were a blur, as I was talked through the medical requirements and my forthcoming stay in hospital. During this time, I received a text from my head of department asking if she could call to make suggestions about timetabling for my return that would 'ease things up' for me; coincidentally, I felt incredibly ill that evening with a rocketing temperature and was readmitted to hospital with what would later be confirmed as septicaemia. I replied to the text on my way to the hospital, explaining that the call would have to wait.

The next morning, my head of department got in touch again, this time to ask if there was any way I could get someone to drop in or post the mock exam papers I had. I felt pressured to reply, so explained that I was still in the hospital and my partner would post them when he could. She suggested that maybe he could drive halfway to school and meet someone from the department with them as she was nervous about their arrival if being posted, and a back-and-forth discussion got underway until my partner just said he would drive them over that afternoon. She asked for him to just drop them into reception, without the awkwardness of meeting anyone. Awkwardness on whose part, I wonder.

I was contacted regularly during my hospital stay: an anxious student believed that I had her exercise book and her parents would like it located, or did I know where my data folder was kept for seating plans. All by text, always caveated by a 'rest up' to close. I was tired, in every sense.

Upon my return, I was unsupported through planning, the behaviour management process felt challenging as my classes pushed back in rebellion of my absence, and I was uncompassionately managed. During my phased return, I was repeatedly asked or chased to plan for the lessons that I was not in for. My year 9 group were positively hostile; during one girl's feedback discussion with me about her latest assessment, she retorted, 'You have no idea of my progress, you've barely been here.' My year 11 group had been given to someone else and refused to meet my eye in the corridor when they saw me or looked at me with contempt. Concerned about the contact that had been made whilst I was off, I asked for a meeting with the deputy head, stating that I didn't wish to raise a grievance at this point, but wanted to voice my worries as I didn't feel it was appropriate to contact people directly in such a situation. In response, he gave me two points that he believed to be relevant: one, the strain that the department had been under in my absence; and two, that I had been known to be looking for employment elsewhere before my absence. My union rep interjected to state that I was 'suffering a bereavement, not off with a headache,' and so perhaps the text messages and phone calls that I received weren't appropriate. I maintained that my mental health – and, consequently, my physical health – would have been less impacted, had it not been for this repeated contact. I wasn't asking the school to hold my hand; I was asking for systems to be in place for all staff so that their mental health would not be under fire as a result of their workplace.

The damage done by a broken system took time to restore, both mentally and physically, but I do at least have these experiences to thank for how highly I regard helping teachers with workload. I felt as though my value system, the reasons behind my desire to be a teacher were being somewhat picked away at, and subsequently compromised as a result. There was a significant disconnect between how I wanted to teach and how I was being asked to teach. It is impossible to be a teacher without this system of values; we do not turn up just to sit at a desk and go home again. I had done that already and it wasn't enough. So, to have those who were in positions of responsibility mismanage me until I reached the point where it seemed like my only option was to give up a place in a profession that I had paid to train to become a part of – well, it was, and is, ludicrous. To feel so undervalued as a trained professional that it seems as though others are actively encouraging you to leave – that is how I, and many others, felt.

Through a series of events, I left the school, and my story doesn't end badly: I still teach, of course. But the year before I almost left teaching, 35,000 other teachers did leave the profession.

Collective purpose

I didn't leave teaching, but I do know that whilst that may be a rare ending, my story is not a particularly unusual one. I returned to a school where I had worked previously, and I thanked the then head for saving my career. When I took maternity leave with my second son, I developed a website for English teachers as an evolution of the shared drive I had created back in 2013: a site that hosted their resources to share, and a guest blog for people to contribute towards. Now, with over 14,000 members, over 30 annual subject-specific regional events a year and an established peer-coaching programme, I wanted to find a strategic way of enabling teachers not only to share without navigating social media, but also to feel as though they belonged to a community that shared their vision for teaching. Litdrive became my way of saying thank-you to all of the people who encouraged me to stay in teaching when I wanted to leave. All the people who supported me when I wasn't really doing an incredible job of supporting myself.

The Litdrive inbox inadvertently (but welcomingly so) presented me with emails from numerous teachers who would tell their stories: stories of almost leaving, anxiety, leaving schools that made them unhappy or struggling to find a balance in what is a profession that doesn't lend itself kindly to the word. Teachers who had just had children or had taken a break from teaching and who now felt completely out of their depth in the classroom. Teachers who were being bullied in the workplace. Teachers that shared their own narratives with me and told somewhat dystopian stories of uncompassionate treatment that, when brought together as a collective, makes that statistic of 35,000 seem like a reasonable response. I do believe that for every awful story, there is one of reason and positive resolution, and of teachers finding their fit within schools. Why? Because when you place people into stressful situations, there are not just negative outcomes. Those people form groups, and share experiences, and use those experiences to form a new definition of what it means to work in a school. Those people become leaders, and run their own schools, and share their purpose, and their why with others. I only want to stay in teaching if it means that I can work within a system that values me as a professional. I have every faith that this is possible if we re-evaluate the way in which the system works. My purpose came so late to me that I bumbled around, finding out snippets of my reason to teach as I went along. I teach because social justice is important to me. Much of this book, particularly the reflections, are what I wish someone had challenged me to ask of myself at an earlier point in my career.

When I first started to write this book, it was as a result of frustration, fuelled by the conversations I had with teachers everywhere as every year, they toyed with leaving – and that's the ones that chose to stay.

When I have been poorly this year through overwork, controversially I am going to say, this was my fault. No one asked me to spend a whole weekend marking the whole year group of mocks at the expense of time with my family. No one asked me to teach over allocation because of staff absence. No one asked me to work most evenings until past midnight answering emails, planning and marking. The reality of the situation is that my personality drives me to fix things and find solutions whilst my pride forces me to prevent any kind of failure. — Zena Chadwick, head of department

We are all guilty of this, but if we continue to run schools on guilt and interpret the fact that there are not enough hours to complete our roles as failure on our part, we are sorely mistaken. If we are to examine workload in a diplomatic way, in a way that drives solutions, it is imperative that we start with why this job is so important to us in the first place. Only then can we start to save it. It wasn't good enough or acceptable to me just for us to throw our hands up and say that others are making teaching too difficult for us. Half of the battle is the broken profession, yes; but the other half is what we as teachers decide to do about it.

I want to propose a manifesto that we as a profession will only be in a fit state to provide the level of education that children are entitled to if we hold staff in the highest regard within our schools. Teachers need empowerment so they can self-regulate their own physical and mental health, through a methodical approach to teaching and operating better. Wellbeing is fulfilling our why, our purpose, of being in a workplace that breeds the capability to teach effectively, build productive relationships, make us feel as though we have accomplished a balance between satisfying all of our life roles. Everything else is superfluous.

- I don't mark at home because I don't feel I should need to.
- I don't work in the evening because I need to sleep.
- I don't send emails late at night because I don't want to read them.
- I don't leave conflict unresolved because it leaves me unsettled at the end of a day.

- I don't write lengthy lesson plans because I don't feel they are valuable.
- I don't make excessive to-do lists because they make me feel inefficient.
- I feed my professional self because I want to feel like I'm becoming better.
- I don't accept that my purpose should be compromised.

This is wellbeing. Not one ounce of yoga.

REFLECT

What is your why?

You will find self-reflection tasks throughout the book, simply to support you in evaluating the section in question, how it aligns with what you are already doing in school, and what you may be able to take forward from what you have read. The tasks are to aid you in processing what you have read, so that you can start to consider how you can make decisions in your professional approach to wellbeing that will support you in a sustainable way. It may be that these act as a way for you to summarise your own thoughts in reaction to the topic, or it may simply raise questions for you about your own situation or context. I have attempted to structure these sections in such a way that they don't form a 'top tips' or 'to-do': they should act, and are intended to act, as a way for you to return at a later point as a reminder, to mull over, and take stock of your own situation.

What made you read this book? What was it that prompted you to read this book? What state of mind were you in when you decided to pick up the book? Do you think that's relevant to note? What are your expectations? When do you currently feel that your wellbeing is most at risk as a result of work-related issues?

Evaluate your current situation:

- Why do you teach?
- Perfect world thinking: what does a true sense of professional purpose look

like? Consider the school, the team, the hours, the interactions. Create your perfect workplace.

Reality

- Which aspect of this perfect workplace seems furthest away from your current reality?
- To what extent do you currently feel fulfilled at work? 1–10
- What do you most enjoy about teaching?
- What do you enjoy the least? Be as precise and specific as possible here.
- How long have you felt this way? Can you pinpoint when this started to change?

Obstacles

- What three elements impact your workload the most? Both inside and outside of work?
- What do you wish you had more time for at work? Which task currently receives more of your time than you feel it should?
- Consider the last three months. How many instances can you recall of times that you have spent – with friends, family or on your own – exploring non-teaching interests?
- What led you to do so? Be as specific as you can.

Way forward:

- What reflections can you take from reading over your responses now? In a week or two, turn back and consider the same question.
- Which sections of this book may provide you with support for your obstacles section?
- How will you find the time to invest in the possibility of change?
- What further support can you already call upon?

The nature of the beast
The oddities of teaching

'The best thing for being sad,' replied Merlin, beginning to puff and blow, 'is to learn something. That's the only thing that never fails. You may grow old and trembling in your anatomies, you may lie awake at night listening to the disorder of your veins, you may miss your only love, you may see the world about you devastated by evil lunatics, or know your honour trampled in the sewers of baser minds. There is only one thing for it then – to learn. Learn why the world wags and what wags it. That is the only thing which the mind can never exhaust, never alienated, never be tortured by, never fear or distrust, and never dream of regretting. Learning is the only thing for you. Look what a lot of things there are to learn.'
— T.H. White, *The Once and Future King*

What is it?

Teaching is like no other job in the world. It fascinates me how disjointed the reality and perception of teaching really are. People view the profession as somewhat of a Marmite delicacy: comments are always 'I could never do what you do' or 'I wouldn't mind it for the holidays!' When the media or external bodies discuss teaching, the narrative swings between a demonisation of the system (as we all rally around to collaboratively destroy children) and general bemusement (and perhaps envy) that we are rewarded with 13+ weeks' holiday a year for our light-hearted, six-hour days. Indeed.

Teacher training is focused on how to drive outcomes from students; we examine the qualities that we would expect a 'good' teacher to have. We explore what it means to teach well, or plan well, or contribute well, but overall, the training that is provided is there to support the child's learning, not the teacher's workload. We seldom provide a platform or forum for discussing or preparing new teachers for the idiosyncrasies that teaching will inflict upon you, whether you like it or not.

Teaching is its own creature with its own language (ALPs, PAN, SISRA, FSM, API, A2L – you name it, we'll abbreviate it), which we use when we collect in pockets to discuss and compare stories, revelling in the fact that we have managed to find other people who understand what it is like to be us. You only truly understand a teacher if you are a teacher. We find comfort in the narratives from other schools, the horror stories and achievements, to be shocked or awed by. We refer to our friends as teacher friends or non-teacher friends; we have different conversational topics stored for each. We know our teacher friends will only commit to social events at the weekends or in the holidays, never following a parents' evening or when reports are due, and never on a Tuesday. When we are struggling at work to find the right words for situations, we seek out our teacher friends for advice, because the non-teaching folk won't understand, or will tell us to speak to HR.

There is no HR. Not in comparison with the corporate world, at least. Or there is, but they have an administrative role and not an advisory one, with the exception of matters of more gravity: disciplinaries, grievances, whistleblowing policy. At times, unions take the place of what would be the services of a personnel department. Often, we hold each other up; and teachers who have worked with one another, and long since parted ways professionally, will remain friends for life. Teaching is a funny being that brings professionals together with common interests that they simply cannot find elsewhere, because there are certain aspects, highlights and pressures of the profession that are unique to, well, the profession. There are several ways in which teaching is uniquely stressful, and I think it's key that we explore them so that we are able to articulate what it means to experience them – and thereby work towards refining or improving particular aspects of education, of course, but also equip staff and school leaders adequately to deal with such oddities. And as a starting point, teaching encompasses some ideas that simply do not make sense.

If you have worked in teaching for your entire adult career, as with any profession or working for any particular company, you become accustomed to working in a particular way – not necessarily because it is successful or works towards change, but because it is how you are used to working. It works well enough, so why change it?

Heuristics in judgement and decision making in schools

Theorised by Tversky and Kahneman,[1] there are several different bias practices that come into play when we make decisions. One is the availability of knowledge and how the process of retrieval can impact our capacity for making good decisions. When we weigh up probabilities within a scenario that impact a decision, we retrieve prior knowledge from our memory to help us to make that decision. However, because we find it easier to recall ideas or concepts that we understand better, we tend to use these aspects to make decisions and therefore tend to make decisions in ways that we have always made them. For example, you have two routes to work: one is less scenic, and longer, but you always go that way because the stages of the journey are easier for you than the shorter but more rural option. Because the first one is on the motorway, you sometimes get stuck in traffic as a result of this choice; but you continue to choose this route because it is just too tasking to go about the task of remembering the other option.

Dependent upon where you teach, you could be in the same role as someone you know at another school, and have an entirely different experience as a result of the decisions around the choices

---

1. Tversky, A. and Kahneman, D. (1974) 'Judgment under uncertainty: heuristics and biases', Science 185 (4157) pp. 1124–1131. Retrieved from www.bit.ly/35A9OSw

of the job specification, support, and time allocation or utilisation provided to you. Moreover, both of you could be entirely satisfied by certain aspects of their role, and discontent with others. Such is the diversity of teaching! It is this diversity that makes certain policies and processes in school so inconsistent when we consider teacher wellbeing. To start a conversation around improvement without making every school identical, we must first acknowledge that it is possible to improve school settings by looking at what works elsewhere and making it your own.

This chapter will look to consider just three key aspects that are specific to teaching (although do present in other professions in similar ways): the physicality of teaching, the impact of extended holidays running parallel with the speed of the profession and the use of time within education.

How do we examine the oddity of schools aid wellbeing?

If we are to understand how to look after ourselves not as people, but as people who are teachers, we must grasp what it is about teaching that makes it both unusual and difficult. We have to understand what it is we are dealing with in order to fathom why it makes us feel the way that it does, and why we emotionally invest so much of ourselves in something in this way. Is what we are doing worth it – for us? Do we feel our ages by the end of the year, or add a decade to that figure? There is growing research available to ascertain that happy teachers provide grounding for happy students, and teachers under strain will pass such mental strain onto students similarly.[2] It makes for just one of several sensible reasons for improving the particularities of teaching – we will do it, even if at times it is a little painful (to say the least). Even if we are tired (even after a new-born, I had not known tiredness like teaching), malnourished after seven weeks of feasting on a mega mix of biscuits, and already a little anxious over the vast expanse of a six-week holiday, we still

---

2. 'Teacher stress and students' school well-being: the case of upper secondary schools in Stockholm' (2019) Scandinavian Journal of Educational Research.

want to teach. What is it that makes us connect with teaching in such a personal way that we are so reluctant to seek out any other alternative career as a replacement?

In Brian Rowan's 1994 article in *Educational Researcher*, he holds up the concept that teachers place craft and labour as particularly unique characteristics of teaching, incomparable to other professions. He states that we struggle to find just comparisons because whilst the labour and prestige may be unique to teachers, 'the occupation of teaching receives lower prestige than its professional status warrants' – its level of professionalism in comparison to other roles is subjective to the person scrutinising it.[3] A doctor or barrister, for example, is seen as a universally valued role in society; while teachers are well-regarded only by those that comprehend the work: teachers value other teachers. We regard teaching highly because we understand the incredible work that goes into being a teacher.

The other aspect of how we determine job importance is through the psychological impact as a result of the job complexity. The more complex a job role is, the more likely it is to have an impact on things like job satisfaction and intellectual functioning. This is often what teachers speak of when they outline the reason they chose teaching, particularly those that came to teaching later: it was a temptation to have a profession that provided a sense of reward. It is this reward that makes teaching such a challenge of its own, unlike other professions, but this does come at several different costs. The higher the challenge, the higher the reward; but equally, the higher the challenge, the more of a strain this will take upon physical and mental health. The most rewarding jobs – jobs that contribute to social and moral purpose, jobs that pay to our role of philanthropist – are often the most challenging. The more we give of ourselves within roles in schools, the more important it is to retain some semblance of balance for ourselves. But it is also 'the emotional intensity of

---

3.   Rowan, B. (1994) 'Comparing teachers' work with work in other occupations: notes on the professional status of teaching' Educational Researcher 23 (6) pp. 4–17.

teaching[4] and training providers' failure to prepare us adequately for this that makes that balance incredibly difficult to accomplish.

Both the mental and physical toil of teaching are multifaceted and come with their own consequences. We take an incredibly uninformed, rather self-sabotaging approach when it comes to our physical health when teaching. In an office, I was used to regular risk assessments for my seat and desk at work, health benefits, car, laptop, systems and departments that would answer the questions that I was not trained or paid to know. My glasses prescription was paid by the company; my physio appointments, if I thought I'd been at my desk too long for the week, also as expenses. If I travelled with work, my travel and food were paid for – with a generous budget. If I felt a little tired after a particularly complex or challenging deadline, I would book Monday off and go for a massage or a shopping trip. Teaching in comparison was like a primitive walk back in time. No one cared if your back hurt, or your chair was falling to pieces. Your laptop took 15 minutes to load up as standard, and the glare on your monitor screen was part of the charm. Delightful.

Teaching is a far cry from the corporate world indeed. We work at full throttle and beyond, 39 weeks of the year. Our self-care fits in around school hours or gets put on hold as each summer, and we tell ourselves that we will make time next year to focus on our health, haircuts and generally staying on top of things. We listen and nod politely at our friends when they chat about company cars and voucher prize draws for spa days at work, and we graciously accept gifts from children – a box of Milk Tray or a 'Best Teacher' mug that we can't walk the corridors with because it doesn't have a lid, but that we treasure anyway because it means something to us. Our meeting times with other adults can be sparse, and we walk away from our working days sometimes feeling a little jaded, or with a hefty to-do list. But we love teaching – oh, how we love it so, even if it can be difficult at times. How we love it so, if only it was a little bit easier on us.

4. Prilleltensky, I., Neff, M. and Bessell, A. (2016) 'Teacher stress: what it is, why it's important, how it can be alleviated', *Theory Into Practice* 55 (2) pp. 104–111.

'You teachers have it pretty easy'

Physical health

Nearly three-quarters – 73% – of teachers say their workload is having a serious impact on their physical health;[5] teaching brings with it not only this mental spinning of multiple plates, but also a significant demand upon physical health. Sitting at a desk for extended periods of time is incredibly poor for our posture, but so is standing for four to five hours a day. Sitting without adequate training, guidance or the relevant risk assessment – something carried out as standard within corporate professions within big organisations – can be significantly detrimental to physical health later in life. Similarly, the extended periods of working inside, without access to daylight or sufficient breaks just to go outside, will also make their mark on physical wellbeing, and these physiological factors will of course in turn have a sustained effect upon mental health. 'But we have breaks,' the cynics may remark, but do you? 'Breaks' consist of a speedy dash to the single staff toilet or getting a drink – never time for both – and my lunch break is 20 minutes of shovelling food down my gullet before returning to my classroom, combined with the heady mix of a detention duty. Perhaps this pace and physical demand is why some teachers will admit that one deciding factor is the removal of time from the classroom in later life: a 22-lesson week is far less strenuous in your twenties than when you reach your forties.

Back to basics

Is this really all that surprising? That as part of a plan for progression, we are ready to admit to ourselves that being a classroom teacher in our fifties and sixties is a concept that we find a little daunting? Whilst it is an uncomfortable idea that this would factor into our decision to move towards a more strategic role, it is an honest one, I believe. Just as the bartender becomes the bar owner, we have to

5.   www.bit.ly/35G3hKZ

find comfort in being transparent that teaching is not a full-time occupation that we feel is possible as we grow older.

We all need education in order to feel both mentally and physically empowered. Knowledge makes it so and is likely to be one of the pull factors that brought us to teaching in the first place, although perhaps not consciously. But in the same way that it enriches us, the physical demands of teaching are undeniably strenuous in both the primary and secondary sectors, each with their own challenges. If we consider the classroom and school as a risk assessment, how many factors in a typical day attempt to encroach upon our sense of wellbeing?

Risk assessment	
Travel to classroom at place of work	Is kettle empty with a queue of at least five members of staff?
	Is staffroom at least seven minutes' walk from photocopier?
	Have additional three minutes been added to journey to drag bag of books up two flights of stairs?
	Is there a contingency for forgetting lunch and leaving it in the car?
Teacher timetabled for working days	Is teacher to run at high speed (in the form of a slow jog so they can reprimand other students on the way) to bus duty in the morning?
	Can teacher then attempt to find drinkable water to take with them to detention duty?
Teacher workplace assessment	Does the teacher's chair have a distinct wobble?
	Is the screen glare bouncing off the whiteboard behind them?
	Are their wrists suspended mid-air as they type, for fear of knocking the keyboard over from its already last legs?

To maintain optimum levels of physical health, first of all, we must find the time to invest in our physical health. View yourself as the most important resource, and recognise that the 30 minutes you put aside to look after yourself on a physical level will enable you to reap the rewards in other aspects of your work.

• **Drink the water.** The damage that you will cause yourself by denying your body one of the very things it needs to KEEP YOU ALIVE is ludicrous. A great many teachers that I spoke to about this drank less water purposefully to avoid going to the toilet because of the anxiety around needing to go whilst teaching. Broach this in an open discussion with colleagues near your classroom: set up an agreement, create a non-judgemental contingency within your department.

- If you operate predominantly in a windowless or blind-drawn classroom, you may want to think about the daylight you are allowing yourself to have. In a recent study, the impact that lacking windows has upon your sleep and physical health overall is startling. 'Office workers with more light exposure at the workplace tended to have longer sleep duration, better sleep quality, more physical activity, and better quality of life compared to office workers with less light exposure at the workplace,' and so the benefits are more substantial than you may imagine.[6] With the time that you shave off your workload as a result of whole-class feedback, centralised resources and putting your energy into effective delivery, find 15 minutes to walk in your working day. Listen to a podcast, read a blog in the cloud shine (that's what we have in England from August to June, by the way), or just eat lunch outside. You can make an entire meal from Joe Wicks's cookbook in 15 minutes. You can walk a mile in 15 minutes, if you're brisk. It will cost you nothing to take 15 minutes out of your day. Review this in a week and I guarantee you'll feel better – if not, feel free to get in touch on Twitter. I'll join you for a walk as payback.
- **Stand to teach;** and when you sit, focus on posture. Spend five minutes each lesson sitting really bloody straight. I use our retrieval practice time to do this. Your spine will thank you for all eternity if you stretch it out now and then.

I know – you know to drink water and go to the toilet and get exposure to daylight and look after your back. It sounds so easy, until the reality is that you don't find time for these things and they don't

6. Boubekri, M., Cheung, I. N., Reid, K. J., Wang, C. and Zee, P. C. (2014) 'Impact of windows and daylight exposure on overall health and sleep quality of office workers: a case-control pilot study', Journal of Clinical Sleep Medicine 10 (6) pp. 603–611.

seem a system-wide priority. We have just accepted a poor working environment as standard in education, sitting on chairs ripped at the seams at best, and designed for children at worst, reaching out over a keyboard and squinting through the screen glare to carry out our jobs, but this is a really under-emphasised area of our working life that we could do with paying more attention to.

There was a crooked (wo)man

In a second Twitter poll I conducted, to give a small taster, 82% of 348 voters stated that they had never had a risk assessment for keyboard or desk use during their entire teaching career. Those that did state that it was normally as a result of an injury that they were still going to be recovering from when coming back into work, or due to pregnancy where the maternity policy demands a risk assessment as standard procedure. This wasn't actually carried out at a desk or by a trained professional in risk management; they were simply asked whether they needed anything.

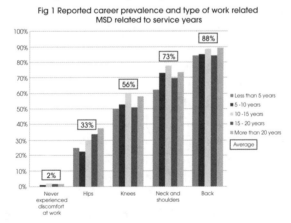

Fig 1 Reported career prevalence and type of work related MSD related to service years

In an online report drawn up by the company Jolly Back[7], which specialises in physiotherapy for teachers, 76.6% outlined that back pain was just part of the job. Whilst the union research survey for this polled primary staff, I think in this context, it is telling of how

7.   www.bit.ly/2Ti47uv

we approach physical health in the education sector in comparison to other industries and businesses. What does a positive working environment look like?

I spoke to Lorna Taylor, trained physiotherapist and Founder of Jolly Back, about achieving positive physical health in schools:

❝ Working with schools as a physiotherapist is a privilege but it's the sector where I see most variation in terms of musculoskeletal health due to the nature of teaching. For example, I support primary teachers in their mid-twenties after back surgery, those with neurological conditions affecting nerves and muscles, early years teachers who are awaiting knee replacement, teachers with neck and head aches from poorly set-up technology at work and secondary teachers not sure how they can continue working until retirement age due to the physical and mental demands of the job.

There are clear, direct links between physical and mental health and so, for most impact, prevention measures should and can benefit both. For example, pain leads to reduced movement, limitation of activities and fatigue, which in turn create a cycle of loss of confidence, fear of pain, fear of future long-term impact, further anxiety and avoidance behaviours. Stress often manifests itself as a musculoskeletal disorder (MSD) – physiological changes occur in the body (e.g. increased heart rate, tightening of muscles, increased blood pressure). We need to look at reducing MSDs together with supporting improved mental health and wellbeing, looking holistically at health.

Activities which create a risk include:
• Bending, twisting or repeating an action too frequently (e.g. working at low heights with young children, moving between classrooms, poor workstation setup – hunching over a computer if lighting is poor or screen too low)
• Uncomfortable working position (e.g. poor workstation setup – low desks or science bench combinations, unsupportive office chair, laptop on a flat desk, inappropriately placed whiteboards)
• Repetitive and heavy lifting (e.g. books, equipment, children, furniture)
• Not acting on symptoms quickly enough (e.g. cumulative strain and niggles which come on over time and are not reported)

- Psychosocial factors (e.g. high job demands, time pressures and lack of control)
- Working too long without a break (e.g. not even having time for adequate hydration and toilet break)

Here are some ways that you can help yourself:
- Keep active – fitness and strength help keep our musculoskeletal system in a healthy condition
- Drink water regularly – our shock-absorbing spinal discs are over 80% water and loo breaks are essential, not a luxury!
- Get comfortable before you begin – the most common cause of getting back pain is already having had it. If working regularly at a computer (at work and home), ensure the top of the screen is at eye level and use a separate mouse and keyboard.
- Take regular movement breaks – every 30 minutes, move for at least 30 seconds. It will make a world of difference in the long term.

Lights out

I reach crisis rapidly when I am sleep-deprived. Without sleep, the most manageable tasks seem formidable. Existing on four or five hours of sleep a night over a period of months with my second and third children, I was known to go through periods of high-functioning output of productivity, then find it incredibly challenging to recall words, complete straightforward tasks, or even manage to drive. Physical symptoms would present themselves in the form of temporary vision impairment, or crippling headaches that would render me pretty useless.

Teaching encourages sleep deprivation, through the endless to-do lists that fight to deprive you of any sense of satisfaction, to late nights at parents' evenings followed by early mornings. Terms are an endurance test in themselves – particularly the more persistent ones in the run-up to formal examinations: we push a little harder, for a little longer, and can forget that, in doing so, we are sabotaging ourselves a little in the process. We can sometimes feel as though we are not in a position to determine how much or little sleep we are able to get; I feel your pain on this one with a two-year-old and one that has yet to celebrate his first birthday! In the early days of maternity leave, I would often feel completely unable to function and my frustration came with having many ideas, but zero energy to put them into action.

You may find that when your crisis point hits, and you attempt to pinpoint the source or trigger, you need to look back further than the point that you felt you had hit the wall to find the real moment that you were pushed further than you should have been. This section offers a series of strategies for not only immediately dealing with the rush of anxiety that comes with crisis triggers, but also the long-term action that we can take to protect ourselves from experiencing such feelings of apprehension and generally being daunted by the prospect of trying to work. Here are some of the responses I received when I asked what kept people awake:

- 'Mainly thinking about my year 11s' coursework – what point they are at, ideas to support them'
- 'Running through conversations I have or will have to check for social faux pas, running through the next day'
- 'Decisions made by a colleague that I disagree with'
- 'Netflix'

It seems that we may be withholding sleep from our bodies to squeeze in the things we wish we had the time for, or because work is very much at the forefront of our minds. And what happens when people tell you how important sleep is? You find it all the more difficult to sleep. Remember the series run by Channel 4 called *Shattered*? If you're not as ancient as I am, I recommend that you look it up, especially if you need a little more convincing on why sleep is literally going to save your life. The series used a *Big Brother*-esque format with contestants depriving themselves of sleep for the longest time in competition for a cash prize of £100,000. They could receive rewards of snippets of sleep but could also be punished. 'Your ability to make rational decisions fails and you become impulsive,' says Professor Russell Foster of the University of Oxford. 'You lack empathy and your social interactions will also be compromised.'[8] Dr Nerina Ramlakhan, author of *Tired but Wired*, explores the idea that we no longer incorporate switch-off moments throughout the day: our constant desire to multi-task means that our minds are busy for longer: 'We have become restless as a society – and that places more demands on us when we get into bed at night.'[9] With the pace that teaching governs you to stay at during the day, it can often be 3 p.m. before some teachers take a drink. The task of keeping an alert eye on 30 children leaves very little room for downtime, and this job simply doesn't allow for quick, quiet moments. Beyond that, have you ever looked back at work that you have completed late the night before? The standard will be significantly different if you completed the work on a decent night's sleep, I can assure you. (That's all well and good but isn't always a realistic possibility, of course.)

This all sounds rather defeatist though, doesn't it? What can we do to ensure that we have the sleep that we need when there is simply so much to do?

> *When you're tired, tasks take longer, difficult situations look worse, rational thinking can become overwhelmed by emotion, and your sense of agency decreases. Others are relying on you: prioritise sleep.* **– Julia Steward,**
> **Founder and Coach at Chrysalis Leadership Development Limited**

One of the most common problems that teachers face (as with any profession that doesn't really have the fixed endpoints you find in project-focused professions) is chronic insomnia or issues with

---

8. Kale, S. (2016) 'Shattered: legacy of a reality TV experiment in extreme sleep deprivation', The Guardian, 4 September. Retrieved from: www.bit.ly/2Owxe11
9. Dr Nerina Ramlakhan *Tired But Wired: How to Overcome Sleep Problems: the Essential Sleep Toolkit*, Souvenir Press, 2010

the quality of sleep. As many as one in two adults experience short-term insomnia at some point, but one in ten adults have admitted to having long-term, recurrent insomnia.[10] Beyond this, sleep is vital to our health, particularly having an impact upon our heart health: neurologist Matthew Walker reports that when daylight saving time is adjusted back or forth, we see approximately a 24% increase or decrease in heart attacks respectively,[11] with similar spikes in road traffic accidents.[12] Sleep is paramount to our ability to remain healthy, commit things to memory, prepare for learning, and ensure that we are able to make use of the things that we learn. We wouldn't expect students to make progress by coming into lessons after six hours of sleep, so why are we trying to do that ourselves?

Twitter teachers reported a variety of reasons that keep them up at night: increasing workload generally, unresolved conflict with students or colleagues, accountability, or planning and marking for the next day. Sleep is the biggest overlooked superpower there is. I still worry when I receive emails from Litdrive members, attempting to access the site for resources at 2, 3, 4 a.m. If people are thinking about or planning lessons at a time that they could be sleeping, what is keeping them up?

Dear Tired Teacher,

- **Avoid sleep binges.** Do not try to survive on five to six hours of sleep and then attempt to regain the sleep at the weekend to 'stock up'. In his recent book Why We Sleep, Matthew Walker shares a lot of advice that we need as teachers. 'Sleep is not a credit,' he states, and we are at our best mental and physical health if we consistently get seven to nine hours' sleep, irrespective of the day of the week. Unpopular but beneficial, by

10. Sateia, M. J., Buysse, D. J., Krystal, A. D., Neubauer, D. N. and Heald, J. L. (2017) 'Clinical practice guideline for the pharmacologic treatment of chronic insomnia in adults: an American Academy of Sleep Medicine clinical practice guideline', *Journal of Clinical Sleep Medicine* 13 (2) pp. 307–349.
11. Sandhu, A., Seth, M. and Gurm, H. S. (2014) 'Daylight savings time and myocardial infarction', *Open Heart* 1 (1) [Online].
12. Smith, A. C. (2016) 'Spring forward at your own risk: daylight saving time and fatal vehicle crashes', *American Economic Journal Applied Economics* 8 (2) pp. 65–91.

rising at the same time and sleeping at the same time, we put ourselves in good stead for dealing with conflict or disagreement, the physical exertion associated with teaching, or even just planning fantastic, knowledgeable lessons that rely on our ability to draw from memory.

- **Avoid problem-solving just before bed.** In a study at the University of Lancaster, subjects were given maths problems and were three times more likely to be able to solve them after sleep.[13] It's the simple reason why it is perhaps best to sleep on a problem! Instead of wracking your brain at bedtime, journal the day that you have had, or the day that you are about to have, and always close with something (or things) that made you happy or that you can express gratitude for. Ending with a positive idea aids the process of closure for sleep – it's a good habit to get into.

- **Prepare yourself for sleep.** Set an alarm or reminder 15 minutes before you want to aim to be in bed. Close the laptop down, brush your teeth, have a skincare routine – all of those things that we rush to do at the end of the night can be done with the time that you have allowed yourself. Think of it as a readjustment of the time: you would spend less time than this travelling to work, folding laundry, sitting on hold, cooking dinner. This is time for you to prioritise the most important thing you can do for yourself: sleep.

- **Prioritise your sleep.** Earlier, I gave the advice that sleep and water are more important than walking in with a lesson plan, and I would be interested in any narrative that could be formed to contest that. As an NQT, I sat up until ridiculous times of the evening, only prompted to go to sleep by what I lovingly refer to as 'the fear' of when my then three-year-old son would wake up, and exactly how much time that would allow me to sleep. Planning lessons, creating PowerPoints with animated outcomes, laminating resources – these should all be superseded by your sleep. Once I realised that I functioned on a far more effective level with sleep than without, I would toy with a projector ban for the week, or a 'no photocopying' rule. Now, I rarely spend excessive amounts of time mapping out lessons, and focus my energy on subject knowledge and sleep.

---

13.   Wagner, U., Gais, S., Haider, H., Verleger, R. and Born, J. (2004) 'Sleep inspires insight', *Nature* 427 (6972) pp. 352–355.

- **Avoid the snooze button.** Not only does a repeated snooze button send miniature cardio spikes to your heart to start your day (which, on their own, are nothing; but imagine that five times every day for an entire working life), but a study at the University of Surrey also found that it has a profound effect on our cognitive function.[14] If we look at sleep as a reward of marginal gains, not spending 20 minutes every morning dozing is one that will ultimately pay off in the form of our physical health.

- **Avoid those that are sent to sabotage our sleep.** Sleeping tablets, alcohol and decaffeinated options of drinks all present the false promise of a fast track to sleep, but the quality of sleep is compromised in the process. The restorative quality of sleep is lacking when we take these things in an attempt to sleep;[15] and often, it is just masking the problem.

- **If you must...** If you find yourself in a position that you work before bed and your brain isn't going to be at full operation level, consider the tasks that you complete at a particular time of day. I avoid all planning and marking at home and prioritize this for my PPA time, because that is my bread and butter as a teacher: I need that to be the task that I dedicate my full attention towards, irrespective of what is on the to-do list. If I were to work in the evening, I would draft emails that I can scan over the next day before sending (or do other tasks that require less cognitive commitment). You are essentially creating more work if you complete a task that is of a poor standard and then have to redo it the next day.

Instead of aiming for quick fixes, focus on the things that keep you awake, and what you can do to remedy those. If you experience repeated or prolonged insomnia, seek medical attention, as the psychological symptoms that present as a result of sleep deprivation will only exacerbate existing problems.

Yours,

A mother of two tiny sleep thieves who has cried out of tiredness once or twice.

---

14. Santhi, N., Groeger, J. A., Archer, S. N., Gimenez, M., Schlangen, L. J. and Dijk, D. J. (2013) 'Morning sleep inertia in alertness and performance: effect of cognitive domain and white light conditions', *PLOS One* 8 (1) e79688.
15. Mander, B. A., Winer, J. R. and Walker, M. P. (2017) 'Sleep and human aging', *Neuron* 94 (1) pp. 19–36.

'You're in it for the holidays'

Whilst we are all incredibly grateful for our 13 weeks off a year, I know I can talk freely amongst friends in the safety of a teaching book. Extended holidays are hard. Term time operates at top speed, with less sleep, less food, less health, less time, less headspace. But holidays operate at the other end of that spectrum, with extended periods of unregulated time, lacking a sense of purpose, and time to mull over the academic year ahead. Results day looms, with the expectation of being there for students in the midst of our holiday, perhaps so that we never truly relax. The elephant in the room, and one we are most certainly not allowed to complain about, is that holidays can be a real beast to wrangle with. One teacher I spoke to compared it to being on a carousel horse: 'Blink, and you're starting all over again.'

Each term brings its own demands. September is spent getting to grips with new classes and new foci for the year. January to Easter is focused on identifying gaps with higher year groups as much of their content is complete, whilst lower years are finally secure in the routine of expectations and the format of your subject. It is also the darkest part of the year, and known, particularly in February, for being the lowest point of many teachers' mental health. Easter to summer is a torrent of speed, getting examination-ready, completing mocks, and we hurtle towards the end of the year with promises of a break within sight. The psychological processes that come with the ebbs and flows of an academic year are fascinating; it seems that when we are almost at the point of running out of steam, a break is handed to us to rejuvenate – only for it to be over before it's even begun. I remember being incredibly excited about my October half-term break in my PGCE year and chatting about it in the staff room, as I had booked a holiday. I was, at the time, teaching eight hours a week. I asked one of the science teachers what she was planning to do with her holiday, and can all too well remember the jaded look she gave me, as if having to indulge a child. 'Sleep,' she said, and walked off.

But what if the holidays actually act as a hindrance to our wellbeing, rather than a perk of the job? Our holidays have become somewhat void of their purpose, and instead we rest up simply to prepare to go back to work. Running with a high level of epinephrine (also known as adrenaline) and cortisol (which is released in response to produce a longer-term strategy for the body) while attempting to adjust to a slower pace after weeks of operating with such a constant awareness of external stressors will of course have repercussions, both physically and mentally.

Mental fatigue is perhaps the most common side effect of good teaching, I would argue; learning in itself is a tiring exercise, and we exert energy in our dual-edged roles as teachers by both learning and teaching day to day. Our role is reliant upon constantly reflecting and gaining new methodology in order to move forward, and our profession encourages you to move on to new challenges in such a way that you never truly master many elements of the role. The advice that is highlighted repeatedly in articles aimed at a corporate, professional market as a strategic response to mental fatigue? Take some holiday.

> Persistent epinephrine surges can damage blood vessels and arteries, increasing blood pressure and raising the risk of heart attacks or strokes. Elevated cortisol levels create physiological changes that help to replenish the body's energy stores that are depleted during the stress response.[16]

All at once, summer comes around, and so follows articles around the depression and general feeling of uncertainty for teachers during the holidays. Teachers describe feeling lost, or that the first week or two is almost a settling-in period before they truly start to feel more relaxed. Many report feeling ill or coming down with a cold or cough during that initial start to the summer as they readjust to a slower

---

16.   www.bit.ly/2Y9qPFv

pace. Professor Vingerhoets of Tilburg University carried out a study into the link between taking holidays or weekends out of work and then consequently suffering from sickness. Those most likely to suffer from what he later coined 'leisure sickness' were individuals that demonstrated characteristics including 'an inability to adapt to the non-working situation, a high need for achievement, and a high sense of responsibility with respect to work'.[17] Sound familiar? Feel like you fall ill as soon as you stop every year? This is also physiology: the over-creation of hormones means that we will often ignore any indication of illness until we either burn out or make the time to get medical attention – whichever happens first.

The mental impact of school holidays is also an aspect that cannot be overlooked. Historic studies explore concerns around the impact of having an extended period of time away from work and the way that this can cause fluctuations in mental health for teachers. In a YouGov poll from July 2018, over 43% of the 811 teachers asked also stated that they find it increasingly difficult to switch off during the holidays.[18] This mental impact has various sources: some teachers reported anxieties over results day, or just the adaptation from a routine to an expanse of time to fill; some teachers struggled with the lack of interaction with others, both students and colleagues.

What is the hardest thing about the summer holidays?

- 'I feel lost, as though I still need the period 1-period 2 structure to break up the day!'
- 'I make sure that I plan something each week so that there is still a feeling of routine.'
- 'With three children to entertain, I really miss the adult interaction.'
- 'I struggle as I feel like I need to be doing something "amazing" with every day otherwise I'm wasting it.'

---

17. Vingerhoets, A., Van Huijgevoort, M. and Van Heck, G. L. (2002) 'Leisure sickness: a pilot study on its prevalence, phenomenology, and background', *Psychotherapy and Psychosomatics* 71 (6) pp. 311–317.
18. www.bit.ly/2P2VYqi

- 'Just a general air of restlessness. It's either the lack of routine or the fact that I spend the summer term thinking of all the things I can accomplish work-wise in the summer then panic when it arrives.'
- 'I feel listless in the holidays. I know I should be resting but I find it very hard to relax. I can usually do one day of "nothing" but then I want a project and end up putting so much into it that I'm not really using the time to recharge.'
- 'Loneliness: not all our friends and family teach, so we spend an awful lot of time alone. And with days out and activities being expensive, quite often it's hard to fill the days.'
- 'I think it's a feeling of needing to be consistently productive and the pressure for everything I do to appear meaningful or a worthy use of my time. Doing nothing (relaxing) feels like cheating...something that should be hidden. I struggle to switch off from the fast pace of term time.'
- 'I can burn myself out just as much in the summer as in term time because I don't want to "waste time" so I try to keep busy. I'm also alone a lot.'

I want to consider how we use our holiday in such a way to self-regulate our health, so that we close the year with clarity and feel positive about the year ahead. I also want to consider how the school systems can operate with an awareness of these issues and put processes in place to assist with what can feel like unavoidable side effects to being a teacher.

There are two questions of enquiry here for us to consider as a profession. Does the school system as a whole need to get with the times and shift towards a way that actually doesn't just make assumptions of staff with a 'think yourself grateful' approach to the demands of a school year as a working shift pattern? And are there strategic things we can put in place individually or at a local level within schools to support staff and students in an anticipatory way for the mental and physical impact of the summer break? To look at strategic change is a vast cultural shift, I appreciate, but is the 'perk' of holiday a poisoned chalice of teaching as opposed to a perk of the role?

It appears we just need to look at the concept of this gift of time a little differently. Here are some things that help:

- **Expectations can be our biggest enemy.** We put so much expectation on ourselves for the summer break – the things that we will achieve, jobs around the house that have long been neglected, days out that social media informs us everyone else is doing with their children, the INSET day when everyone will run that obligatory question, 'Have a good summer?', and you may not have anything to say. One teacher mentioned the pressure of how they imagined summer versus the reality: 'I feel like the summer holidays are a target to get to and people (me included) think, "Phew, a year is finished – yay!" Then I get here and think, "Now what?"'

  Tackling the beast of six weeks of time can seem relatively daunting, particularly when your monthly income in teaching doesn't include a 'summer of fun' bonus! However, once broken down into segments of time, or when specific tasks are given a regular slot each week, the time can feel less overwhelming. When I had my eldest son, we would draw a circle of 30-mile radius and find six places within that circle that we would visit. It was a nice way to discover new places (as opposed to spending hours on the internet, looking for cost-friendly activities for children) because there was no sense of expectation of what the day should look like, warped by bright-coloured, busy websites with children laughing at what a fantastic childhood memory they had been given for only £59.99 for a family ticket for four (no family tickets for lone-parent families, of course). We were just heading on our own little adventure of discovery. If you are alone, then find a task to be completed each week that will either act as reward or give you a sense of achievement.

- **Find your tribe.** If you feel listless or as though the days are a little empty, set yourself small goals to keep you ticking over. I tend to find that seeking out other teachers is the best way to spend some of the time: it can turn the loneliness and feelings of isolation into a sense that you are in fact on the best skive of the year in the most delicious way, eating lunch at 3 p.m. whilst the rest of the world beaver away in their offices. Gather other local teachers for coffee mornings, or picnics, or whatever takes your fancy. There are several groups on social media to help gather local teachers, or you could even start your own local group. The MTPT Project (Emma Sheppard, founder of MTPT, features in a later chapter) carry out a series of regional networking coffee mornings and events for parent teachers at any stage of their journey, so if you have children to entertain, they are a great shout.

- **Find your summer flow.** If you want to work over summer, that's OK. If you want to watch every box set mentioned to you by non-teacher people in the last nine months when we've been slipping on our pyjamas at 8 and the prospect of a 9 p.m. period drama is perilous to our sleep schedule, that's OK too. Whatever works for you is fine. As Freya O'Dell states, 'our own contentment can only be defined by us', and once you find a balance that leaves you feeling rested, inspired and motivated for the year ahead – and this will most certainly be a learning curve – then you will find yourself closer to your own ideal that works in your context. I tend to find that the longer I teach, the more prepared I am for the summer dip. No one is expecting anything of your summer, other than you. Think of it as a time gift in response to the year that you have had in school. You've earned it.

But what about schools? The responsibility of an employer does stretch into the summer, and schools ought to ensure that the environment that their staff work in supports them in the lead-up the holidays, but also enable them to enjoy and benefit from the holidays, and ultimately, help them to feel adequately prepared for the return to work. There are ways in which schools can address the concerns highlighted, and a number of soft touches that can be put in place to exacerbate common issues that have been broached.

Closure and completion

What do the final weeks of term look like for your staff? Are you currently using the time to acclimatise staff to six weeks of zero productivity by having a 'slow down' period? Instead of less successful strategies for staff to 'slow down' – including teaching the following academic year's timetable (essentially starting September in July), teaching and data drops in the final week – find ways to bring your school community together in a way that isn't overburdening staff in those final weeks. One school reported that the entire school takes a local walk in the final week, visiting different areas of the local community. Other suggestions include plays, discovery workshops where teachers share their interests and hobbies, taster training sessions for the following year, and local volunteer-led drop-in sessions.

Nothing like that happening in your school? Create your own sense of completion. Each year (or at the end of term if it has been a particularly tough one), I always make sure I find the time to send thank-yous to those staff that have really helped me on difficult days or when I have had to make challenging decisions: TAs who have regularly worked with me to motivate students, or premises staff that have had to put up with my endless questions around logistics when planning in-house events for students.

Summer and solitude

Are there any informal groups that staff could create for those interested in maintaining contact with other teachers over the summer? Whenever I broach the subject of daring to admit that summer is difficult, the overarching, consistent message that teachers return to is the struggle with solitude – particularly those teachers that have groups of non-teaching friends or are lone parents, or just teachers that have partners that aren't in education and so struggle to empathise with the negative feelings that can arise from having a prolonged period of time to fill. Is it possible to explore summer meet-ups with particular groups of teachers in your local network? At a time when the only people you bump into are students, retired people and frazzled parents with children, getting together with a group of like-minded teachers would be a welcomed way to spend time during the week. Libraries and local community centres also offer bus trips, days out or meet-up groups, and it may surprise you to find that there are people out there during the day who also like to seek out those with common interests – self-employed, part-time workers, shift workers, etc. – and who find time to run or attend walking groups, running clubs, short-term arts classes, craft meet-ups, book clubs, orchestras, dramatics clubs, and everything in between. If you can't find one that suits, why not start your own? Drag a sympathetic friend to come along to the first few and keep you company (this is an MTPT Project coffee morning favourite strategy) and you may create an entire network as a result.

Anticipations and anxieties

How is gained time used to prepare staff for the year ahead? Sam Strickland's interview (later on in the book) demonstrates an engrained, productive approach to utilising staff time in those final weeks in a way that not only benefits the school but also alleviates staff anxieties around planning and preparation through department away days where the department is covered as a standard expectation, and the department staff plan collaboratively to resource for the following year. This enables staff to feel a sense of accomplishment and peace of mind (before they leave for the six-week break) that they are fully informed for the first few months. It can be incredibly disheartening to leave in the final days of term with a draft timetable and a rough outline of what is being taught for the next term, but with very little preparation beyond that. Not only does it lead with the expectation that staff should plan over the summer break, or the first few days of the new term (dependent upon time given at INSET, of course), but it leaves staff with a sense of uncertainty rather than the ability to leave next year's schedule in their classroom (safe in the knowledge of what they are to teach the following year), close the door and rest that part of their mind until they return. Senior leadership can encourage a culture of restful minds by enquiring into the extent to which their staff have been equipped to leave work at work. Has time been provided to departmental leaders to allocate to staff for collaborative planning or clearing rooms? Can administration staff be freed up using the timetable reduction from year groups leaving or trip days in order to refresh display walls so that teachers have a blank slate rather than a to-do list for the first day back? Could student lists and the relevant data be printed centrally for staff to include in planners for when the new year begins? Are there any policies that could be shared for staff to read for the next academic year in the time available before summer?

In the same way, as summer comes to a close, how can school leaders take the opportunity to create a supportive school culture?

Jennifer Webb, assistant headteacher and author of *How to Teach English Literature: Overcoming Cultural Poverty*, shares her school's approach to equipping staff at the start of the year for the hotspots to come:

❝ In September, all of our staff receive a brown paper bag stuffed with goodies as a welcome back. There is nothing expensive or fancy in there: chocolate, hand sanitiser gel, tissues, tea bags, a teaspoon, post-it notes, highlighters, pens, an invitation to staff drinks on the first Friday after work. This year, our academy trust also donated some school-branded travel mugs for staff, and little pin badges of our logo for everyone. We also put in anything which might be helpful in navigating the year, such as timings of the new school day, lists of important offices and phone numbers, and a list of which pastoral staff are assigned to each year group.

Every single member of staff gets one of these, from the principal to the attendance officers. It is really important that everyone feels equally valued, and that they are all a team from the outset, regardless of their role. Staff really like the packs – they don't seem to mind that they are super cheap to put together – it's the time, thought and humour which goes into them that counts. There is something about giving every single person their own teaspoon which says, 'I understand that sometimes it's the little things which make your day difficult. Here's a solution to one of those little things.'

- -

'You only work 9–3, Monday to Friday'

The school calendar makes efficient use of staff time. What other profession do you know that counts up their working hours at the start of the year, concocting entire spreadsheets to measure it out as work gets underway? But we all know that this document is propaganda and doesn't speak for the extra hours teachers give. Alongside the more official direction of time – open evenings, parents' evenings, twilight CPD, meetings – there are fluctuations to our working year that result in working hours which tip the scale.

Martyn Reah, as part of the #teacher5aday movement stipulated a #lessthan50 hashtag, encouraging teachers to work less than 50 hours a week. It's concerning that we need to create an initiative to get under 50, but even more concerning is the fact that teachers in response gave the fluctuations of late-night INSET and school events as a reasonable excuse to exceed the hour count. The lure of summer acts as more than a hefty perk, but if we send the message that in fact 50 hours a week is a reasonable expectation in between, I'm not sure it makes for a fitting retention campaign.

If teachers are our greatest resource, time is a teacher's most useful commodity. If we want to ensure longevity in what we do, there needs to be a consideration of two strains: one, how time is being used in a way which could be avoided; and two, how we can spend that time in more meaningful ways.

Using time

If we think of time as a commodity in schools, how are we balancing the books?

- Assume a classroom teacher's day rate of £150.
- Reduce to approximately £25 an hour, and then to £6.25 for 15 minutes.
- Let's say that a school delivers two briefings a week, lasting 15 minutes in total. One is necessary and involves key members of staff to share the schedule for the week, any key messages and safeguarding concerns about individual pupils. The second is delivered because 'that's the way it has always been done' and doesn't seem to have the same impact, tone or pace as the other meeting, which feels far more productive for staff messages.
- 100 teachers attend both meetings, totalling over £600, which is an incredibly expensive way to waste time.
- Multiply that one wasted meeting by 39 weeks of the academic year, and you're looking at almost 10 hours, and over £12,000.
- Still want to carry out a meeting because of tradition?

Imagine the different ways in which this time could be spent utilising staff through teaching development. One hundred teachers and ten hours a year could be the foundation for an established CPD programme, or focus groups with children, or a mentoring programme. Not only would it be putting school money to a really precise, well-thought-out alternative provision, but these actions would re-engage people to develop in a job that they are so keen to fall in love with all over again.

Will Smith, CEO of Greenshaw Learning Trust, states that in his schools there are,

> *no meetings. We're just talking about professional development. The only time we come together is to talk about improving. We don't come together to sort out rooming and to sort out cover and supply and ordering books, all of which are important, they can be done elsewhere. We come together to talk about professional development.*[19]

How can we ensure that the times we bring people together feel purposeful?

- **Is this meeting necessary or habitual?** The purpose of the meeting should be clear to all who attend before they walk into the room. All attendees should receive agendas for meetings at least 48 hours in advance so that they can take the time to consider their place in the meeting. If they do have ideas to share or concerns they want to raise, the agenda will let them know when they will have an opportunity to do so. Remember, we are easing the uncertainty of these situations in order to give staff a sense of relief about what to expect. Furthermore, if you have staff with part-time working arrangements, what provision is there for them to access detailed accounts of meeting discussions, agendas and minutes? If you have a flexible working arrangement, it can be quite infuriating to spend the first

---

19. www.bit.ly/34Qd2qg

day of your working week trundling around the building, trying to find out what happened at missed meetings.

- **Is the meeting agenda clear and timed?** The meeting agenda should make clear who is leading which section of the meeting, with the time allocated to each element. This ensures that people's expectations are managed accordingly. Ideally, different members in attendance should lead different sections of the meeting, as it affirms why they are there: to be heard. It is often effective to start with any other business (AOB) as opposed to closing the meeting with it; it ensures that those not as actively involved with the original agenda still have an opportunity to raise anything they consider to be of note.

- **Is it solution driven?** How many meetings have you attended with a lot of talk but without any concrete action points by the end? Use the timings provided on the agenda as a guide; all contributions should have a clear action point attached to them. Invite contributions from those that are not forthcoming. It is those people whose opinions will be most valuable, as they could be silent because they are hesitant to be honest, or they have listened to others and can provide a different perspective.

- **Are you leaving admin at the door?** A meeting where teachers are giving up their time should be focused upon teaching and learning, not passing around the ESPO catalogue. It's the most expensive way to order stationery and does not require a meeting.

- **Are you finishing on time?** The chatters can stay behind, should they wish, but be clear that the meeting has ended for those that want to leave. Send minutes out promptly (delegate minuting to someone in attendance who can type as everyone discusses so that this is not a job leftover post meeting).

- **Are you just repeating yourself?** If it's been on an email, you don't need to reiterate it. If you are following up an action, or something that is past deadline, then by all means use meeting time to do so – but be careful not to use the time to chase people for a deadline that's yet to pass because it's on your mind. In a similar strand, ensure everyone present needs to know what is being shared. For instance, does Jackie need to talk about her year 10 non-attending students with everyone present? Does Colin need to share a year 8 student's personal circumstances and how it's left a hole in his data? Probably not.

- **Are you saying thank-you?** Thank everyone for contributing and attending. And for the love of God, bring cake.

The inconsistency of the whole-school briefing

The other way that meeting time is sometimes poorly spent is on whole-staff meetings or briefings. In keeping with school tradition, most schools have a whole-staff meeting once a week to share information, allow members of staff to address the whole staff with any news or updates, and it also provides an opportunity to thank staff for particular successes over the course of the week. Over 3000 teachers responded to a Twitter poll to share their school's approach, and not only did this variety offer great insight, but it showed that the ways in which information was disseminated differed massively. The majority (62%) had a weekly briefing, but several others reported on a multitude of ways that schools communicated with them. What was particularly fascinating was the disparity of time usage. For some, a 15-minute meeting every day; for others, a weekly or monthly meeting of no more than 5 minutes.

What does your meeting time look like in school?

- 'I worked in a school once where we had a briefing every morning. It was awful – especially as the first thing Head/SLT said was, "Welcome to x-day," whichever day it was. Felt patronising: I don't need to be welcomed to the day; just get on with it.'
- 'Every morning, and it's noted who misses it as well.'
- 'Weekly before school but often cancelled at the last minute – by email at the moment we're walking from our classrooms to the staffroom...'
- 'Did a brief stint as executive head of a school that didn't have daily meetings. Really missed seeing everyone at the start of each day. One morning the fire alarm went off by mistake and it was so lovely to see everyone.'

- 'On Friday mornings, we read through the things on the Google calendar. These are also written on the board.'
- 'We also have a whiteboard that details the upcoming fortnight up in the staffroom, and then meet Wednesdays after school for staff meetings.'
- 'Not in directed time.'
- 'Twice per week at break time.'
- 'Twice a week, I think. Both before school, but on days I don't work.'

Briefings differ significantly from meetings because they are usually an opportunity for the leadership team to convey key messages and for staff to share information for the week ahead. When is it key to bring a whole staff body together? Is it important that we recognise ourselves as part of a collective with a common interest? Certainly.Linda Emmett, in her interview with Niall Alcock,[20] explains that meeting on this level with staff is key to driving any sort of change:

> *[Tell] them that they need to tell us what's going right and what needs to improve. They need to be able to tell us if there's anything that needs to change in the school. Otherwise, the school wouldn't have transformed so quickly. If we can tell staff it's OK to speak up when things aren't OK, then that's really, really important.*

I would agree: if we consider the relationships that we build with other staff through the small connections that we are able to make, staff briefings are essential to feeling that sense of collective purpose. However, it needs to hold value, and it needs to feel unobstructive to the work, because the work is paramount. You cannot hold staff to ransom through the exasperating process of reminders of deadlines when it is meeting time that keeps them from completing the task about to expire. However, it is also frustrating as a part-time member of staff to feel as though you are on the back foot when in work,

---

20. www.bit.ly/2r83CHT

missing vital information or having to find extra pockets of time to catch up on minutes for meetings that you will never be able to make. A balance is essential.

Reviewing all of the responses to that poll, it is clear that meetings need to fit within the context of the school, and with what staff feel that they need: some reported very few meetings, and this felt sufficient; some reported daily meetings and felt that this was necessary. Dean Lewis, a teacher at a pupil referral unit (PRU), shared that he attended a debrief meeting every day after school, but that it was required because of the nature of the school:

> *The daily briefings and debriefs are essential to working in a PRU. Management and staff can update everyone with any message or contact with parents/ carers or multi agency that might provide insight into pupils, triggers etc. All briefings are recorded and, where appropriate, actions for specific staff included.*

In this particular context, decompression after a day of what could be incredibly challenging behaviour and the mental impact of that means that staff need an outlet to discuss the effect upon them, maybe professionally but also personally. By sharing the events of the day, we learn to rationalise and self-regulate our reactions, and become reflective through this process.[21]

The spending of a time budget – in the same way that we examined marking allocation minute by minute and time within our curriculum design to account for responsive teaching – is absolutely paramount to fit the setting for which it is designed.

Fascinatingly, two senior leaders approached the topic from entirely different viewpoints:

---

21. For a really interesting read that gives an insightful start to an exploration of the power of talking to others, see Stiles, W. B. (1987) 'I have to talk to somebody' in Derlega, V. J. and Berg, J. H. (eds) *Self-disclosure: theory, research and therapy*. Boston, MA: Springer, pp. 257–282.

How does your school hold whole-school briefing meetings?[22]

❝ **Peter Richardson:** Wow. I must be missing something here but I really don't see the need for one. Online calendar and emails. Unless there is something significant going on (which can wait until weekly staff meetings), why take up previous time of whole staff?

❝ **Clare Sealy:** Daily before school. Five minutes tops. Nice bonding experience apart from anything else. People won't read their emails until after school or maybe a day or so. And it's nice to see each other. We're a very small team though.

What particularly interests me is Clare's final comment about the size of the school. How can we create a culture around whole-staff briefings so that all schools feel 'small' and we can enrich our schools with the feel of a community, irrespective of size?

As a senior leader, consider these questions:

- Is the duration of the briefing essential to what is being communicated? Is there an expectation of a time duration based upon the mantra of 'It's directed time'?
- Is the information merited for a briefing, or could it be communicated in a more efficient way? For example, if the same updates are being repeated, then it could be included in a workspace calendar, for example.
- If the entire briefing is actually just telling people things and talking at them rather than providing a forum for them, does that information really require a briefing? Often, these types of meetings are justified with 'People won't read emails' or 'People won't get the message'; but if it is important, I would argue that it needs a written reminder rather than a rushed meeting in the morning when people's minds are elsewhere. If it is a matter that will result in questions, it deserves a full meeting.

---

22. www.bit.ly/3a4spOK

What can schools do to value time?

- **Time cost:** Time cost your own working week using the resources provided. This will give you a really objective outline of how you are spending your time, and how high the impact is of that time being spent. Consider how many hours are required to carry out your role versus how many hours are available to you. Are assessments being time costed? Calculate what you are asking staff to do in the time that's been given to them.[23] For a guide to keeping track of the time cost of your workload, see the appendix.

- **Timing:** Consider your school calendar in a way that is thoughtful to staff first and foremost. One school provided parents' evenings on a Thursday to ensure it was not tiring for staff, but also didn't operate a single parents' evening until the spring term. This allowed staff to get to know their classes, but also to get to grips with duties and workload in those longer terms through the autumn and winter. A simple but incredibly impactful logistical measure. In the same vein, when we know the traditional dips of the academic year, what time-constrained events are put into November or February, and how can this be altered or improved, so that staff feel like they have the capacity to contribute?

- **Time sequencing:** when putting a calendar together, there needs to be a sense of mindfulness as to why things are placed in the sequence, frequency or placement that they are. Consider the placement of parents' evenings in accordance with data drops: are teachers being put in a position to have nonsensical conversations with parents around outdated data?

'You are always on an INSET day'

When sharing the frustrations that come from wasted time in schools, teachers will say that the way INSET is utilised infuriates them. Introduced in 1988 by Conservative education secretary Kenneth Baker, the five additional working days for teachers were intended as a provision for training and sharing important information regarding

---

23. www.bit.ly/2LjLvFJ

the school systems. Coupled with the introduction of the national curriculum, INSET days were given as 'a luxury most professionals don't get'.[24] However, the way in which this time is used is fantastically open to interpretation, without the guidance of a particular framework or remit for the requirements: 'They were originally called Baker Days, which soon became B-Days, on the basis that school managements didn't know what they were or how to use them.'[25]

A protected element of our professional development time that cannot be lost to other duties, INSET is one of the most treasured ways of bringing a school together to develop the sense of community that we know is so instrumental to building a set of shared values through professional development.

INSET, a peculiarity in every school, has a mixed reputation with teachers for its effectiveness and the way the time is divided up across the year. Traditionally – and you may recognise this model in your school – INSET is spent with two days at the start of the year to set up key messages for the year ahead, perhaps sharing results and using the opportunity of all staff being in one place to share successes and the testament that such results are down to the staff that supported students to attain them. Thus follows a day of training run by an external consultant, a teaching leader in a previous life that wants to share a range of tools that will help with a particular teaching and learning strategy. The pedagogic thread that runs in the backdrop of the training perhaps lacks relevance to the school setting or all subjects in attendance, but it feels like pretty light work and you just have to sit and listen, right? Looking around, you see people checking their phones, writing out seating plans, and the maths teacher next to you has a rather intricate doodle in development. Again, I'll refer back to my cost analysis – only this time, scale up the price.

Whilst there are several whole-school CPD training programmes on offer that give a detailed opportunity to reconsider the knowledge

---

24. www.bit.ly/2Yi6SMX
25. www.bit.ly/33QkVuw

and depth of curriculum planning, or expand on a practical implication of cognitive science, that is not the INSET I recall in my example. Examples from teachers around the poor use of time on INSET days include (and I sincerely hope that you are not nodding your head in agreement):

What have your previous INSET days involved?

❝ **@Lauratsabet:** Dressing another member of staff in newspaper (actually happened)

❝ **@Strickomaster:** The best one I ever endured was clapping and singing the words 'management' and 'leadership' with a group of middle leaders. The Head at the time walked in and looked embarrassed.

❝ **@MaverickGrammarian:** 4-6pm session on 'wellbeing'... that included trying fruit tea, yoga and colouring in mandalas. My comment that a much better thing for my well-being would be to have gone home at 3.20pm was not well received by SLT.

❝ **@ChemMcDougall:** We've also been asked to massage each other's eyebrows as a way to relieve tension (I wasn't at all tense until I was asked to massage eyebrows!)

❝ **@NotoffPineapple:** At a previous school, we had a bouncer come in and explain how to manage behaviour. Once of his pearls of wisdom was to 'get in a cussing match' with students, as they wouldn't know how to respond, apparently.

❝ **@LPLFlippedEng:** The one where we had to visualise our Happy Place, then step into it. The Growth Mindset one. The Thinking Hats one. So many... Austin's flaming butterfly... I need to go and lie down.

❝ **@TeachEnglishHOD:** ...Then NEVER hear anything else again based on ideas...until the following September when we are asking to repeat activity for same issues that were fighting fought AGAIN rather than prevented

❝ **@katyjvella:** Every department sits and watches their head of department fill in a curriculum intent document – that really only one person could do – that could have been done beforehand and that we all had to 'pretend' to have input on. 1.5 hours of my life I'll never get back.

Are we using these five days in the best possible capacity? Can we honestly say that bringing a team together so that they then have to spend the day finding camaraderie in mutual despair is the best use of professionals' time? If our system of CPD was particularly flawless or efficient, then we wouldn't see the rise of movements such as ResearchED, a meeting of minds between educational researchers and teachers. As the shape of education changes and the landscape broadens, should we look to use these days in a way that 'fits' better with what we want to know?

The fundamental flaw with whole-school training is that it assumes that we are all at a similar standpoint when it comes to what we need to know and how we wish to develop. It's like planning a lesson where everyone's knowledge is exactly the same: categorically impossible, and pretty poor practice on our part as teachers. Administration work, members of staff in positions of responsibility sharing what they do or want to do in the year ahead, or even the whole-school display of a lunch duty rota – these are not ways in which we as professionals can make the best use of this time in a manner that hands over the independent direction of professional development to staff and provides them with the autonomy that they need to carry out their roles. By using time in a way that means execution of ideas is well meaning and well structured, with well-actioned impact so we know that what we are doing is effective and satisfying, we can start to feel as though time has been spent well.

CPD that nurtures staff

Some suggestions and studies of how CPD is being used in a way that drives staff forward raised the following questions:

- How can CPD support individual staff development in a way that is truly meaningful?
- Does CPD need to be a one-size-fits-all in order to make an impact?

- How is CPD revisited and reviewed at a later point to evaluate its impact – not that staff have made use of it to measure their accountability, but that the CPD itself was of use?
- How can we ensure that we spend CPD time so that it is the best use of time, at the right time?

Take the metaphor of CPD as a dress. I've rolled in a dress as everyone's answer to their wardrobe requirements for the year. It has a lace frill, is fitted for flattery and a midi length, for all those that appreciate the schoolteacher's struggle with extraordinary hem lengths that get passed off as 'workwear'. But June doesn't like dresses, and could not be less engaged with the idea. She's already on her phone, checking through Facebook. And Lydia bought the perfect dress last week, because after 20 years of intensive dress shopping, she knows what makes a good dress already, thank you very much. And Serena is not even sure what makes a good dress so doesn't want to air her views on it. And Moira – Moira has tried dresses and they're really not the way she wants to live her life.

Can we honestly present something to a whole staff body with the caveat of 'You all need this because the school needs this' and expect not to be met with a little professional withdrawal? In my jobs outside of teaching, training took place at the start of the role, then was revisited according to the needs of that individual. Whole-staff training was non-existent, saved only for major update messages from the organisation that would be subject to staff consultation: a change to working hours, or major policy. If we want to upskill staff to the point that they want to stay, can we really be so insulting to professionals as stating, 'You all need the same thing'?

CPD that works

There is a great deal of fantastic practice going on inside schools that we could learn from, particularly if we want to retain staff through training them to be experts in their field. Staff don't resent this time: their frustration stems from disappointment that the time often doesn't live up to their hopeful expectations. How we shift to productive, meaningful INSET not only demonstrates to staff their value and their place in school improvement, but also sets up the stall for the year ahead: 'These are the great things we can achieve, and we would really like to bring you along to help us achieve them.' If we look to serve our staff, CPD is one of the most purposeful ways to do just that.

Professional development should aim primarily to support staff with their particular focus at that time. One school I spoke with provided a day for staff to visit another school where their practice aligned to the member of staff's particular development points. A Google document was then set up for that member of staff to jot some quick takeaways from the day to share with the whole school body, and the document became a bank of reading for staff: time-efficient and easy to dip into for reflections later in the year. Other great examples included funding staff to attend conferences around research-informed practice or opening up their own doors to share best practice with other members of staff. As an exemplary way of making the most of in-house CPD, Hannah Wilson upskilled her staff by training and empowering them to open up their CPD programme to neighbouring schools. Taking a 'lean-in' approach is also mentioned frequently by headteacher Jeremy Hannay as a demonstrative way of opening your doors to other schools to say, 'We've not perfected it, but we would love to share what we do, and see what we could learn from you in return.'

CPD takes two approaches if we consider the definition and distil it further: subject-specific professional development, which is paramount to improving our practice within the classroom, and our pedagogical approach. It is through these two aspects of CPD that we can make steps to improve and look forward to what could be done differently – better. We can all get better – always.

We are experts
One model is subject-specific training that develops our ethos to be experts of our specialism. It is this very mantra that formed

the thinking behind Litdrive CPD events. The regional events run by Litdrive work to fill a gap for CPD where English teachers lack an outlet to fill their subject knowledge but also need to make use of the extensive subject knowledge that is already in existence in schools, but not necessarily tapped into as a resource. We have so many incredible experienced English teachers, but when you move schools, or change exam specification, it can mean getting to grips with a text that you have never taught – even a decade into your career. Litdrive CPD uses the model of teaching teachers around specific texts or genres, using modelled strategy, annotations of texts or lecture-style sessions around character, plot or literary theory to really lift the quality of subject knowledge around a text. Experts deliver a series of mini sessions that focus on underpinning the knowledge required to teach a text well. Feedback from teachers is very positive, with one stating, 'After 25 years of teaching, it's great to find something new to challenge and inspire.' If we are going to hold up knowledge of our specialism as central to moving teachers from proficient to expert, then we need to create opportunities for staff to spend time in schools harnessing the components of their subject.

This could involve visiting other school departments or delivering a series of mini lectures within the faculty for others to glean information from. It could be signing the team up to a subject association or digest for the subject in question and using department meeting time to share this information. If we are using the curriculum as a fluid document, we must treat staff to the same process of enrichment to ensure they are aptly prepared using the time available.

Finally, moderation meetings within schools are incredibly powerful in ensuring that we don't leave the less experienced teacher to feel that they are only one step ahead of the student. That's important: if we are not passing knowledge to the next generation of teachers, and wearing it like a badge of honour, what narrative are we passing to those teachers in classrooms after us? The process of moderating is another exercise that has been manipulated over time to take place for box ticking and not genuinely developing staff knowledge, and so I would advise a short, one-exemplar discussion so that staff can work towards being completely confident in their craft: 'What does a grade 9 look like? How do I know? How can I use this in my teaching to ensure I teach to this specific standard of understanding?'

Dialogue as development

Another model of CPD in action that breathes trust and autonomy for a teacher over their own development is a structured coaching model. With many schools now utilising coaching programmes as a really effective way to provide a tailored use of CPD time for staff, coaching is not a new or revolutionary idea, but it does move schools away from this blanket approach to CPD that could perhaps be far better executed. Through a refined programme that reduces large group CPD, the focus becomes far more specific to the needs of the individual and encourages dialogue that feels valuable to them and their own personal journey. Short, focused and regular discussions that centre around the individual can really empower that member of staff in developing practice and considering the steps in their career, whatever that may look like. If we want to fast track everyone at a hurtling speed towards the same roles, towards the funnel neck of senior leadership, then we are taking a blinkered approach when it comes to the development of people.

Coaching enables teachers to do less, but do it better, by being goal focused and not trying to embed large, unmanageable change into their practice – something that a less experienced member of staff may appreciate when the start of a teaching career feels rather overwhelming, and the complexity of teaching can often mean that areas of focus become quite vast. In the same way, a more experienced teacher may have a more refined idea of the type of teaching they want to adopt in their classroom but want support in doing so. It may be that they have become less reflective; in which case, the coaching process can support with a sense of self-distancing so we can see how and where we can improve. Coaching is able to provide staff with a far more personal, bespoke approach to what they want to do with their career, and how exactly to go about it.

- -

Kathrine Mortimore, lead practitioner for English at Torquay Academy, explains how to reduce the workload of teachers using a coaching model, and how her school provides a brilliant outline of the allocation of CPD time in a more effective way for teachers, taking a research-informed approach to focus on the process of improvement through dialogue, and not endless reams of paperwork with a one-time-use shelf life:

❝ Coaching has had a far greater impact than I think anyone could have envisioned back in 2015 when our CPD model was launched at Torquay Academy. It has been such a powerful vehicle for change within the school. As a team of coaches over the years, we have gained a valuable insight into the strengths and weaknesses of teaching and learning at any given moment across an academic year. Initially, we needed to tackle calm and silent starts to lessons, eliminate low-level disruption and create consistency across the school. As time moved on and behaviour improved, we found that some students were 'passively non-compliant' – sitting silently and seemingly well behaved, but actually following a minority of instructions and getting little work down on paper. Our twilight training sessions responded to these changing needs, and coaching could then reinforce that focus in an effectively cyclical process of school improvement.

Alongside the obvious benefits to teaching and learning and the improvements to staff wellbeing this brings, there are also the cultural benefits that are more difficult to even pin down, much less measure. The relationships that staff have – not just within departments but also across the school – are more positive than I have experienced elsewhere. The cross-departmental coaching encourages dialogue between departments, which aids communication and empathy. So many lessons are seen and discussed on such a regular basis, it stands to reason that the number of anecdotal conversations held across the school increases. We can all appreciate the challenges faced by our colleagues in different parts of the school and celebrate their successes as we see the small but significant wins that are achieved on a day-to-day basis.

Finally, our children see the regular and supportive presence of other members of staff in their lessons. Rather than the tense and forced atmosphere which often results from a rare performance management observation, our children see that our teachers often have other members of staff dropping in to see how a lesson is progressing. In previous schools I've worked in, there was a definite sense that you as a teacher were alone – and your ability to manage a class rested solely on your own resources. Looking back, the students definitely knew this, and the most vulnerable members of staff suffered as a result.

Whilst it took a significant investment of time and resources to implement, I firmly believe that if there is one thing school leaders can do to improve staff wellbeing, it is to replace one-off performance-management observations with coaching. It is heartening to see how many schools are already heading in this direction.

- -

Our mental and physical state are not fixed; there are ebbs and flows to both. At a starting point, caring for ourselves is difficult because it requires regular, conscientious care and, of course, time to do it. To equip ourselves for the nature of teaching, some of the factors outlined as unavoidable are going to make a significant impact upon our mental and physical health, should we let them. Simply being aware of the effect of such factors is in itself a resolute step in caring for ourselves. It is only when we start to inform and equip ourselves with the knowledge we need to look after ourselves that we are in a position to teach effectively in schools.

Time is one of our most precious commodities in teaching; coupled with teaching itself, it defines the value of what we do, and how we spend our time can be an expensive affair. So, as we add up colour photocopying, or make cuts to stationery budgets in schools, perhaps it would be advisable for school leaders and budget holders to consider the cost implications of how we use staff within schools. If staff aren't making it to duty points, there's a reason for that. If staff are struggling to teach lessons promptly and to their full degree because placement between two lessons is a ten-minute walk, that needs to be accounted for. Teachers' time to prepare of a morning is possibly the most valuable part of their day (we all know the sharpened elbows for the photocopier queues all too well) and so it is often not the time duration of the meeting, but what it is taking that teacher away from that perpetuates the issue. What can be an incredibly small amendment on a strategic level will make a monumental difference to staff and holding time as key is our starting step to greatness.

Martyn Reah (deputy head of Eggars School in Alton, Hampshire, and founder of #teacher5aday) cultivated an idea that grew into a movement around the world, supporting teachers during both term time and the holidays to ensure that they keep their mental health – well, healthy.

#teacher5aday started as a small collection of teachers, sharing initiatives and ideas that they used when they were aware of crisis triggers, or as a way of maintaining positive mental health. What started as a grassroots whisper across social media has spread to a strong, established community across the world of teachers connecting in their common belief in the importance of looking after themselves and others. I spoke to Martyn about the concept of #teacher5aday, and wanted to get to the mechanics of whether this would be a pragmatic response for schools to implement to support their staff, or even for individuals looking for a structured approach to their workload with mental wellness at the forefront.

Talk us through the concept behind #teacher5aday.
I was listening to Mark Healey, a school leader, talk about the proposal (which we now know to be heavily embedded in evidence) that happy staff mean happy students. The presentation was based in part on the New Economics Foundation report *Five Ways to Wellbeing* (2008)[26] written by Sam Thompson, Jody Aked, Nic Marks and Corrina Cordon. I recognised how fundamentally powerful these five aspects of mental health regulation could be in maintaining a healthy balance between work and rest for teachers.

#teacher5aday consists of five components that outline ways in which we can all ensure that we look after our mental wellbeing. The five aspects consider

---

26. www.bit.ly/2FNxc9s

the impact of human connection, exercise, observing the world around us, developing ourselves and giving back to the community as key areas of focus for us to ensure we look after our mental health and avoid common issues that can trigger poor mental health, such as isolation and loneliness, or a sense of feeling overwhelmed.

What explicit impact have you seen as a result?

The anecdotal evidence and connections that have been made by teachers speak for themselves. Thousands of teachers have taken on the initiative, sharing their experiences via social media, and supporting one another through discussions, collaborations and meet-ups. As a result, the #teacher5aday community features a monthly focus, run by a range of hosts, and has a number of spin-offs that members have driven – such as #teacher5adaycook, #teacher5adaysketch and #teacher5adayrun – where the almost 7000 members can share their downtime pastimes and enjoy connecting with people who share their passions.

#teacher5aday has prompted fundamentally vital conversations about wellbeing in the workplace, and how we must take responsibility for our own mental health and the mental health of others to create healthy, happy employees who are fulfilled both inside and outside of work. Teaching as a profession is under a great deal of stress, with concerning retention rates in areas of the UK and the demands of school roles known to be incredibly high pressure. The #teacher5aday initiative has not only made great change to alleviate this but has helped to change the climate of schools everywhere, in a way that promotes wellbeing beyond the tokenistic qualities of previous initiatives that cost more money and make little impact.

How does it work?

There are five elements to #teacher5aday as a way of self-regulating your mental care.

Connect (#connect)

- Collaborate with others in your department, in other departments or within your network. Build a support system that you can give to and use when you need other perspectives on ideas or situations.

- Attend a networking event to help you connect with others locally and nationally.
- Set up a club or group at work where you meet with a like-minded cause: cake, books, chess! Connecting with others that share your interests is a really healthy way to disconnect from stress and maintain mental wealth.

Be active (#exercise)

- Get off the bus one stop early and walk the final stretch.
- Go for a walk before or after work or at lunchtime – even if it's just around the car park!
- Set up a work-based sporting activity like a work football or netball team.

Take notice (#notice)

- Keep a photo journal.
- Go for a phoneless walk or run and notice your surroundings.
- Use a meditation app (Calm or Headspace are just two examples, both free for teachers!) to spend a quiet three minutes.

Keep learning (#learn)

- Write creatively, at the same time every day for five minutes.
- Learn how to blog and share your stories.
- Find a local course that inspires you or check out organisations like FutureLearn that offer free online courses in collaboration with universities around the world.

Give (#volunteer)

- Offer skills out to people free of charge – for example, cooking, creating audiobooks, proofreading or making cakes.
- Start a volunteering initiative in your local workplace.
- Volunteer regularly in the wider community.

Why do you think wellbeing has become such a prominent topic in education recently?

It is a topic that is really prevalent in lots of other sectors but has become equally so in many schools as a result of Ofsted's focus on wellbeing, but it's being done inconsistently. Some schools have made significant changes; but in a range of settings, people don't seem to register that there is a different way of operating. Young, inexperienced or poorly mentored leaders come into educational leadership after an alarmingly short time in schools, and they don't have any (or only limited) understanding of what effective leadership looks like. Fast-track promotion leads to holes of exposure where the experience isn't there. Young heads can also be easily manipulated by trust leaders, governors etc. to deliver performance strategy that is actually just overloading staff.

We have caught up with other sectors in a range of ways: flex working, working conditions, valuing staff, providing opportunities to perform to high standards of care. The previous mantra of schools across the board was 'work hard and work huge hours – and that's how you succeed'; thankfully, this is starting to erode and some schools are no longer measuring their success against a performance table. The holistic development of staff is really important; teachers are adaptable, but there is a point where enough is enough.

One of the nicest things to have come of #teacher5aday was that people have come together and supported one another in the absence of decent systems in school. If social media is used properly, there is a huge community of people waiting to help others. The idea of belonging to a community and the value of that collective voice is what will help to drive change.

Wellbeing has become tokenistic on two levels: one, as a tick box and not really backed up with ways to make a dent in workload at classroom level; and also used as a badge to get out of things – mental health become a PE note. But it's not fluffy, and you simply have to eliminate stuff in schools to put new stuff in – that is key.

What is it about the nature of teaching that means it causes such stress? Is it really just external agencies at play? What individual ownership can we take of this?
There are classroom-based stresses – communication, behaviour, targets, expectations, the responsibility for students' futures – but so much stuff that is uncontrollable: Ofsted as a big stick, grades, a lack of support, not feeling good enough in what you're doing, the school ethos. Ultimately, good enough is good enough, but it can take years to come to that realisation, and sometimes it's only possible when surrounded by people that practise it in their everyday.

What makes the teaching calendar a key stress indicator?
The first few years of teaching are an emotional journey. Until you get well

versed, and even after several years, there are certain times of the year that heighten anxiety and stress. The time period from fireworks to daffodils is also difficult in schools. The impact of behaviour in schools during winter is immense. Teacher performance during this time needs to be incredible on students' behalf due to examination preparation and the impact that will have, but teachers' stress around that will feed the children's stress as well. Christmas also brings a lot of anxiety to teachers and students; and as a school community, we soak that up. Can we anticipate that fluctuation and try to combat it? Maybe. We need to try to manage the workload that happens in those months and minimise it if we can. Things like having a well-organised calendar are second only to a brilliant timetable. When are your parents' evenings? Have you provided time for a job well done or only enough for a job half done? Reduce the load on staff to ease pressure points. Space out significant events not only to save your teaching body's energy but also give time to do the prep work needed for those events. Recognise that you can't do it all – you need to get rid of stuff to add it. What can we do without? What is there for no other reason than the fact that it has always been there?

We need to operate on three- to five-year improvement plans that aren't just reactive to what's happening, that don't get distracted by headlines. Making an impact by considering improvement of outcomes and how we can support that – that is an effective culture for workload. You need to work on a project for an extended period to see the fruits of your labour, and good schools will have staff running projects that have longevity, and are thoughtful responses to their environments, instead of knee-jerk reactions.

Do you think there is a place for schools to adapt our working year to ease workload stress points? What would that look like and do you have any examples of this in action within schools?
Yes! We have control and autonomy. Reducing data drops to two a year; joint planning with increased department time; remove written reports; make feedback policy bespoke to departments; supportive behaviour systems – for teachers as well as students; effective email communications with nothing sent out at weekends; or finding a way to take frequent litmus tests to see how staff are. Defuse the pressure around outcomes and don't use Ofsted as a

scaremonger or the starting point for your reason why; your results come from your effort, not because Ofsted say so.

REFLECT

As a leader:

- Consider your school setting. What would you say are the three strengths of your school in accommodating and anticipating the oddities of teaching that this chapter discusses? It could be as simple as providing breakfast in winter months, free tea and coffee, or staff sports on a Friday. Perhaps you can find a more strategic example.
- What do you hope to work towards to add to this list? Again, three key examples. Are there aspects of the year that show a distinct lack of provision currently?
- If you were to ask your most dissatisfied member of staff how they feel supported at pressure points of the year, would do you imagine that they would say?
- How could you use this feedback in a positive way?

As a teacher:

- How do you currently prepare yourself for the various pressure points of the year?
- How does your school currently support you to do this? Consider when your timetable and school calendar are shared and the method used, or perhaps how timescales for completion of assessment work are structured.
- How could you contribute to driving a more solution-focused ethos within your school?

Imposter syndrome

'I have written eleven books, but each time I think, "Uh oh, they're going to find out now. I've run a game on everybody, and they're going to find me out."'
— Maya Angelou

Named by clinical psychologists Pauline Clance and Suzanne Imes in 1978, imposter syndrome isn't a registered medical condition, but the phenomenon is well known within any profession that relies upon self-assurance, confidence and leadership. Imposter syndrome in its simplest definition is thinking you are not capable of carrying out a role that you really are capable of. It is a condition of self-limitation, as you think that your achievements are all as a result of luck, and you are merely waiting for the day you are exposed as a fraud. Up to 18% more likely to occur in women than men, imposter syndrome plays upon self-doubt and a lack of self-worth in an attempt to hinder the sufferer's productivity and sense of success.

In a recent study reported by *Forbes* magazine, women reported using much more proactive strategies such as turning to their support network to reinforce and reaffirm their capabilities, whereas men used more avoidance-related tactics to cope, ignoring the symptoms as opposed to acknowledging them. It raises the question as to why fewer men suffer from imposter syndrome in a range of studies; does this mean that ignoring a problem eradicates it? Basic psychology would argue otherwise; but as imposter syndrome relies upon the beholder paying it some attention to think in a negative way to begin with, there may or may not be some merit to the tactic of ignoring it. With this in mind, when it comes to reviewing the research, my advice speaks to those who wish to be more consciously aware of their imposter syndrome – I wouldn't endorse ignoring the presence of something as a way of dealing with it.

Structural features of gender difference in society lend themselves to being key indicators of the syndrome in women: we know that women are paid less on average; we know that women are frequently the family members presented with the task of caring for children and taking gaps of leave from their professional duties; and we certainly know that women are responsible for growing babies. Extended periods of time away from the opportunity to establish yourself professionally can lead to feeling as though you lose a sense of professional identity. In addition, Dancy and Jean-Marie[1] (2014) found that the condition presented highly in women where the women in question felt underrepresented within their profession or that they were under fire from industry-specific bias. This explains why the more senior the position, the more prevalent the syndrome in women: we are still massively under-represented at senior level within schools, with female headteachers making up only 38% of the headteacher workforce at secondary schools within the UK.[2] Being a zebra in a field full of horses is going to make you feel a little out of place.

Additionally known to be highly prevalent in the medical profession and academia, imposter syndrome seems to present itself in professions where it is a necessity to operate in a consistently challenging environment. To elaborate, the educational sector is malleable and progressive, one that demands people look to improve, to continually develop as professionals, to be open and considerate of findings and research that could seek to overturn previous thoughts, beliefs or values. We do not stand still. We read to have

---

1.   Dancy TE, Jean-Marie G. Faculty of color in higher education: exploring the intersections of identity, impostorship, and internalized racism. *Mentoring Tutoring*. 2014;22:354–372.

2.   DfE, School workforce in England: November 2012, accessed at www.bit.ly/34V0pu2

our ideas challenged, so that we can take stock and reassess; that is who we are as teachers. You know that, by reading this (or any other educational publication), you are opening yourself to the possibility that you may read something that contradicts previous opinions that form your belief system as a teacher. Remember that time you found out that people weren't really on board with learning styles, and you pretended that you never believed that auditory learning was a thing? That. And so, imposter syndrome is prevalent as we constantly reform our professional identities to fit with the task at hand, or in response to changing staff structures, for instance. As an entity that relies upon comparison of your own capability to that of others, a change in the dynamics of a working team can reignite the nagging voices of the syndrome and bring them to surface, even after extended periods without so much of a whisper. Any profession that is informed by theoretical evidence and knowledge is likely to come up against this challenge. We are changing and evolving as a profession all the time and forming and reforming ideals is a by-product of that; imposter syndrome is just one of the outcomes. Where your position relies heavily upon intelligence and scrutiny, there is of course a strong possibility that you would be led to doubt the extent of the first when held under the microscope of the latter.

Ways that imposter syndrome can act as a hindrance

- It attempts to force you to label yourself.
- It attempts to quieten you when it comes to your achievements.
- It attempts to change the way in which you use language to define yourself.
- It attempts to encourage the idea that you are a fraudulent, less deserving version of yourself.
- It attempts to drive perfectionism.
- It attempts to cause you to react in the same ways to the same types of events.

Notice the word 'attempts'. The symptoms as they present can be inconsistent or infrequent but restrict us in how we identify and define our successes – or beyond this, influence us so that we confine ourselves to only being able to achieve at a certain limit, or within a certain remit. As opposed to recognising our personal qualities as strengths or enabling features, we allow them to force us into ourselves, so that two significant things result. One: we start to believe that these limitations are real and tangible; but even worse, two: we move beyond a thought process where there is safety in inaction, and our behaviour starts to mirror that of the limiting thought processes. Simply? We start to believe our own imposter syndrome hype, and do less than we are capable of, or less than we desire to do.

There is much talk about 'ignoring your inner voice' and 'tackling the monster head on' when it comes to feelings of insecurity or uncertainty around our own achievements or capability. Search 'imposter syndrome' on any reputable bookshop website and you will find many pithy titles that use aggressive, masculine verbs to help you to 'tame that beast!' or talk of a 'cure' or 'remedy'. Far from endorsing a somewhat combative approach, I would argue that the characteristics of imposter syndrome make us who we are; to pinpoint further, these symptoms are just niggling by-products of what it means to be human. Do I want to stride into a room, liberated from my inner voice? Well no, not really. To be frank, it would push the limits and lines of balancing knowledge with humility; but above all, I rather like people to understand that I'm not a massive pillock. And so, how do we set about the task of navigating through these feelings, which are real and restrictive and inhibiting, without resorting to declaring self-love in the mirror each morning, or just ignoring it and hoping it will just go away?

I argue that the symptoms that identify with the key features of imposter syndrome are actually rather enabling and empowering rather than a hindrance, if you choose to harness them in such a way. Teaching (and teacher training for that matter) calls for you to adopt a professional 'self', a persona that you don't connect with or apply within your personal life; you are performing as someone that you do not recognise as yourself to teach: your 'teacher-self'. Coupled with the frequent reflection on your own practice, with a constant and relentless drive to improve what we do, teaching has no endpoint; it is never mastered. Whilst this is incredibly exciting, it does nothing for our confidence in mastery. Such is the context in which we work. This process is necessary to developing what you want to emulate within the classroom and is an unavoidable part of the journey to becoming an effective teacher, in my view. The issue is that part of your role within your life then becomes a daily habit as you need to slither from one self-made personality to the next, in the presence of students, to colleagues, to your own children, to friends, to your partner, and back again. It is inevitable that, at times, you may find self-doubt at your authenticity comes creeping in. However, Hutchins and Rainbolt suggest that this is a fundamental part of what it means to work within academia, and that, rather than view imposter syndrome as something to confront and conquer, it is better to 'posit it as a formative part of career learning and development that shapes how faculty develop their professional identity'.[3]

Ways that imposter syndrome is an enabler of success

It attempts to force you to label yourself

Imposter syndrome allows you to mould and form the type of person you want to be. We all move through life trying to shape and reshape ourselves, in an attempt to close our lives on a final chapter where we have, at the very least, attempted to better ourselves as people. Developing the ability to make a transparent version of yourself – a layer to all of these different selves that then allows you to be your true self in the company of everyone – helps you to affirm who you

---

3. www.bit.ly/2DP4FiB

really are. It makes you feel both personally and professionally more comfortable. It is the reason why school selection is so important – because you need to ensure that you are able to present yourself authentically to be most content (more on identifying the right school for you later on). I'm Kat, I like good coffee, spending time with my children and listening to Penguin podcasts. There isn't a single group of people that I would be reluctant to share that information with. Imposter syndrome moves you to a place where you are one person to all people.

It attempts to quieten you when it comes to your achievements

This is healthy for all of us. Us Brits look rather disdainfully at anyone blowing their own trumpet unless it's done in the correct fashion, at the best of times, to the right people, for the right valuable reason. If praise – even self-praise – feels bogus, we reject it anyway, and so this quietener helps us to regulate true achievements, and what is truly valuable to us with regards to what we achieve. If there is a whisper in your ear that keeps you in check when sharing success, it makes you share the success of only the things you feel you should be most proud of. Beyond that, if you are sharing success only to be met with reactions other than praise, it provides an insight that perhaps the people you are sharing such news with are not the people who support your success in the first place.

It attempts to change the way in which you use language to define yourself

The thing that annoys me the most is when I look back on bios or job application forms that I have written only to realise that I have used pretty negative words to describe my purpose or achievements. Imposter syndrome will influence the words you choose to describe your actions; like an evil thesaurus, it will search around your vocabulary bank and select those poor limiting adverbs – 'I just...I only...I sometimes...' – to define you and leave you feeling cold. Take the time to look back over the last supporting statement/appraisal document/job application you wrote. Imposter syndrome acts as a handy guide to help us to retrace our words and replace them with more purposeful verbs that accurately describe what you do every single day: 'I am...I deliver...I oversee...I lead...' Once selected, you just need to familiarise yourself with being brave enough to utter them. Do it once and it becomes easier every time.

It attempts to encourage the idea that you are a fraudulent, less deserving version of yourself

You are ever-changing. You are not the person that you were last week, month, year – but you are also not the person you will be in a week's time, a month's time, a year's time. As your identity to starts to lose shape, your emotional resilience, cognitive power (and I mean that to refer to not only the knowledge you have, but also your capability to apply it) and sense of belonging will change and grow. You are not presenting as a fraud by what you do; you are simply shifting the various facets of yourself to suit your environment or master a situation at hand. You shift gracefully from parent, to teacher, to friend, to colleague, to public speaker, to meeting facilitator. The teacher you present to 30 students is a different teacher for each and every child in the room. Far from fraudulent, this is versatile and actually rather masterful, if you think about it. Every single person's interpretation of who you are is under your control. As you invest in the time to equip yourself with the tools that you need to adapt to those situations – ask for a day to shadow a member of staff, work collaboratively on a project, team-teach an intervention session – you become more empowered.

Imposter syndrome simply helps you to figure out what experience or expertise you need to flourish in whatever it is that you are trying to achieve. When I built Litdrive, I knew nothing of copyright law, website development, accounting, fund bid writing, managing people remotely and on a voluntary basis, marketing, social media management, SEO, analytics, or the rest. Some of those I didn't need to know much about but ended up falling down a rabbit hole full of them along the way. However, they all served a purpose: to arm me with knowledge. The more you do this, the more you self-affirm that failure isn't the ultimate point of no return, but a necessary part of the process of becoming better. Far from being fraudulent, you are learning to be your future self, and every deliberate step that you take towards becoming that person means that you are entirely deserving of it.

Being able to mentally walk through future events is a talent that you can thank your imposter syndrome for. Mental rehearsal has so much value for preparing you for what could happen – but in this case, it prepares you for what will most certainly not unfold. Imposter syndrome presents all sorts of horrendous possibilities that cannot compete with a rational, pragmatic mind that has already contemplated what sort of outcome it wants. I recall one teacher stating that her imposter syndrome was so overwhelming during learning walks or book checks by senior leadership that 'I just imagined someone turning up at the classroom door halfway through my year 8 class to hand me my P45'. Now, she knew that whilst it would make for an amazing sitcom, that was never going to happen for two key reasons. One, people don't operate schools, on the whole, like a gladiatorial arena. Two, her books were exemplary because she was (and is) a brilliant teacher. She cannot fail, because she has the self-reflection to know when she's doing a fantastic job. She has also equipped herself in anticipation for feeling this way. Failure is only possible in your imagination with imposter syndrome, because the reality is never as challenging or as nightmarish. And even when things don't go to plan, you learn so much about yourself as a result.

It attempts to drive perfectionism

Perfectionism gets a bad press, and in a multitude of ways, so it should. Exploring the relationship between motivation, procrastination and perfectionism, Akpur and Yurtseven consider that each is essential to success, with perfectionism as a key driver of motivation.[4] The drive to improve or achieve relies upon your own worst critic – yourself – in order to truly feel any sense of accomplishment.

This process of doubting ourselves and expecting too much is the very act that ensures humility, a human condition whose absence would make self-improvement impossible. There are only two places for putting humility back in its box: interview days (start stockpiling those empowering verbs – 'I assert, I manage, I lead') and when you've done something that (by your measurement – not someone else's) is amazing. There's nothing to be lost by occasionally keeping yourself in check and deliberating over your capability; it just demonstrates that you want to be better, without any other motive but a self-governed one. Just don't let it eat at you, because humility is powerful and priceless.

It attempts to cause you to react in the same ways to the same types of events

This is where we stop imposter syndrome in its tracks: by predicting its movements. It rarely creeps up on you when you least expect it; unlike a panic attack, or other psychologically driven conditions that don't always give us a polite, five-minute warning before they take the spotlight, imposter syndrome skulks in the shadows trying to make itself known backstage, knocking over a prop or two and muttering under its breath that if you were any good as a human being, you would have noticed it ages ago. It invites us to guess its habits, so we can start to build an anticipatory profile of when we can expect it to drop in. The more aware we are of how imposter syndrome presents itself in a way that is unique to us, the more we can prepare for these moments accordingly.

Personally, I enjoy pushing my imposter syndrome's buttons when it comes to public speaking. For years, I attended educational

---

4.   Akpur, U. and Yurtseven, N. (2019) 'Structural relationships between academic motivation, procrastination and perfectionism: a modelling study', *Cumhuriyet International Journal of Education* 8 (1) pp. 95–112.

events after putting myself forward to speak, sometimes months before the event. The day would arrive and I would feel like I was actually going to pass out from the anxiety of talking in front of other teachers – and I would always try to make a swift exit afterwards to avoid the painful prospect of encountering feedback, but particularly positive comments. It wasn't that they were going to tell me it was an utter shit show, and ask who on earth put me on the line-up – usually quite the opposite (which I find equally uncomfortable, for the record, but I do try to deal with it like a normal human being and say thank-you) – but I simply couldn't bear listening to my imposter syndrome crank up its simultaneous internal monologue, as it told me that they were lying through their teeth and could I please stop sweating. You see now, I can recount the exact sequence of events that leads to my imposter syndrome showing up – and as a result, I'm ready. In fact, I piss her off by sticking around and talking to people. It means that I actually meet some lovely folk; but above all, she can't lie to me the whole way home and tell me that everyone thought that what I had to say was pretty beige, because I took the time to listen to feedback from people. It breaks her heart.

Section summary:

- Focus on the white space, not the black dot. Realise that what your imposter syndrome will emphasise and caricature for you will always be the minority of what you do, and not reflective of all the wonderful things you are doing in school. Celebrate that regularly.

- Choose your crowd. Not a yes-group – that's not helpful or productive, and in fact can reinforce the perception of a low sense of self-worth, because you sometimes struggle to feel the feedback is genuine. Choose to surround yourself with honest yet supportive people who will recognise the time to praise and celebrate, but also provide a great sounding board for when you are at points of crisis.

- Maintain a sense of integrity – be true to yourself. That sounds very airy-fairy, but for imposter syndrome sufferers, it is so important that you decide on a direction, or a vision of what is important to you, because the syndrome will try and move you away from that and dilute any clear sense of perspective at its worst moments. Kathryn Morgan highlighted in a recent workshop that 'we all wear masks'; but when you feel as though you are trapped behind one, it is essential that you invest time in establishing to yourself the kind of person you are, and the kind of person that you want to be, so that if and when it is questioned, you know how to deal with it. It may be useful to write this down, giving yourself a reminder for when imposter syndrome attempts to cloud your judgement.

REFLECT

What is your strongest thought as an imposter?

Find an honest, well-trusted colleague or friend for this. Ask them for three evidenced reasons that conflict with your strongest thought to provide you with a strong base for a counter argument.

Challenge this – embrace the imposter. Does your imposter syndrome have any ammunition for its claims? Can the feelings that you experience actually enable you to change your thinking here?

Consider the last time you experienced imposter syndrome. What in particular exacerbated it?

- The task?
- The circumstance?
- The timing of the event – lack of preparation? Lack of knowledge? Lack of experience in the task?

Write down two things that you can do to counteract this experience next time (this doesn't need to be immediate) to prepare yourself for the same situation. By anticipating the fear, you can equip yourself against it.

Hunting and gathering
Marking, assessment and feedback

'The only important thing about feedback is what students do with it.'
– Dylan Wiliam[1]

On average, teachers work 14 more hours per week than they are paid for; and the majority of that time is spent on 'preparation, planning, and particularly ... marking'.[2]

Marking: 'If it is not making children make better progress, then it's not worth doing.'[3]

What is marking?
Ask any teacher about the marking they've got to do, or the marking they've not done.

Marking has been repeatedly highlighted as one of the most time-consuming pressures on teacher workload and I know I am telling you nothing new here. Marking represents one of the most prominent points of contention for us. It appears on every wellbeing forum, every union workload survey, every key discussion looking

1.   Wiliam, D. (2016) 'The secret of effective feedback', *Educational Leadership* 73 (7) pp. 10–15.
2.   Weldon, P. and Ingvarson, L. (2016) *School staff workload study.* Australian Council for Educational Research. Retrieved from www.bit.ly/2rb2fbB
3.   Claire Sealey in *Tes*, 2017.

for 'the answer'; but for many, we are still no closer to finding that answer – not by a long stretch. An English teacher might have six classes. If it takes two hours to mark a class-set of books, their marking workload – on top of their 22 hours' teaching, lesson planning, working with students outside lessons, etc. – is simply unmanageable. Teacher Tapp has reported that over 38% of teachers spend more than five hours a week marking.[4] With almost a whole extra working day dedicated to looking at students' books, does what we do here have any value? 200 ticks later, has that process in any way made me feel like I am adding value as a teacher?

David Didau states that marking and feedback are not the same thing,[5] and if we start to look at marking, we are barking up a bit of a diseased, delusional tree in the sense that we've lost sight of the purpose of marking itself. 'Feedback is universally agreed to be a good bet in teachers' efforts to improve student outcomes whereas marking appears to be almost entirely unsupported by evidence and neglected by researchers.'[6] This speaks of both reason and logic. So why are we still talking about marking and not feedback?

In order to start to explore the answer to both of those questions, we need to consider the misconceptions behind the value and process of marking and feedback. We also need to consider why we mark books in the first place.

Many schools operate a marking policy as opposed to a feedback policy, and in the context of understanding the mechanisms of such policies, marking is the verb and feedback is the result of the verb. We need to consider the fact that when we look at marking, we are reviewing a key area of a teacher's workload that, thanks to policy, they have very little autonomy over. We understand the value and necessity of feedback for students, but that does not mean we have to enjoy it – indeed, teachers will secretly share this information with trepidation, in the same way we might feel guilty disclosing that

---

4.   'Marking like no-one is watching', accessed at www.bit.ly/2LukjnJ
5.   David Didau, accessed at www.bit.ly/366xpQ0
6.   David Didau, accessed at www.bit.ly/34XgBLh

sometimes, *sometimes* we dislike our own children. You're a teacher; you're meant to like marking.

However, when we start to try to tackle meaty time-drains like marking and attempt to provide solutions, they are viewed with a level of scepticism. Dylan Wiliam once described marking as 'the most expensive public relations exercise in history'[7] and I'm inclined to agree; do we mark for student improvement, or policy adherence, or re-affirmation? Is there, dare I say it, an undercurrent of martyrdom around marking and we have reached a point of discomfort where we cannot say we loathe it – because that would not pay homage to the work of children – and we cannot see an ounce of value in the process itself? There is a great deal of ownership around marking policies, and by some, it is viewed as a rite of passage that a teacher must undergo. Are you really a teacher if you don't have a pile of marking awaiting your perusal that you can complain about? However, we know the value that decent student feedback holds for us and our practice: in the same survey as above, Teacher Tapp found that a great deal of teachers would still mark to the same degree even if they were not bound to do so by policy. This suggests that far from it being a mark of martyrdom, a comfort blanket or another way in which we can display medals of honour for our hard work, we recognise that good, solid teaching comes from holding a high regard for the work of students and providing expert advice on where to take that work. It is not that feedback doesn't have a place, of course, but that we need to find a way of making feedback a sustainable, consistently valuable process. Why are we permitting marking to be a task that we simply dismiss as the nature of the beast, a necessary evil that comes as part of the deal when we sign up to teach?

Learning is a cloud of smoke but marking and assessment are the soot marks which we can attribute to our graft. Herein lies the problem. The debate moves to considering whom the marking is for, because seeing the outcome of teaching through students' work

---

7.   www.bit.ly/2PheSd7

can be incredibly rewarding – but it should be exactly that, and not exist as a method of measurement as it has become. As soon as we start to view feedback as something that needs to be governed, instructed and monitored, it is no longer a tool for teachers, but a tool for leaders. The Education Endowment Foundation (EEF) report that there is a huge disparity between the presence of effective marking and what is being carried out in schools.[8] And so who is using marking, and for what purpose? An overwhelming 78% of teachers in secondary schools believe that marking practices are unmanageable,[9] which implies that it is the policy and not the process that is flawed. Remember, we think it's worthwhile as part of our practice; it is the way in which it is orchestrated that doesn't seem to add up.

Marking and feedback provide students with a pathway to improve, but also enable us to gather data to allow us to report on what it is that we want to know. If we start to gather data that we don't need, the process will have less value. The less value that something contributes to your day-to-day role, the less you will feel motivated to do it. The less relevance that the work that you are marking has to what you actually wanted to achieve, the less you are going to want to gather that data in the first place.

Why does adapting marking aid wellbeing?

If we are going to scrutinise teacher wellbeing under a constructive, pragmatic lens, it is only logical that we look at one of the key ways that we are spending our time, and whether this is the best use of it. The fruit of our labour – children learning as one – is evident through marking, and the process should ultimately be the way in which we can identify what students are capable of, but also what will inform our thinking for teaching them. When marking books becomes anything other than those two things, it becomes a source of both resentment and anxiety.

---

8.   www.bit.ly/2OUrKa6
9.   NEU Workload survey, accessed at www.bit.ly/2roCu7F

Marking is yet another way in which the role of the teacher has been poorly designed. Looking objectively at the role, there are insufficient hours in which to carry out the basic requirements of the job, and marking is a big part of this inability to claw back the hours required to do your job to a minimum adequacy. When the time frame becomes smaller than the hours needed, we not only shift the precedent for teachers to work well over and above the standard working day, but we start to prioritise the things that don't need to take priority. To just mark and plan requires all and more of the time available to you, so what does that leave room for? When we move 'nice to have' tasks into expectation, but don't give people the time to do the essential tasks for their role, how can we honestly expect them to want to do even the essential tasks without a level of despair and perhaps resentment?

The psychological impact of always feeling 'not quite done' takes its toll. When I talk about workload to teachers, I repeatedly explain that this is something that you have to make your peace with. Many roles within academia require the pragmatics of being a lifelong learner, and that includes mastering a sense of incompleteness. But this feeling shouldn't come as a result of marking. Marking isn't particularly progressive, or necessary to a teacher's mastery of subject development; it is mastery of being able to identify what has been learned by students. Whilst I believe that the skill of marking needs to be learned like many other areas of expertise outlined in this book, and in terms of a learned skill within academia, it is something that a teacher should feel that they are becoming better at; there should be scope to feel a sense of accomplishment from marking. However, marking instead sometimes becomes recognised as an administration task.

Once we start to look at marking as an administration task on par with checking emails or photocopying resources, it loses value, and we become more reluctant to do it. Schools fuel this misconception further by implementing marking policies that set us up to fail, and that are poorly designed to reinforce the idea of marking as administration and not marking as feedback. Policies that provide stringent guidelines on marking frequency (that often don't align with assessment points or the data that a teacher wants to gather about his or her classes), guidelines on particular pen colours to use, or clauses regarding literacy coding or layered marking (you mark, students respond, then you respond to their response) become further and further removed from what they were originally designed to do. We want marking to inform us of where our students are in their learning. Nothing more. As a classroom teacher with an allocation of a small amount of time per class, marking in the midst of a busy day of teaching, and then required not only to find the correct pen, look over the work once for the content, once for literacy coding, once for the student dialogue and responding to each aspect in a different way, what would really encourage you to do it? Because it is certainly not improving outcomes for you or your students. Not at that cost of time.

And so, books start to go home with teachers. Books creep into cars and sit in on our journeys from work, silent car-poolers that sometimes don't even manage to get out of the car when we reach our destination. Alternatively, books sit in our lounge, or on the kitchen table for the weekend, slumped in a corner, watching us eat, have a glass of wine, have breakfast with our children; they lurk with a sense of intent, evoking waves of unnecessary guilt in the process. If, for any reason, they do manage to convince us to lift them out of the purpose-built bag that we hang on to just to transport books (every teacher has a specific book bag. It is a meagre attempt to minimise the fact that we hate carrying books), we sit in front of the television of a Saturday evening, book in lap, uninspired. Teachers torn in two, balancing a weak attempt to watch a film with looking at a book every 20 minutes, neither task being done well or with any semblance of enjoyment, therefore defeating the object. We start chasing our tails, always marking – or even more commonplace, always trying to mark and failing to do so.

Why do this to ourselves? What is it that we set out to achieve? What value does marking hold when it is being done to such a poor standard (albeit with absolutely the best of intentions) and doesn't set out to do what we need it to do? The motivation behind the task becomes blurred between knowing that we need to do it and actually wanting to do it because we just don't buy into the narrative of how and why we are marking. And what happens as a result? We grow to loathe it. It takes up far more time than we ever felt inclined or warranted to give it – and we wouldn't mind, but even after all that time, we don't feel like we are giving it the attention it needs or, at times, deserves, and we don't feel like it is ever complete. In essence, we have subsequently managed to make what is a key part of our role unachievable.

If we are going to improve wellbeing, we really need to start by looking objectively at how the hours of our day, week, term, academic year are spent, and whether the hours required are the hours that are actually available. I don't need to fill in a timesheet to tell you that these two things don't add up for any teacher I know. According to an article in *Schools Week*, Tim Oates states that his own upcoming research 'will show teachers are "relieved" and better their understanding of pupils' learning when "neurotic, bureaucratic marking processes" are removed'.[10] The issue is not the marking but what marking has become.

Returning to my two questions: why are we still talking about marking and not feedback? And why is this one of the most significant sappers of our working week? Teachers will argue that there are two elements at play here: what is in your control as a teacher working within policy, and what is not. If the process to which you are bound in schools doesn't make sense, we need to start having objective discussions around marking policy in order to make it an effective, sustainable practice that is fit for purpose. Otherwise, it becomes up for debate as to who the process is for: you; the student (who should be equally as interested as you are in the result of your marking, but often isn't) or actually, senior leaders and regulators, who will not

---

10. Staufenberg, J. (2017) 'School where staff mark "how they like" gets government approval', *Schools Week*, 17th December, accessed at www.bit.ly/2I.C6QKW

have the context or overview necessary to understand what needs to be achieved by looking at books.

If we want to change the climate around marking, we need to deconstruct the mechanism of what currently resembles marking practice and reassemble it in such a way that it begins to look like something that we can work with, that will be of benefit to us and then, perhaps at a secondary level, of benefit to students. In addition, we need to look at marking with fresh eyes as feedback; one is far more informed than the other in regard to what will contribute to a teacher's role as a whole. Finally, we need to rebrand feedback so that instead of it appearing on the to-do list in the form of an unhelpful, persistent after-thought, it is a pre-planned, conscious part of our working schedule that we need in order to carry out the central core of our practice. In addition to this, we need to work with school leaders to reach the understanding that more script does not equate with a better quality of feedback. More script from the teacher does not make for better-spent time. More script from the teacher does not mean better results. It is only with this understanding that we might stop searching for a silver bullet to end our marking woes and start to see it as a part of a teacher's role that actually reaps rewards, as opposed to just killing time – and our professional souls in the process.

Marking should be feedback, not marking

For the sake of a definition, marking is an administrative task adopted by teachers of yesteryear, comprising filling the pages of an exercise book with endless annotations and finished off with a sprawled, elaborate comment at the end of the piece of work, outlining its strengths with perhaps some specific reference to the work itself, and a comment on the effort made, in the teacher's eyes. We don't use the cane anymore; why are we still torturing ourselves with traditional marking?

Feedback is something that will fuel further strategic thinking for a teacher; it is a dialogue, from expert to novice, informed through consideration of misconceptions made and content grasped.

Where marking is the noun of the evidenced script, feedback is the verb of action within the classroom, the dialogue between student and teacher. And if we consider this theory, how do we fit policy to a conversation?

Previously we have opened the door to not only feedback policy (which I do believe has a place in schools – but we will get to that) but, as a secondary measure, even to verbal feedback stamps – of which I was once an owner – to evidence conversations. If we are to assume that we are only marking for ourselves or the student, are we being so arrogant as to state that our students need to have discussions time-stamped in order to remember them? Will a generic stamp placed in their book ensure that they recall the key elements that they need to improve? The short answer – no. We all know that the feedback stamp was never for the participants of that conversation. It was to ensure that something was happening for external parties.

Another practice that can perhaps occur is the teacher that insists that extended marking is essential. The written feedback is an extended piece of writing providing personalised feedback for the student that outlines where their work evidenced areas of achievement and success to complete the task and lists a series of areas to look to improve, perhaps with suggestions as to how that might be carried out. As a result, marking each individual book takes some time, perhaps 10–15 minutes, making a class set of books not only difficult to fit into the schedule of a working day, but in essence, impossible to complete or maintain. Even at five minutes each, a class set would take two and a half hours if carried out in this fashion. Six classes: 15 hours a week. If we park that for a moment and look simply at the value of marking in this way, does it lead to better progress? Again, the short answer – no. But it makes the rest of us look bad, because it implies that this is not only a superb way to demonstrate busyness, but that excessive is best: the more ink, the better the progress. We all know it isn't true, and yet this evokes guilt in all of us because we cannot compete with it.

Feedback should act as a support mechanism between the student's current point and where you – and they – would like to be with regards to how successfully they complete a task and, in addition, their confidence to do so. Once outlined, modelled, and supported, creating a piece of work independently for the first time after initial instruction, they may feel incredibly vulnerable (as any author worth their salt will tell you!). Feedback exists to harness student confidence and capability to complete the task that has been set. Without this guidance, they will never really know how to improve.

However, research demonstrates that to be personalised, feedback doesn't need to take the format of long, extended commentary – and actually this is unproductive for the teacher and doesn't serve a purpose as effectively as we might hope. Students look for a summative grade and, if this is present, seldom look for the commentary that follows or accompanies it. Students will also often struggle to understand the feedback that they have been given, which is, I am sure, a familiar story as teachers carry out feedback lessons, surrounded by children that are unable to make sense of what they are being advised to do to improve. In fact, in a study of over 4000 students, it was concluded that students perform better when their performance is not formulated or linked to a particular grade.[11] To help students improve, we should form language around task-related steps to improvement, not end goals.

Whilst battling over the terms 'feedback' or 'marking' may seem just a case of semantics, perhaps it is productive to consider the connotations and associations we have with these terms as a profession. 'Marking' is the term which we have grown to loathe because it doesn't define what we are trying to do as part of the process, and what we hope our students gain from the process as a result. Conclusively, I think it's safe for us to put marking in the metaphorical bin.

---

11. Clark, D., Gill, D., Prowse, V. and Rush, M. (2017) 'Using goals to motivate college students: theory and evidence from field experiments', *NBER Working Paper No. 23638*, accessed at www.bit.ly/2YtqgH0

Feedback should be the start of a dialogue so students can bring their argument to the table. What have they learned? How have they demonstrated that? Feedback also acts as an opportunity for the teacher to provide explicit guidance to students about how they can improve or refine the process to ultimately improve the quality of their work. Sounds easy, right?

Students often don't use feedback in the way it was designed, which is half the frustration. It either doesn't get looked at at all, or not in its entirety, rendering the time spent on it completely fruitless – which in itself is damaging to a teacher's sense of accomplishment. You spend almost half of your working week doing something that receives absolutely no recognition and doesn't do what it was designed to do? How entirely demotivating.

Even if feedback is successful in receiving the eyeball time that it deserves, the additional issue then becomes establishing whether students have understood it enough to then be able to apply it and thereby improve their work. With a personalised comment that may differ for students each time, in a language that is only familiar to them through marking dialogue and in no other context, it may take time to teach the process of feedback as a practised skill with its own merit. That's not to say this doesn't deserve consideration, but how often do units of work allow time for dedicated feedback, let alone time to teach the expertise of how to take on feedback and apply it successfully?

If we are going to make the process of feedback effective so that it provides some semblance of reward (which is essential for us to feel a sense of success at what is 'the work'), we have to look at the model itself through the student lens.

Feedback needs to be taught; it is a capability that we assume of students but that is completely alien to them, particularly when we look at the disparity between primary and secondary. As an example, I do not recall a single – not one – experience of reading marking from a teacher during my secondary school education. Books were looked at, I assume, but marking was seldom documented and assessment mentioned even less. Instead, I recall sitting as the teacher led the class through worked examples on a blackboard, or instructed outlines of how to respond, or corrections of spellings to copy. Explicit instruction was key, and we followed. This didn't detract from independent thought or interpretation, but actually freed up the time required to have meaningful discussions around responding to texts. I can only assume that some bright spark felt that those conversations had to be monitored, and so let's get it down on paper – because if it's written down as marking, it must work, right?

Feedback is possible without marking every book; and moreover, it is effective for improving outcomes for students, by making them active participants. The feedback – successful feedback – was not a product of onerous script by the teacher, but instead as a result of the verb 'feedback' – the conversation, the discussion, the delivery of how to do it.

There is the discussion point around learned helplessness with marking processes that are currently used in schools; the excessive scaffolding means that often we simply end up with a regurgitated version of what came out of our mouths as teachers. There is a fine line between students acting on feedback given and teachers giving feedback so finite that they have written the improvement for students. However, several examples from various schools have indicated to me that perhaps the process and policy surrounding marking was no longer following sensible strategy for the two groups of people that needed it to work the most: teachers and students.

Feedback does not need to be personalised to an individual student level. It doesn't require a series of pens, colours, shading, codes, symbols or hieroglyphics to work effectively. It doesn't need to have a layered exchange of dialogue on the page, like a note passed between friends. It doesn't need a stamp to prove that you had a conversation. It just needs to be a conversation. Feedback is the dialogue that acts as a starting point for students to understand what they have mastered and provides guidance as to how they can then master the next step in the process of their learning. It really is that straightforward, and anything else is superfluous and not really curated with either teacher or student at the core. It is just one of many tools that a teacher has that acts as a tester of the current climate so that we can start to plan the route ahead.

- Written marking is not wholly valuable so stop doing it – even if it feels nice. Being less exhausted feels nicer.
- Feedback should be developed as a metacognitive process: teach the language of feedback as explicit content so students get better at the process of evaluation.
- Strip policy back to the core of what feedback should set out to achieve: how can you find a balance between what the school wants and what you know will work better?

Feedback should be a 'value versus time' equation

I am fascinated by the variation in time dedicated to marking from one school setting to the next. How is it that an English teacher in one school, with the same number of classes and the same key stage coverage, can still have such different experiences with the outline, frequency, policy and process of marking? I would argue that feedback is a policy that can transcend context, setting and student demographic. If feedback is going to be truly sustainable and successful in the same instance, we need to be having objective and honest conversations in schools and admit that some are doing it better than others, and learn from this.

Setting a frequency for marking acts not as an intrinsic component of effective feedback, but as a tool of accountability; it sets the somewhat uncomfortable tone that in order for something to be done well, it must be given a certain number of appearances over the course of the academic year, and it can then be measured by external agency. It also implies that without overview, teachers won't do it. I do not dismiss the accountability factor; policy has a place to support and manage where standards are not where they need to be. But to follow the 'high challenge, low threat' mantra of Mary Myatt:

setting the precedent of a marking interval does not lend itself to high-quality feedback, but potentially just more feedback. It does not provide a guarantee of quality. If the most prominent feature of your feedback policy is how much needs to be done, it's pointing in the wrong direction.

Feedback should be time efficient and time mindful. It should be curated in such a manner that teachers are able to consider their working schedules and see the possibility of being in a position to view students' work regularly and provide regular discussion around improvement. We should be able to incorporate feedback into medium-term planning for teachers, so that it does not become the afterthought to teaching, but the 'before thought' to help us in whichever direction we plan to go next.

If we are mapping out units with specified periods of feedback, we equally need to find the time for teachers to be able to look over books and identify what that feedback needs to be. We need time to identify key misconceptions and to write modelled examples of what we want students to work towards. Ask the questions: where is the time to review work to provide feedback? If students are completing skills practice on Thursday and their teacher is teaching all day Friday, is it reasonable planning to expect a review of this work before their next lesson on Monday? The danger of setting out feedback frequency is that it doesn't match up with the nature of the unit of work that it supports or the teacher that utilises it. How often have you been party to shoehorning a 'mini-assessment' into lessons because you need to mark something? It's madness at its finest. Frequency can act as a benchmark; but if it is unachievable, it becomes wasted policy. Horror stories of 24-hour marking turnaround, two-week 'deep marking', colour-coded systems that students cannot decipher – these all distract us from having a tool that makes a useful impact.. If we give some thoughtful consideration to the data that we want to gather, the time available to acquire it and the time available to share it with students, it's a far more pragmatic process of curriculum and assessment working in tandem.

Consider the following example:

Students have four lessons a week to cover a unit of learning that will span a ten-week period. Of these 40 lessons, there is the following to consider:

- Students are taught Monday to Thursday.
- Once a week, students will complete a regular writing practice lesson.
- Students will be expected to be able to recall, at a minimum expectation, the knowledge outlined for the course.
- Students will practise three key skills to enable them to demonstrate an application of such knowledge.
- The content consists of contextual study, reading a novel, and exploring plot, character and theme throughout.
- Students will complete a summative assessment at the end of the unit.

Therefore, feedback should form an integral part of the curriculum planning:

WEEK ONE: Writing lesson	Content	Content	Skills practice
WEEK TWO: Writing lesson	Content	Content	Feedback completed by teacher
WEEK THREE: Writing lesson Review feedback with students	Content	Content	Skills practice
WEEK FOUR: Writing lesson	Content	Content	Feedback completed by teacher
WEEK FOUR: Writing lesson Review feedback with students	Content	Content	Skills practice
WEEK FIVE: Writing lesson	Content	Content	Feedback completed by teacher
WEEK SIX: Writing lesson Review feedback with students	Content	Content	Skills practice
WEEK SEVEN: Summative assessment of knowledge	Content	Content	Feedback completed by teacher
WEEK EIGHT: Summative assessment review with students	Content	Content	Summative assessment review completed by teacher

If we consider this as a model, it helps us to reach the realisation that actually, around skills practice and a dedicated writing lesson for the first lesson of each week, content knowledge lessons only have 50% allocation of the entire time provided. It's a truth that we perhaps all subconsciously know: you start term with a six-week unit that you already know will become more and more rushed as you progress through it, because such things as specified time for feedback have not been pre-planned. It sets teachers up to fail. But by mapping out in this way, we can shift from this sense of never quite managing to do everything well to providing equal value to feedback and the delivery of knowledge. It is one of the key arguments that I would make for a reduced curriculum as opposed to the previous model of a unit per term at key stage 3 particularly – it doesn't provide the time required for feedback to be done well. Do your curriculum maps account for the hour-by-hour outline to ensure that you can complete feedback effectively? Where is the time to consider working exemplars and improvement processes, as opposed to just getting through content?

The second layer of this process is to be time-mindful. The feedback to be provided to students cannot be long, elaborate comments – not just because they don't serve the purpose, but because the working week simply does not allow the time for them. I shake my head in despair at marking schedules when the marking is too substantial to squeeze into the schedule. Reviewing books – looking over what has been executed well, and what still needs to be done – should take less than an hour per class set. That's two minutes to review each book. With regular, timely feedback, for a main-scale English teacher, that's six class sets of books a week, and six hours. An hour each side of the working day plus three hours PPA time gives 13 hours, of which almost half is reviewing for feedback, and the other half is planning and administration. *That* is time mindful: it is an objective, unapologetic perception of the working week, and the tasks that are expected to be completed within that time. Anything over and above that is expectation and not goodwill, and it is only through a dialogue that we can start to adopt the mindset within school structures. I will look at ways to encourage this dialogue in later chapters.

- Prioritise time for exemplar models and feedback.
- Allocate time for feedback into units of work so that 'pauses' are present for you and the students.
- Create a system that gives time back to you for the meaningful stuff.

Feedback should be quality efficient

Once sufficient time can be given to making improvement through feedback, we need to ensure that the feedback that we do provide is effective in what it sets out to achieve. By driving the standard of feedback, we can be certain that the time that we dedicate to it isn't fruitless. I know I can recall feedback lessons full of frustration and not a lot else: instructing students in what I expected them to do with the feedback in books, only to find myself circulating to 30 hands in the air to decipher my writing, decipher the meaning of the feedback, check what they had written for reassurance, or simply to intervene when students who had not understood the feedback itself then chose not to action it and wrote something else entirely. Feedback has to be taught in the same way that you teach, well, everything else. The vocabulary of teaching is complex enough that it is insufficient to use exam terminology and expect students to make sense of it. This is why discussion and dialogue are so much more powerful than writing a note in a book. Like all other entities of learning, this needs explicit instruction and practice in abundance.

What isn't efficient:
- Long, written feedback without the time to explain or contextualise. If you can manage to write in 30 books and then find the time to explain each set of writing to the relevant student, I would challenge you on the value of that time use.

- Verbal feedback stamps. If you are having to document conversations, I would ask who the feedback is for, or if you do this with all of your daily discussions, time stamping each person's head as you go.
- Stickers to gauge/measure/correct. If we are adding a red/amber/green to students' work, it doesn't give any additional context or empower them with the information to improve their work.
- Stickers for literacy. Pointless. Just because you tell a student the correct spelling does not mean they will spell it correctly the next time. Spelling, like most things, takes regular revisited practice. Correcting without understanding the process or the rule of the error means this is a short-term fix.
- Different coloured pens for separate components of marking. Again, as long as the student can locate your feedback quickly and without deciphering, I would ask if you regularly write in a variety of shades for line management meetings – you know, to make it memorable and so they know it's your writing.
- Marking that stipulates a written dialogue with students. You mark; you write, 'Please try harder'; they write, 'No probs, Miss, will do ☺'; you date their response (yes, this feature is becoming more and more commonplace, along with date stamping. In order for him to know that I had adhered to policy, an observer once suggested I use a date stamp to 'save time'). The only task being achieved here is a mutation of a student-teacher, text-talk, emoji-ridden back-and-forth – albeit one where you can remember the exact date you wasted your time on it.

Instead, here is an evidence-proven example that will (along with regularly revisited modelled examples of what you are asking pupils to complete) deliver feedback effectively when accompanied by discussion and puts feedback into context for students. It will also not take up your entire life and enable you to watch television, read, cook, wash, eat and sleep.

Whole-class feedback

Many schools have now adopted whole-class feedback as their sole approach to providing formative feedback to students. With several adaptations taking place, and Michaela leading the way by no longer marking books in the traditional sense and instead adopting whole-class feedback as policy, feedback in this format not only alleviates workload but is more effective in demonstrating improvement. I'd like to consider working examples, and the reasoning behind particular formats, but also how each component of the feedback form can work to improve not only the quality of your Saturday night without a bag of books, but also the quality of feedback that you provide to improve student outcomes. Most importantly, it's feedback that doesn't feel futile.

The teacher takes a look over the class books and identifies what that class have learned and any misconceptions or gaps in learning that may result in revisiting specific areas of content or deliberate practice. They can make a remedial plan to ensure that everyone is where they need to be – and significantly, as close to where they should be as a collective group, learning together.

Greg Thornton, chartered teacher and head of history at a school in the North West, explores his development of whole-class feedback (WCF), and how the process not only makes a significant impact upon workload but also improves the very act of feedback itself.

Talk us through your thought process when you came up with your method for whole-class feedback. Were you informed by any particular research or experiences?
The creation of the WCF 'crib sheet' in the spring of 2016 arose due to a number of reasons and I'll admit that a chief influence was nothing research based, but simply being a husband of a heavily pregnant wife and needing to drastically improve my work-life balance.

Our current marking policy, which I had inherited and continued, was focused on deep, triple marking with lots of coloured pen. This, alongside planning for the new history GCSE, meant that my workload was rather high.

At first I just made a basic sheet of four boxes (WWW/EBI/To do/Spelling, punctuation and grammar) that I scrawled notes on, which accompanied my deep marking, so I could get a big picture of each class as I sometimes felt I was too 'micro' and not 'macro' enough in my view of class progress.

However, this was still too intrusive on my time (almost three hours in some classes); so to simply get all my marking done in my PPAs or after school, I began to trial just using the sheet and no written comments in books whatsoever with a GCSE class. Funnily enough, no one died, their progress was not negatively affected and I felt that I was looking at their books more often and noticing patterns, common misconceptions and whole-class issues that I had not previously noticed due to being head down in 'personal comments' and not the bigger picture. Having trialled it for a term, I presented to my line manager and head (both historians and open to change, which was great), who loved it, and we rolled out WCF to the department from September 2016 onwards – and it has stayed this way since, with a number of departments across the school using the same model.

As this was only my second year of teaching (and my first as head of department), I will admit that at the time I was not the most research orientated or even aware but my line manager and headteacher at the time (@lizzy_francis and @ewenfields) always sent out blogs and articles, including the recently released EEF some time after I began to trial the sheet. Almost by coincidence I also found the wonderful blog post by Joe Kirby 'Marking is a hornet'[12] which discussed how Michaela Community School had been using the sort of methods that I had been trialling for a while. Moreover, I was also introduced to blog posts (by Harry Fletcher-Wood and David Didau, such as 'Less marking, more feedback'[13]) about the feedback loop, which, alongside the 2016 EEF report A Marked Improvement?,[14] confirmed that what I was trialling was the right thing to do. Since, I have read more heavily into feedback and its power through the usual channels, particularly Dylan Wiliam's 'The secret of effective feedback',[15] and Harry Fletcher-Wood's Responsive Teaching.[16]

12. www.bit.ly/36wLk2f
13. www.bit.ly/2PvXHoj
14. www.bit.ly/2P7ocBb
15. Wiliam, D. (2016) 'The secret of effective feedback', Educational Leadership 73 (7) pp. 10–15.
16. Fletcher-Wood, H. (2018) Responsive teaching. Abingdon: Routledge.

How does WCF work? How does it benefit students?

I had the opportunity to present WCF at my school's (Meols Cop Research School) first research conference in 2017. During a conversation about why I used WCF, I likened it to a 'tuning fork' which allowed me to quickly assess my students' progress quickly and then take action to address any concerns or misconceptions.

Essentially, WCF replaces traditional methods and allows you to take a snapshot of a class through looking at a number of lessons or a piece of written work without the need for any written comments in books. It is also used as a tool to highlight the clear and high expectations of the teacher.

The process goes as follows:

- Staff complete a generic WCF sheet per class after an assessment, specific piece of work or number lessons.
- They focus on identifying common mistakes – spelling, punctuation and grammar – and misconceptions from the whole class, noting down any proposed actions to take in the feedback and any student models that can be shared (good or bad).
- Praise and EBI is also noted down for student effort and presentation, thus 'sweating the small stuff'.
- Once done, the sheet is used to inform a feedback lesson which focuses on closing the gap in subject knowledge, disciplinary skills and anything else pertinent. This lesson may involve filling subject knowledge gaps through direct instruction and student collaboration, going over and practising skills, modelling and redrafting or simply covering presentation and literacy skills.

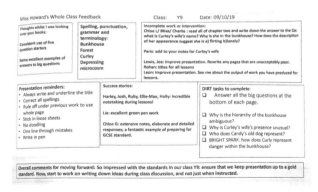

The clear benefit for the students is that staff know them better and are well equipped to improve their learning and progress in the class. Students continue to receive personal verbal feedback, but the class move towards improvement and refined practice as a result of what is tailored, specific feedback.

How does this impact staff workload?

Across the department, it has vastly changed workload and evolved the way we work and plan. Using premade WCF sheets, staff can go through student assessments or classwork in 10–30 minutes, jotting down misconceptions, praise, planned activities etc. and this forms the basis of their feedback. This is a significant drop on the 2–3 hours per class that I was doing in history in our old deep, triple-marking style.

This was transformative with regards to our department marking (especially with those who taught eight or nine different classes) and it allowed us to spend more time being responsive teachers. We certainly spend a little more time on planning 'feedback' lessons based on the WCF sheet, but this is a much more valuable use of time and has certainly been streamlined over the years by generic templates for the feedback lesson.

Recently I have moved to simply using just the WCF sheet itself and some photocopied pages from student books under my visualiser to provide feedback on certain written tasks, meaning that the process takes 30 minutes in total.

This method has accompanied our move towards coded marking of assessments, which again has removed any written comments and has reduced workload as we have a generic bank of codes based on knowledge/ skills that we amend and apply to each assessment at key stage 3 and 4.

What advice would you offer to teachers who are interested in using WCF or want to approach senior leadership to improve marking and feedback policy?

WCF focuses on moving from a marking culture to a feedback culture, which has greater proven impact on students' progress. Marking has almost become a dirty word, linked to high workloads and time-consuming activities and we need to really amend our policies to simply 'feedback' policies.

To start, schools need to think about the why, as with all strategies. Why are their staff marking? What is it for? What do they want to achieve? And this should always come down to moving the child forward. Then, look at the evidence on how to do this best. It points to effective feedback![17]

In the growing evidence-informed culture, there is such a wealth of blogs, books and reports that challenge the myths about marking and emphasise the learning benefits of feedback. Initially, I would point them in the direction of the EEF's A Marked Improvement' from 2016, which was the first proper document that I was introduced to when I began to look for evidence. The findings of Hattie and Wiliam, alongside many brilliant books out there, specifically discuss using the feedback loop and being responsive practitioners.

Furthermore, look at or even visit those schools which use WCF – for example, the case study of Michaela Community School, who have achieved outstanding results and do nothing but WCF.

Lastly, give it a whirl – what do you have to lose?

We hang on to the notion of extended marking with nostalgia and martyrdom, but it is a time allocation that we cannot realistically commit to. The entire process benefits no one: we are doing the same thing over and over again, and it is fruitless. If it doesn't benefit students and it impacts staff ability to carry out their role, why do it?

Unconvinced? Still want to use your scented, glitter roller ball numbers? Let me point out a few concepts that will convince you to convince your SLT, and allow you to watch television again, or walk the dog, or do whatever job you are being blocked from doing by a marking pile longer than that story that Bastian started reading in his school attic:

- **The students need personalised feedback,** Kat. Yes, yes they do. *This is personal.* By providing feedback in this way, I can ensure that every student in my 30-strong class will be mentioned at least once a half term. They will also get to see the work of others, my modelled exemplars and small-group or one-to-one intervention far more frequently than if I provide individual feedback to every student, which then needs to be deciphered,

---

17.   www.bit.ly/2FNqSyt

interpreted 30 times over, inevitably with my support. As Joe Kirby states, 'Marking a book is useful for one pupil once only.'[18] When what you are doing has meaning only for a moment, what is the point of doing it?

- **The students won't receive specific praise in their books.** Yes they will, because they will receive a copy of this that they stick into their book. But also, what is more useful is that they will have specific feedback that recognises what is valuable in being learned, and what is still to be learned, rather than a smiley face with an insistence that they did really well, or must try harder, when they don't actually know what either of these things looks like.

- **The students will receive feedback that doesn't apply to them.** The process of identifying common misconceptions rarely means that you are identifying the gaps for some, but that they are the gaps for many. Students will all gain feedback as a result of this process; I have never provided feedback and subsequently had a child unable to find a part of the action tasks that enables them to improve. If a student could grasp everything the first time, we'd all be out of a job. This also informs you as the teacher how did you outline this part of the content? What was the focus of your delivery? The ability to check the temperature as frequently as you see fit (rather than always feeling like you are chasing your tail to mark books) ensures that you can become far more informed of your class's capabilities.

- **It will look like I haven't marked the books.** To who? The student? They will have a contextualised discussion with you and the class, or the form stuck into their book. An observer? They will see a contextualised discussion with you and the class, or the form stuck into books. SLT? They will see a contextualised discussion with you and the class, or the form stuck into books. Ofsted? They will see a contextualised discussion with you and the class or the form stuck into books. The window cleaner? They will see...OK, I'm done.

18.   Joe Kirby's blog, accessed at www.bit.ly/2t7a7eI

- **I enjoy writing personal comments.** If you like to spend your weekend sharpening the end of your feather quill, sighing emphatically in your sense of purpose for the task ahead, and curating delicate prose to each and every student, who am I to stand in your way?

Assessments are testing, testing

Assessment is another entity that lacks resemblance to what it is that teachers should be gathering as a litmus test of what they have taught. Part of the reason that teachers are reluctant to embrace marking is the form of the policy; but equally, it is that the assessment doesn't deliver. In a nonsensical bid to build up to higher key stages and align to GCSE grading, students now sit assessments that aren't actually testing what it is that we want students to know – or we want to know about students. In English, we have been encouraged by previous curriculum models to teach transferable skills, institutionalised to believe that this is even possible and that if students can analyse one text, they can analyse all texts, in all contexts, for all exams. Any English teacher will scoff and tell you that they would be out of a job if such a myth were true. Daisy Christodoulou uses an outline from Simon and Chase to stipulate, 'How does one become a master in the first place? The answer is practice – thousands of hours of practice.'[19] And yet I hear of English departments compiling assessments that do different things entirely, with brand new content, and then expect children's progress to take an upward trajectory, which it won't because learning is not this linear.

And so then, schools try to design a system to manipulate assessment data, so that the data creates the illusion of linear progress, and a semblance of what we were aiming for in the first graph. Here is where we start to haemorrhage common sense and lose sight of what the assessment is designed to do. Instead of measuring what children have learned, the assessment becomes something that will make it look like they have learned, irrespective

---

19.   Christodoulou, D. (2014) *Seven myths about education.* Abingdon: Routledge.

of whether they have or not. This isn't done with malice; it is a consequence of holding accountability alongside progress.

In addition, the style of the assessment is very much dependent upon the style of the teaching. If the curriculum map lends itself to the theory of teaching transferable skills, the final assessment will just be a clone of the previous formative assessments where students receive feedback for the same task, and are essentially just replicating the same format of assessment but post-feedback to inform their improvement. Such an approach is flawed for a multitude of reasons, least of all that we are teaching children that assessment will get easier, not through practice, but by doing the same thing over and over, which isn't true assessment. We're not testing knowledge; we are testing the ability to pass tests. It is despairing to teach children, with the best of intentions to equip them with knowledge of your subject, only for this to become a dilution of knowledge as students complete tasks that will make them look as though they are getting better.

Formative assessment does not need to resemble the summative assessment that it precedes in order to be successful

I have two issues with the midpoint-endpoint approach to assessment in terms of effectiveness, but fundamentally, in regard to workload. If students have been unable to successfully grasp the components of an assessment in its entirety at a halfway point through a unit, when they are yet to have a full grasp of the knowledge required, then the final assessment will be an application of just-learned or recently learned knowledge that they have yet to apply to an assessment-type task. It also means their capacity to practise application of this knowledge will be diminished as a result of their learning content shortly before the assessment. This means that essentially, the teacher will mark two sets of the same assessment that I can assure you demonstrate very little improvement, because students have not had the time to practise getting to grips with the knowledge learned. It makes for a poor use of teacher time, but also sets children up to perform poorly – demotivating for all involved.

We need to understand that the disciplinary knowledge for our subject can be deconstructed into several smaller pieces, and these pieces can then be tested. If I want a child to be able to write critically about how Shakespeare presented love within *Romeo and Juliet*, they need to understand several definitions of love, where love is presented within the play in alignment with the definitions but also where there may be evidence of various aspects of love. They then need the vocabulary to articulate as much and possess the rhetoric consideration of the argument as such. If this were everything that year 11 should be able to successfully achieve, then mapping formative assessments might address the key components of all of these areas. They would still be successfully addressing the matter of assessing the student's ability, but in a staged, considered, scaffolded approach, not just regurgitating GCSE questions with key stage 3 texts. If we truly want students to understand the key components of assessment at the end point, we must do less but do it better. What would that look like?

We've fallen into the trap of thinking that assessment needs to match in format (not in content) the end result. Perhaps when we are at the mercy of external examination, practice papers serve a purpose, and I do believe in deliberate, repeated practice; but this doesn't mean that the practice always needs to replicate the format of the test, only the content. Instead, we can test knowledge through repeated low-stakes testing and it fulfils the same purpose. If we are to hold knowledge up as the key indicator of student learning, then we simply test that (particularly at key stage 3) when it is vital that we spend time with a clear, unclouded view of what the students do and do not know, not whether they have mastered a skill. Attempting to get students to operate with an endpoint in mind when they are only at the beginning of that journey is frustrating for both the teacher and student (as is evident across the country). Dissect your endpoint into key milestones and consider how you can design an assessment that stages that process over the long term. Test what we need them to know. Not all at once, not matching an exam paper, but just what we need them to know.

Here's an example:

Year 8 have studied gothic literature, using a range of extracts but with a repeated focus on *Frankenstein*. I want them to be able to define the gothic genre, outline the key authors that are recognisable as prominent in this genre, have an understanding of the art and architecture of the time, and be able to identify where Shelley incorporates these within the plot, character and themes of *Frankenstein*. This is huge! Do I need to see evidence of all of this in an assessment that is formally marked? I would say no. Would a GCSE exam paper successfully measure their understanding of all of these elements? Also, no. I can identify the extent to which the knowledge has been learned through regular, low-stakes testing and select one key aspect of these elements of the unit that would be valuable to explore in sufficient depth so that if needed, the student could recall the information and attempt to apply it in future. In order to make assessment valuable, I need to ensure that what I have chosen to give prominence to in the assessment itself *is* valuable.

The deliberate practice method is where the final assessment does not resemble the scaffolded lead-up assessments, but instead we practise retrieval and application of knowledge. This could take the form of multiple-choice questions, or short-response questions, which are less onerous once created and have greater longevity but more importantly, indicate explicitly where the gaps are. From this, I can then identify what exactly needs further teaching or intervention in a very concise and methodical approach.

- Move away from over-testing using extended responses that act as a drain on marking time.
- Avoid using an assessment system that tries to track progress as though it is linear (it isn't!).

- Prioritise knowledge over exam format. Ditch testing key stage 3 as though they are key stage 4 or key stage 5.

Assessment should be a collection of the data you want to gather – nothing more

As subject specialists, we often collect data that we do not require. Think back to one of your class's last assessments: what information did you glean as a result of that assessment? Did it provide you with a pinpointed account of what that student did or did not know, or were you left with vast areas to improve that give an overview rather than a concise picture of what you need?

If we use my previous consideration of the Gothic genre: I want my students to be able to recall elements of the genre, but looking ahead to my key stage 4 curriculum, I want them to understand Shelley as a writer, as a visionary within Romanticism and as an anonymous female writer of her time before then identifying herself. There is also the unorthodox use of narrative within *Frankenstein*, giving the reader an insight into the monster's mind that reveals the status that he feels he deserves. We can test all of these things sufficiently through the use of multiple-choice questions. This enables students to demonstrate the knowledge learned in an efficient way both for their next steps and for teacher workload, and gives us a clear path to refine and improve content to ensure that we are adequately preparing students, inside and outside of the confines (should you see it that way) of the curriculum. Using multiple-choice questions in this way will also help to inform departments of where the possible gaps are within the content being taught – gaps that might not present themselves if we use other methods of assessment. Imagine a document for an entire cohort that identifies the exact areas of content that students struggled to understand, which can then be utilised for meaningful, short bursts of intervention, and which took a sliver of the time to compile? More to the point, imagine the impact upon workload to approach the assessment of students in such a way?

Simplifying assessment means that your assessment method should consider and respond to the following questions:

- What have you taught and why?
- How do you know?

A series of multiple-choice questions will test the climate for the majority of what you have taught. For English, when I use short extended response questions, I can ensure that pupils are given the opportunity to practise the habits of analytical writing for this particular text, but then I can ascertain the state of play – the extent of student knowledge – through multiple choice. It is the knowledge and recall of that knowledge that will put students in good stead for the next stages of their education. We currently underestimate the value of such a tiny, yet powerful process.

- -

How to compile fantastic multiple-choice questions, particularly for English teachers (of course)

The advantages of multiple-choice questions? They're a fast, effective, low-impact (staff and students) way of gauging knowledge learnt. Why is this then not the way we assess in schools all the time? Because such questions are perceived to not allow for critical thinking and are hard to construct well, particularly in more arts-driven subjects, where responses are less binary. However, when compiled with care, they can act not only as a form of regular retrieval, but also as a key indicator of learning for summative assessment. *And* be peer assessed. How do we curate fantastic multiple-choice questions?

Choose what you want to assess across a department. This may sound incredibly straightforward, but to create a multiple-choice question that tests what has been learned, you must ensure that it has been learned. As a subject leader, how can you ensure that the content included in your test has been taught in your classroom? I would return to knowledge organisers for this in the first instance, along with discussing with classroom teachers so that key teaching points are consistent. This is paramount to collating the data that you need, as opposed to all knowledge of a topic.

Create answers that are all identical in length: aim for long stems, short responses. Avoid 'all of the above' or 'none of the above' responses because this will encourage students to fall back to guesswork, instead of critically approaching the question for a positive response.

So instead of:

Who killed Macbeth?

a) Macduff b) Lady Macbeth c) King Duncan d) none of the above

We can construct something of greater value:

How does Macbeth die?

a) suicide b) in battle c) by hired killers d) illness

The information becomes more valuable: if students understand how Macbeth is killed, they can use it as a springboard to discuss his delusion that he would receive immunity from death. Not only is the first question pretty limiting in its ability to test knowledge, but it requires more work to tease out the logistics of the death and relevant motive.

Use them as an opportunity to embed subject-specific vocabulary. Again, this must be vocabulary that has been taught. Aim for understandable language to ensure that students can access the question, otherwise the response will be useless. However, if you are confident in your team's ability to impart and revisit tier-three vocabulary for your subject, don't shy away from it. It is sometimes worth making the response with the most straightforward language the correct answer to demonstrate that more complex vocabulary does not make a more effective response (we all know those students!)

Work to include responses that provide the how rather than the what. As a teacher of English, I'm not interested in turning my subject into students regurgitating terminology that they cannot apply to texts or analytical thinking, and so it is advisable when dealing with less binary subject matter to focus on answers to multiple-choice questions that examine the how, as opposed to the what.

For example instead of:

What is pathetic fallacy?

a) Comparing something to something else

b) Stating something is something else

c) Repetition of language

d) Using weather to reflect mood

This would be more meaningful:

How does Shelley use pathetic fallacy in 'dreary night in November'?

a) To depict the time of year

b) To convey the monster's mood

c) To create a sense of boredom

d) To reflect the narrator's misery

All responses are plausible, but the final response is most accurate in its use of 'reflects' and consideration of the role of narrator. The student must understand that the description of the weather is a manifestation of the narrative.

Include four plausible answers and avoid responses where there is one conspicuously incorrect answer. This not only drives up the standard of your questions, but again, avoids guesswork. It's a good idea to spread the right answers between a) to d), making sure that each option is used an equal number of times across the assessment. It is also ideal to include terminology in incorrect answers, to incorporate other information learned.

Choose questions that act as a springboard for brilliant post-assessment discussion. In essence, any assessment before an externally marked, summative assessment is a practice run, and we must keep this in mind when setting students up to succeed. This is why well-planned questions are fundamental to success.

A perfect world for me? Staged assessments that accumulate knowledge that has been taught, followed by short, repeated response assessments that remove the scaffolds of support over time. So, if we teach year 7 Greek mythology, followed by medieval literature, followed by Romanticism, followed by Victorian literature, each unit incorporates an element of the knowledge taught before it in retrieval, teaching content and the final assessment multiple-choice questions themselves. This can then be accompanied by an extended response. The work within the unit is focused on repeated practice, and we can test the knowledge through precise questions.

- Collect the data that you need to close knowledge gaps.
- Collect the data in a way that you can identify what knowledge students have learned successfully and after a sustained period.
- Collect the data in a way that is efficient for you.

Summative assessment should be fit for purpose for you and them

To then establish this approach to assessment, you need to have humility in changing direction if required. This is why post-assessment discussion is so key to the model of deliberate practice; no cohort is the same, and it is not what we test, but how we use the information to evaluate what has been tested that is important. Again, this is why multiple-choice questions can be beneficial to the process; it is a straightforward way to get a whole-cohort view of gaps and misconceptions and to refine processes. What needs more emphasis when you return to quality-first teaching? Which teachers demonstrate patterns of effectively teaching a particularly complex concept, and how can you harness that by using them to train at a departmental level? Which areas of the curriculum will you need to return to before unit 4 in order to ensure that students are able to grasp unit 4 content? And what have they learned along that journey that they will draw from? Assessment is not the finish line, but simply a water stop. It should inform what we do and act as a tool of evaluation so that we don't just race towards more content, dragging children behind us as we go. We should test enduring knowledge as opposed to exam knowledge as 'exams only sample from wider domains, they are no direct measures of the domains'.[20]

Whole-school solutions

An English teacher has five classes that they see four times a week. In any given term, all books need to be viewed and feedback provided twice. In addition, all classes will complete a summative assessment. In key stage 4, these classes could then complete mock exams which will require marking too. Mock exams could take the format of one language paper and one literature paper per class. That's a minimum of 60 papers for each class. Ten minutes per paper, that's 600 minutes, if you only have one class of course. That's 20 hours' marking in addition to book marking. With gained time often used as justification for this extra workload burden, we then expect teachers to mark mock papers following the physical and emotional pressures of putting year 11 through exams, and often with incredibly short turnarounds. Some faculty leaders report turnaround times of seven to ten working days. This again chooses assumption and expectation over goodwill and puts teachers in the tricky position to mark vast amounts of work, reliably and accurately, in a very short space of time. What then happens is that it is done to a poor standard, or it isn't done at all. If we are going to change the whole-school culture to improve workload, we need to consider how to make an assessment system that is both accurate and achievable, so we can move towards feeling as though there is some purpose to what we are doing.

- -

What does your school do to support the marking of mock exam papers?

❝ 'We had three weeks for year 11 mocks, and it was the same time as year 12 and 13 mocks. I cancelled meetings and covered duties for my team.'
– Lavina, Sheffield

20. Christodoulou, D. (2017) *Making good progress? The future of assessment for learning.* Oxford: Oxford University Press.

66 'Having only a week and a half to mark full English GCSE – in the final three weeks of the academic year – was the icing on the cake of unreasonable requests this year. When I questioned it, I was told that this data would be used to inform setting, which my 2ic and I had already spent painstaking hours fine-tuning. I told my department to get one paper marked and double the marks to get the grade.' – Nora, Yorkshire

66 'We had three days to mark mocks and on the fifth day, all data had to be inputted into centralised spreadsheets (so moderation was included in day four). This was for year 10 and 11 so that they could have mock results day the following week. Bear in mind, for year 11 we do two GCSEs; learning walks and book trawls for all other year groups continued as normal during that time.' – Chris, Wolverhampton

Comparative judgement offers a pragmatic and sustainable alternative, that I would, along with substantive research, argue is a far more efficient and reliable way to grade work. The process is based on a long-standing psychological principle that humans are better at comparing two objects to each other than they are at judging one object against specified criteria. By putting two papers alongside each other, the judgement is made as to which one is the better piece of work. Papers are re-exposed to other markers until a linear format can be made of work from most to least effective. As experienced markers will tell you, this is the process we are effectively using when we mark, but in a less reliable way: we mark, using our memories of marking as a benchmark. However, memory is subjective and 'works a little bit more like a Wikipedia page: you can go in there and change it, but so can other people'.[21] This is why such practices as marking pupil premium work first or marking lower prior attainment students' books before higher prior attaining students' books don't work: we are warping our own system of what a good standard of work looks like. Our memory becomes polished and embellished as we work, and so our own judgement improves.

---

21. Elizabeth Lotus, *How reliable is your memory?* TED Global 2013, accessed at www.bit. ly/34d3Jzr

Comparative judgement hijacks this fundamental flaw in our memories by putting the two pieces side by side, and our working memory tries to ascertain which is superior in quality.[22] This process not only takes half the time to do, but also provides a more standardised account of a cohort as a result. It produces results that demonstrate high mathematical reliability, and with the prospect of marking existing as an incredibly subjective system in schools, also removes this bias to as great an extent as we can without losing the human input entirely.

A far cry from student ranking, this process eradicates the less effective components of the marking process and allows us to take a distilled, whole-picture approach to assessing pieces of work using systems that are not only accurate, but as close to the real-life context of the examination system as we can get. We are essentially creating our own, well-reasoned response to considering the merit of students' work. How we then translate that to students and other stakeholders is something which we then have to take charge of, but the essence of the grading system makes for a really precise starting point.

The system provides schools with a method of effectively assessing student work in a way that is fair but also provides teachers with a significant reduction to their marking time. Is this a realistic solution? Beth Black, Director of Research and Analysis at Ofqual, recently wrote an article that outlines the cost implications that such system overhauls could have.[23] I would ask whether the cost implications of effective marking systems would be comparable to the reduction in absenteeism or staff training as a result of retention. Is this a system that would effectively pay for itself, perhaps?

The impact of this process is life changing for teaching; the organisation No More Marking (NMM), founded by Chris Wheadon

22. Thurstone, L. L. (1994) 'A law of comparative judgment', *Psychological Review* 101 (2) pp. 266–270.
23. Black, B. (2019) '11 things we know about marking and 2 things we don't ...yet', *The Ofqual blog*, 5 March, accessed at www.bit.ly/36tOt2B

and assessment genius Director of Education Daisy Christodoulou, uses comparative judgement software to work with schools to embed such an approach within their marking policy.

As with all implementations that are effective in both time and value, these strategies tend to fall prey to a suspicious eye from the educational sector: we can sometimes be martyrs, and the systems created in schools, particularly around marking and assessment, breathe, 'more work is better work', which comparative judgement challenges – and makes no bones about it. Executed with thought and care, comparative judgement could be the way in which we start to use assessment processes in schools so that they work for us.

I spoke with Daisy Christodoulou about the impact that NMM has made within schools, why she endorses the system with such conviction and where it could take assessment in the future.

Can comparative judgement really make a profound impact on workload?

Yes, definitely. At primary we have found really astonishing time savings. Teachers can judge a year group's writing in 20–30 minutes, when the traditional marking and moderation process was taking hours. At secondary there are still time savings, but they are not as dramatic, and the exact time saving will depend on the subject and the teacher-pupil ratio in that subject. Also, regardless of the time savings, judging is easier and more accurate than marking and a lot of people say to us they find it fun. So even if you are in a subject where there aren't enormous time savings to be had, it's often still a better process.

How does it work?

The reason why comparative judgement is quicker is that the human mind is not very good at absolute judgement. We're much better at comparative judgement. And so traditional marking is absolute judgement. You're looking at one thing and you're trying to say you know what it is on an absolute scale of quality. Imagine someone walks into your room and I say to you, 'How tall is that person?' That's an absolute judgement. The brain is much better at comparative judgement and we find it a lot easier. This time, imagine two people walk into a room and I say, 'Who's taller – the left or the right?' That's a much easier task.

What have been the previous issues with marking policy in schools up to this point?
When people approach No More Marking, we talk about time costing. We tell people to time cost their current marking procedures; and actually, I think a lot of schools realise that their assessment policy isn't doable. I'd say time cost your assessment policy and work out if it's realistic or not.

I think at the root of it is an issue around who the marking is for. For me, the issue is around proxy. The big issue with all education is that it's invisible – learning is invisible. That is the most difficult thing about education. And because it's invisible, what we do, quite rightly, is try to find visible proxies for what's going on in a kid's head. You know something is changing in that kid's head. It means they now appreciate and understand a simultaneous equation. You can't tell that by looking at them. All you're trying to do through marking is say, 'I'll get the kids to produce something that is visible that will be a reflection of thinking that has or hasn't changed in their head.' The problem is that there's a number of ways that your proxy can go wrong.

The big problems happen when accountability comes into this because the accountability is saying, 'If I can't see on paper, it hasn't happened. And if it is on paper, it has happened.' And neither assumption is true. There are things that you can record on paper but have never happened. People can record numbers even though it doesn't actually reflect any underlying change in the kid's mind. Conversely, you can have a kid's thinking genuinely change and nobody records it so people think it hasn't happened.

The problem is that a lot of our proxies have become detached from the thing they're measuring. To me, the classic example of that was triple marking. Triple marking arose from a really interesting impulse when levels were no longer used – which I think was a good thing – and then everyone was worried: 'Well, how am I going to show progress?' And actually, I don't think that's necessarily a bad question; I think we do have to ask ourselves how we're going to show that people have attained and made progress. But then, that question got bound up with Ofsted accountability, so it's about showing that there's evidence. And it became a performance thing as opposed to actually wanting to record that the progress happened.

Then Ofsted said, 'We'll look at books'; and then school leaders said, 'What we need to do is we need to show a dialogue in the books.' And then you have this situation where you've got a teacher writing something, so you can say, 'Look. These three comments are proof that a dialogue has taken place.' First of all, that's taking forever. So that's now turning something that could have been a five-second conversation into 15 minutes of work. That is a huge increase in workload.

If you are going to have an enormous increase in workload, you've got to show that it is really adding value. And it doesn't improve the conversation; it actually makes it worse because when you're writing all those things, it becomes quite mechanical. The feedback dialogue goes 'Well done. Maybe next time you could think about tense'; 'Good. Oh, thanks Miss, I will do that'; 'Great attitude!' This gets to the heart of why written marking is more time consuming. What is it about it that's unhelpful? It's that a lot of the time, when outlining the ways we need to improve, prose is not a very good medium for expressing it. This is why whole-class feedback is better.

What does comparative judgement do to improve the experience of feedback for teachers?

Comparative judgement is quicker because it's easier. People often say to me, 'It's quicker in that I kind of prefer judging. It's just a nicer experience.' And again, I don't mean that as just subjective. I think that's because it is easier and I think we have underestimated in the past just how hard absolute judgement, traditional marking is. It really is tough. Comparative judgement has made me reflect on my own practice as a teacher. What I realized is that I actually always really liked reading children's work; reading their work is fascinating. What I didn't like – and I think what a lot of teachers will say is the thing about the job that they find really tough – was marking it. And I used to think, 'Oh it's just because I'm not very good at it' or that it's a kind of moral weakness; but actually, I think the reason why teachers complain and moan about marking is that there's just something about it that's very hard to do accurately. It just goes against the grain of the way our minds work.

I think the really nice thing about comparative judgement is that you get all the benefits of reading the children's work without that grind of attempting to place it on this absolute scale that you're not sure about. The other thing that people say they like about it is that you actually get to read the work. So again, when you get these very pernickety mark schemes that you often get at GCSE or at the end of primary (where you end up reading the mark scheme more than the kids' work and feature spotting), you're not really reading for meaning. Have they got that, got that, where is that, has it got historical context? Tick, tick, tick.

But with comparative judgement, you can read for meaning. Having said all of that, you know it will give you benefits. Now that we've been doing this for a couple of years, we've also noticed that to get the best use from it, you have to think a bit more deeply about what you're trying to do with the assessment, particularly at secondary. Like all these things in life, you know it's not a silver bullet. You know it's not going to be an overnight solution to your assessment woes. You have to think: what are we trying to achieve? What do we want to do? What kind of information do we want to know about our pupils and when?

How does this work within school settings?

I would say the best use of comparative judgement is where it's part of an overall rethinking of how your school assessment system is going to work. And actually, I'd also advise you not to overuse it. So, I'm saying we have some schools come to us and say, 'This is amazing, we want to use it six times a year' – and definitely when I started teaching, that was the sort of standard way of assessing. I've seen this borne out by surveys – many people would assess every six weeks: once every short half term. You would have a topic in English or maths and you'd studied the topic for a half term; at the end of the half term you do an assessment and maybe even do a little pre assessment – you know, prepare them for the assessment – and then you'd repeat it all again six times. And actually, I think a lot of schools are moving away from that, and have been for a few years now. I think levels are going to make them rethink that. And I think that attempt to get six grades a year is just really flawed, whether you're using comparative judgement or not.

You could use comparative assessment for that, but we would say it's not the best use: those grades, those graded assessment points, they don't need to be done too frequently because they're big assessments of complex skills and pupils take time to improve on them. My ideal would be two of those a year, so I would use comparative judgement twice a year.

Then the question is, 'But if I do that, how will I know?' Senior managers (as well as teachers) ask, 'If I'm only assessing twice a year, how do I know whether the kids are falling behind between those assessments? I've lost half the year before I found out that they're struggling.' And that's where I think multiple-choice questions come in, along with the day-to-day formative assessment that you're doing minute by minute in the lesson. To me, that's one of the things that actually got forgotten about when we were trying to grade six times a year. What you've got to remember is the true formative assessment – that's the thing where you're getting the real live information on how the kids are doing.

I think the other challenge is: how do you create formative assessment in the moment in the lesson systems that are low workload and easy to interpret? As I say, I think multiple-choice questions could form a good part of that; but I think there's a whole discussion to be had there. So, for me, I would actually drastically reduce the number of big open tasks that pupils are doing that need those big assessment moments. And then I'd use comparative judgement for them. And then if you did that, you would probably be decimating the time spent on some of the marking that's happening at the minute. You would be really bearing down on it. Increased marking frequency is really quite ineffectual in terms of bang for the buck: 'We need to see the books marked every two weeks.' The way that gets interpreted is that there needs to be some kind of red or green ink in every child's book. I've seen teachers who are coming up to an inspection or book look and are frantically going back through the books, getting in the marking. And I wonder, has anyone sat down and worked out how that is sustainable?

It's very easy to bring in a multiple-choice question from two weeks, a month, three months before and say: do you remember it? Can you remember these comments? But it is much harder to do that with an essay. You can't ask them to repeat an essay – that is just so time consuming. So, the point about multiple-choice questions is the efficiency, the speed they give you.

What I find really interesting is that comparative judgement takes less time and is more reliable – and we can prove that, right? The other thing I find really interesting is that whole-class feedback – which I'm also a big fan of – takes less time. We haven't proved it in the same way as with comparative judgement, but I think whole-class feedback takes less time and is more effective. It's amazing that there are things like comparative judgement and whole-class feedback because it's very rare in life that you get things that take less time and are more effective! But it also makes you worry about the current system. If you think the fact that there are things that can come in and take less time and be more effective, then it's a huge problem with the current system; there are all these things that are happening that take so much time and aren't effective.

What advice do you offer as a post-mortem to comparative judgement?
When you finish judging, sit down with a group of teachers, talk about the common weaknesses and the common misconceptions you saw. Talk about the actual activities you're planning for the next lesson – and in fact the next series of lessons – that are going to address the issue. And so, the feedback you're giving to pupils isn't in the form of improving your tense; the feedback is in the form of, 'Here's two sentences from someone's piece of work. Can you read these sentences, spot the error, and correct the error? Can you find a similar error in your own work?' If you go down that route of feedback, it's not a compromise. It's not making the feedback worse; you're actually improving the feedback as well.

Some final thoughts on feedback and assessment

We have over-complicated feedback and assessment in education. It is one element of traditional teaching that we struggle to let go of; it has become a key example of the misconstrued idea that more work equals better work.

It is also the one aspect of teaching that I know is likely to be most governed by policy in schools, and the part of your workload that you probably feel least in control of. What I do want to reassure you of is that everywhere that now uses whole-class feedback in their policy started at a place where more traditional marking format was in existence. We all have to start somewhere, and change comes from people making suggestions to try something that works better. So, if nothing else, look at this chapter as a blueprint for you to see what's possible, and a blueprint for your leadership team to see the opportunity that they have to utilise staff far better with the time that they have available.

REFLECT

If you are responsible for strategic overview of feedback:

- Time cost one assessment at departmental level. Do your staff have sufficient time to carry out the feedback policy in place, alongside their teaching timetable? If not, where is that time gleaned from?
- Do you provide examples of what effective feedback can look like so that the expectations of your policy are clear? Are all staff fully informed not only of what the policy is but also the reasons behind the mechanism of the policy itself?
- Do you set a frequency of feedback to be provided in line with assessment cycles? Do the two elements bear relevance to one another – are you asking staff for data when it is readily collected and available?
- Have you incorporated the required amount of time within each unit of learning to complete meaningful feedback with students?
- Does the feedback ensure that the student works harder than the teacher did to provide the feedback?
- Does your policy demonstrate progress and time efficiency for both staff and students? In other words, do you collect data in a timely manner?

If you are an active participant in your feedback policy:

- Time cost a sample assessment. Do you have sufficient time to carry out the feedback policy?
- Are you provided with examples of what effective feedback can look like so that the expectations are clear?
- Are you provided with time allocation within medium-term plans to complete feedback?
- Are you expected to work to a set feedback frequency, and is there a justification for this?
- Does the expected feedback format ensure that the student has to become an active agent with the feedback dialogue and steps to improvement?
- Does the policy support you to help students make progress with an efficient use of time?

Sustainability and substance
Resourcing

Education allows individuals to choose a fulfilling job, to shape the society around them, to enrich their inner life. It allows us all to become authors of our own life stories. – Michael Gove, *The Importance of Teaching,*
The Schools White Paper, 2010.

Detailed lesson and weekly planning were identified by 36% of the respondents to the Workload Challenges Survey as adding an unnecessary burden to teacher workload (DfE, 2016b, 6). However, what is mindful to consider is that only 72 teachers were part of the follow-up study and so the action taken had an incredibly small impact group to act as a measuring stick. Instead, I have tried to draw from a range of sources to try to pinpoint what it is that has made resourcing, generally one of a teacher's favoured tasks, such a drain on teacher time that it has been given the label 'unnecessary burden'.

According to the NASUWT survey, 82% of teachers say lesson planning is too often unnecessary and unproductive.[1] What is it that has made planning – a core duty to the classroom teacher and fundamental to teaching – unproductive? There is sometimes bureaucracy at play here: horror stories of reams of lesson planning requested – teacher training a prime example of this – as each minute of a lesson is meticulously poured over. This is prevalent not

---

1.   NASUWT workload booklet, 2018 accessed at www.bit.ly/2Rbpmvw

just throughout training years, but beyond that, and the evidencing of paper is a phenomenon that has become much more visible, notably in the last ten years. Schools believe they must make learning measurable to appease regulatory bodies, irrespective of what those regulatory bodies require.

However, it seems that the burden of planning remains a drain on teacher resources long after training is complete because it remains in the top three identifiable issues behind workload, along with marking and assessment. The insight that teachers working in excess of 60 hours a week in some cases implies that time, not planning, is the real issue here. As a classroom teacher working in the UK, timetabling demands that you teach 20–22 hours of a 25-hour teaching week, which means to carry out planning effective lessons, if only using dedicated PPA time, teachers have on average eight minutes a week to prepare each lesson. This is working on the assumption that marking, assessment, administration and all other related duties are parked for either end of the bell. Is that a reasonable way to lay out workload expectations?

But what does it look like to create, construct and resource a lesson? Teacher training delivers conflicting messages on this. Time

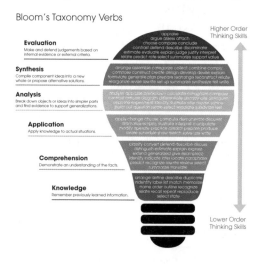

Bloom's Taxonomy Verbs

is spent in approaching the building bricks of learning within the timeframe of a lesson; lesson plans move awkwardly through the verbs of Bloom's taxonomy, selecting one key thing that students should learn how to do, with a small selection being able to master such a thing, and a smaller selection of the small selection able to evaluate how they went about it.

Applying Bloom's taxonomy in this way is unproductive to maintaining vocational purpose for several reasons. It promotes the idea that we should have (and are better teachers for having) lower expectations of our students, and consequently, our own ability to teach. It also promotes the idea that we should be tailoring all lessons for all classes, and so everything that we create has an incredibly short shelf life because it is great for one-time-only lessons. Additionally, it focuses on the doing and not the learning: if we are not directing students to learn, apply and consider the extent to which they managed to grasp the knowledge imparted, but instead assume that only some students are capable of some things, then it's not an ideal way to spend time: time that is limited.

Over-creation and under-reward

For me, teacher training was spent trying to work out how to spend time, as opposed to how to conserve it. In an approach that can only be referred to the '*Brewster's Millions* effect', the doing of activities took precedence over the learning. I used starters and plenaries to rid us of content as fast as possible, creating neat edges of a learning hour, and fitted tasks inside to buffer between one and the next; students were busy with doing, not learning, which again did not aid my own sense of professional fulfilment. We would be wise to observe that the 'allotting of time' approach to planning is dangerous for two reasons: if we plan lessons like this, it encourages us either to fill the time with one idea when it doesn't need it, dismissing the presence of essential knowledge, or alternatively to rush through it so we can start afresh with an entirely new element of the topic when we see our students next. Students are occupied, but as a distraction rather than a direct, conscious purpose that contributes to learning. More so, the activities lack substance in the sense of accumulation of skills and take far more time to formulate than for students to complete. Card sorts, laminated sheets, worksheet after worksheet as a trainee created as some sort of metaphorical comfort blanket to make me feel like I knew how to demonstrate learning. In an age of accountability and evidence, it felt logical and well thought-through to make a sheet to show I'd done it. Lessons became a rainbow of pastel-covered differentiated work, and the reprographics lady was my best friend as I sorted out which work would be lemon, and which would be lavender. Like this was the important decision.

This mindset is still rife within schools, and it is clear to understand the rationale: resourcing makes us feel as though we are in control. As we design mistakenly for our students, we mistake doing with productivity (I will talk about this a great deal later). Starting at a training level with this misconception and then possibly finding yourself in a school that enjoys a paper trail can lead to a vast misunderstanding of what is good for your student – but also, of paramount concern, of what is good for you. Schools that request weekly lesson plans are still in existence. (I recall feeling triumphant at getting a lesson plan down to four sides of A4.) Move forward and we have movements towards one-page plans, taking a streamlined approach to planning; but the act of planning itself hasn't changed here, it just takes less ink. The planning and resourcing still takes an inordinate amount of time – time that hasn't been made available. It means that the one task of teaching that we appear to enjoy is being demonised as yet another thief of our time. But why is this?

Planning lessons has been taught as the blocking of time: conjuring up a component that we would like to cover from the knowledge required for our subject, and then setting about the task of covering that in the space of an hour. We know that learning knowledge doesn't work like this, and yet lesson planning keeps trying to put us back in our metaphorical boxes by insisting that we pick a thing and teach it. Simple as that. This creates a lack of value in the task: how can you be invested in something when you know it doesn't work?

The process of teaching can then become unsatisfying, because you are doing a great deal while the reward is poor in comparison; students are working far less than you are and aren't learning what you want them to learn. Resourcing can take a similar path, as we invest time in creating things that don't reward in time saving, and I would like to explore the various reasons why equipping ourselves for lessons can take up so much of our working weeks.

Shifting goalposts

A vast number of teachers will outline the major changes in exam specifications as a requirement to revisit and revise resources in schools. In the last six years alone, English has waved goodbye to key stage 3 assessment foci, coursework, a far more structured framework to speaking and listening tasks and the introduction of linear assessment at key stage 4, alongside the shift to 1-9 grading and an overhaul of A levels in the same breath. It felt like starting again, and the benchmark was higher in all cases – not necessarily a bad thing, but raising the bar all the same meant that hoards of resources felt worthless, and the concept of adaptation was as laborious as creating new material altogether. The language papers in particular forged a completely new face; legacy papers made way for far more astute questioning, and the accompaniment of blended thematic extracts dating back to the 1800s was a daunting matter to prepare for.

Preparation, planning, procrastination and probable justification

The comfort blanket of teaching; I think we can all relate to planning as a method of procrastination. A hindrance to wellbeing, it can actually act as a way of making us feel proactive or productive when the to-do list seems unmanageable. We create resources because we enjoy it and we'd rather do that than the other work that is less enjoyable. There are not many teachers that hate creating content for lessons. Why? It's the creative aspect of our profession; it allows us autonomy over our craft, even in the most prescriptive of circumstances; and next to delivering lessons, it enables us to work at our most free, making decisions over our approach, as the leader of our own classes. So, it seems logical that the visionary act of resourcing should be the very thing that encompasses the majority of our time; but to categorise it as 'burdensome' is a disappointment.

Not quite on par with martyrdom, resourcing can bring us a sense of self-validation in that by demonstrating something on paper, psychologically, it means we are teaching it effectively. In the same way that verbal feedback stamps were all the rage (imagine time-stamping every conversation you have! Hey, you thought it was a great idea at the time...), as teachers, resources are our only tangible tools, and so it makes sense that when things feel like they're not working, or we want to feel a sense of rehearsal in advance of an event, we create. When this is the motivation behind our sense of creativity, it can sometimes transpose that rather than resourcing for purpose, we are resourcing for preservation. As a natural consequence of this, resourcing can become more throwaway instead of sustainable and meaningful because it isn't fit for the long term; it's for that moment, with that class. But I would argue that resources don't need to have such a personalised tailoring system in order to be effective.

The undercurrent to this is the source of validation: who do we need to justify ourselves to? In schools where teachers have autonomy, by scripting our planning in advance, it gives us a concrete point of reference to consider our thinking at the moment of a lesson that we want to recall and reflect upon. Again, this means that the purpose of the plan isn't for the lesson itself, or the learning, but for either a blueprint to use in advance or a prompt to use to support our memory recall, which in turn would imply that we are not sure of what was truly meant to happen in that lesson. All of these observations still don't address the idea of preparing a lesson plan for someone who isn't going to use (but just peruse) it.

Neither plan nor prompt are conducive to what the original premise of the lesson plan set out to do, which is surely to map out what is to be learned, and how this will be executed. This brings its own challenges. Couple the observation hoop jump with the increasing amount of time that teachers spend working in isolation, rarely observing other teachers' practice, and the planning process has become quite the dilution of its original form. I would even go as far as stating that the way that planning has become an accountable feature for others over the teacher would mean it has become somewhat void of its original purpose. We don't use planning in the way that it would work best for us.

Why is this having an impact on my wellbeing?

Planning, the one task we are meant to adore, has become one of the top three-time sappers for teachers. As with any hobby, pastime or creative outlet, that means if we are forced to squeeze it in between all of the other jobs at hand, there's a strong possibility that we're not going to do it true justice, which is going to leave a sour taste. Similarly, it runs the danger of becoming a busman's holiday: we feel we have to do it instead of wanting to do it. We feel sated by the thought of planning when it comes at the end of a rather large to-do list.

When it's 10 p.m. and you're trawling the internet for something to help to teach the following day (because you have run out of time that was intended to plan and are now irritated that you are being forced into possibly not doing as good a job), you resent the job as a whole. How can we hope for satisfaction if the thing that satisfies us is beyond our reach? Teachers talk in droves about the box-ticking, audit trail of teaching, and the paper mountain is seemingly absent from the 'Those who can, teach' adverts. Teachers tire from the size of the workload, certainly, but equally so from the substance; if you go to work and only manage to participate for the least amount of time in the element that you enjoy the most (next to engaging with children's minds, of course), then it will feel like quite the thankless task.

Why are we still planning and resourcing then?

We need a plan; that is irrefutable. Even the most effective of teachers cannot work through a set amount of content by holding a finger to the wind and predicting it will take 18 hours to ensure that year 10 master *Macbeth*. But as pointed out, we need to shift the mindset around planning to ensure that it has a sense of fulfilment to it; that it is fit for purpose, but that it takes the precedence that it deserves in our day-to-day, week-to-week routine. Planning is our bread and butter. An English teacher can see five to six classes some four times a week, and there must be an established starting point to avoid an unmanageable funnel effect of work at some point during the working week.

There is little research that explores effective planning; small-scale studies demonstrate how many times particular formats have been downloaded and how they were used. I don't feel confident that this is a key indication of what works. If a sheet has four boxes to complete on it, the teacher will fill it with four episodes of teaching. That does not mean that the four boxes have magically become more effective. There is an abundance of advice for new teachers regarding planning, and I would argue that this is not the time to overload teachers with information or, indeed, provide false help. 'Planning is most properly regarded as a means to an end (i.e. effective teaching and learning) and not as an end in itself',[2] and if we start to consider how to dissect planning for learning rather than planning for lessons, it becomes a far less frustrating task.

It is only once we start to engage with how children learn that perhaps we understand the process of planning ourselves. 'Teachers themselves must be more active in using evidence to determine what works in the classroom,' stated Kathryn Greenhalgh in the Report of the Independent Teacher Workload Review Group,[3] and rightly so. Whilst bureaucracy will always be at play in some schools, in order for the landscape to change we need to take ownership of the things

---

2.   NASUWT: Lesson Planning, accessed at www.bit.ly/2FIRmBi
3.   Quoted in the NFER report, Using Evidence in the Classroom: What Works and Why?, Julie Nelson Clare O'Beirne, 2014.

that weigh heaviest on our working days for ourselves and make them function to our advantage.

To plan and resource lessons effectively in a way that works for us and ensures a pleasing outcome, we need to streamline both processes, taking a 'value versus time' approach. What is the learning? What do we anticipate for learners to grasp, and be able to do something with independently? Does our planning process stand the test of time? Ultimately, what is the purpose of the plan – to document the future, or evaluate the past?

Resourcing should support the teacher to deliver the curriculum
Ofsted's myth-busting poster requested that high-quality resources and medium-term planning should be in place and easily accessible for staff; middle management provide a curriculum plan with a thorough provision of the resources as the tools. In theory. The teacher is then responsible for ensuring that they equip themselves with the guidance required. Is this a reality? The government response to the workload challenge survey states that teachers didn't feel able to challenge or address their workload, because they didn't have the tools available to them. Put simply, resourcing still isn't in place in schools.

Is it that medium-term resourcing is now actually the curriculum map in some settings? Experienced teachers' lesson plans vary widely and may not be written down at all;[4] while formal lesson plans tend to follow a prescribed format, practising teachers appear to plan in idiosyncratic ways. The study also gave a hat tip to the fact that teachers plan mentally before a lesson takes place, which enables them to participate in a mental rehearsal that was adequate planning for them to be able to anticipate how the lesson might go.

Learning through a robust curriculum narrative means the learning cannot be dictated by time alone, but by the speed with which a pupil can grasp what is to be learned. So, in order to be authentic to this approach, what do we plan for, and to what

---

4.   McCutcheon, G. (1980). How do elementary school teachers plan? The nature of planning and influences on it. Elementary School Journal, 81, 4-23

extent? How can we streamline the process so that it is just a small extension of our mental rehearsal, and not a cumbersome job that actually tales away from teaching?

Take the long-term plan to teach a unit as an example:

Episode	Quotation Title	Key Question	Bright Spark Challenge	Vocabulary	Discussion questions
1	'Old fashioned by not cosy and homelike'	How do the stage directions give the audience a premise of social class?	Why is class both relevant and significant?	Imposing Portentous ornate	Edna's role Extrovertly higher class
2	'Lower costs and higher prices'	How does Mr Birling convey his opinions of business and current affairs?	Why does Priestly create a polar opposite of his own views and opinions?	Socialism Capitalism Steady the buffs Dramatic irony for purpose	How are we meant to react to Mr Birling, irrespective of our political views?
3 Analysis of Mr Birling modelled live	'as if we were all mixed up together like bees in a hive'	How is birling a character of deliberate provocation?	Why is Priestley's political background vital here?	Crank Naïve Prophetic irony Misogynist	Why does Mr Birling demonstrate so much distain for the Labour Party? The connotation of bees: insects, inferior, small, fragility, working to the death
4 Analysis of Mr Birling	'(Cutting through, massively)'	How do the characters attempt to maintain authority?	Does wealth equal power? Why does the Inspector not adhere to this rule?	Euphemism Caricature Officious Emotive	Significance of interruption as an aspect of the human condition
5	'I'd been so happy.'	How does Sheila evolve through her interrogation?	Why does Priestly demonstrate such a range of reactions in her?	Exploited Gender Narration as distraction Insecurities Justify	Where have we seen evidence of S's insecurities as a woman? Did E just magnify these? Is she authentic in her admissions?

The knowledge is the resource, not multiple worksheets or PowerPoints; episodes are planned; and there is a clear direction in the very baseline of content, vocabulary, and a big question to inform this direction. It can be added to during reflection after a series of lessons (perhaps points of interest that were flagged up in class discussion, or places that would prove useful to provide or increase the exposure to modelled examples, for instance) but this approach enables the teacher to have a blueprint with the emphasis on the knowledge of the subject – as it should be. Revisiting this blueprint will never be reductive; working alongside the curriculum, it informs the teacher of what content will be covered, and the points along the way that this can be revisited. Activities are defunct, because whilst the teacher can choose how to impart that knowledge, the planning is for learning to take place. It also works in correlation with a teacher audit, as it highlights to the teacher where the gaps in their subject knowledge may lie.

Auditing teacher knowledge is key for effective planning. During my teacher training, I found it difficult to plan, because I focused on filling the lesson time as opposed to what students might learn. Imagine what kind of teacher I would have been at the end of my training year if my priority had been to equip myself with the subject knowledge needed, or to read around the subject, and treat my curriculum as I would an undergraduate degree. It would take less time and be so much more valuable. To take an example:

I am teaching conflict poetry for the first time. To audit myself, what should I be required to know?

- Reading through a lens: genre, relevant reading of similar or contrasting genres to place alongside my interpretation of the texts
- Context: authorial information, social and historical context that could be applicable to the genre and the writers chosen
- Subject knowledge: key areas of analysis, tracking the concurrent threads, intertextual application
- The technicalities of the texts and how these prove to convey meaning

Equipping ourselves with the knowledge of the subject is the most time-efficient and empowering process to aid teaching. Subject knowledge-led development has somewhat fallen to the wayside for teaching strategy, and the two should work hand in hand, rather than one steal time from the other. I would stand by the view that this is one of many ways that we can halt the large turnover of teachers leaving the profession: by giving them the tools they need to feel confident with content.

Streamlining the way in which we approach the content itself is also paramount. As with the successful components of the curriculum, we must be decisive in what knowledge we choose to teach. When it comes to resourcing, we must select what our non-negotiables are to enable such teaching to take place. A far cry from worksheet-sticking to plaster over the cracks, on the whole, curated and printed resources should only be required as a final resort. You are the resource; take care of yourself. Your knowledge will be the most efficient resource in the room, and sometimes we are in danger of forgetting that amid photocopying and hoards of cards in envelopes that we convince ourselves are useful. They're not as useful as you.

Audit to knowledge

A unit audit will also provide a rationale to then create a knowledge organiser for students to use. Again, this is about creating resources that will hold longevity, and not just a one-time function for a particular teacher in their particular setting. By teaching all students better, we raise that bar to start with high expectations for the knowledge that we hold dear.

As a working example, a knowledge organiser for a topic may resemble this:[5]

Eduqas Religious Studies A Level - *Ethics - Utilitarianism*

Key Words				
Consequentialist	A theory which is only concerned with the outcomes of an action	Intrinsic Good	Something is good for its own sake without looking at further consequences
Deterrence	Seeking to put off other countries from attacking with a threat of force	Propinquity	How remote happiness is – how long you must wait until it starts
Dissection	Taking apart dead animals in order to learn more about them	Quantitative	A measurable value – e.g. using the Hedonic Calculus to measure happiness
Fecundity	How much pleasure an act will lead to in the future	Relativism	A theory with no absolutes or rules which are formulated in advance
Harm Principle	Mill's idea that we should not stop actions unless they are causing harm to others	Secular	A non-religious theory or idea
Hedonic Calculus	Bentham's way of calculating how much pleasure an action will create	Vivisection	Experimenting on animals whilst they are still alive
Hedonism	Being concerned only with creating the most pleasure and avoiding pain	WMD	Weapons of Mass Destruction e.g. nuclear, chemical or biological weapons

Key Ideas		
Act Utilitarianism	- An ethical theory put forward by **Jeremy Bentham** (1748-1832) - Ultimate aim is to pursue pleasure and avoid pain - It is **relativistic** (there are no rules that can be formulated in advance) and it is **consequentialist** (focused on the consequences of an action)	**The Principle of Utility** - Simply put: 'the greatest happiness for the greatest number' - The aim of Bentham's Utilitarianism is to promote the maximum amount of happiness for society
Bentham's Hedonic Calculus	- Bentham's Hedonic Calculus is a 'scientific' way of calculating how much pleasure or pain an action will cause - Bentham felt we can weigh up pleasure **quantitatively** (measurably). - Bentham has seven measures for pleasure 1. Duration – 2. Fecundity – 3. Purity – 4. Propinquity – 5. Intensity – 6. Certainty – 7. Extent	
Rule Utilitarianism	- An ethical theory put forward by John Stuart Mill (1806 - 1873) - Mill focused on pleasure being **qualitative** rather than quantitative – that not all pleasure is of equal worth and value - Rule Utilitarianism is a hybrid of ethical theories as it establishes a rule (**teleological**) but once that rule is established it becomes a duty to uphold it for maximum happiness (**deontological**)	**Higher vs Lower Pleasures** - Mill argued that some pleasures were **higher** because they were intellectual and separated us from the other animals e.g. reading, art, spirituality - **Lower** pleasures, like sex, eating, drinking, were not as valuable as they are animalistic - Higher pleasures therefore have a higher moral value even if lower pleasures bring more happiness
Mill's Harm Principle	- Mill developed the Harm Principle as a way of protecting happiness and **individual freedoms** and rights - It states that we may never limit the actions of people, except to prevent harm being done to others - All people should, therefore, be free to act how they wish if they do not harm others - Exceptions would be children and the uneducated	
Application: Animal Experimentation	- Animal experimentation refers to the use of animals to learn how to medically treat humans - It can include dissection (taking apart the bodies of dead animals) or vivisection (experimenting on live animals) or treating animals with drugs to check their safety	
	Bentham's Act Utilitarianism - "The question is not, can they reason? Nor can they talk? But can they suffer" – Jeremy Bentham - Bentham believed the animal's capacity for suffering overtook their capacity for reason and language – this was the unsuperable line	**Mill's Rule Utilitarianism** - Mill grouped animals with children: they need to be protected as they cannot care for themselves - On one side animal experimentation leads to the pursuit of human pleasures and protects sick people from harm - On the other side it violates the harm principle
Application: Nuclear Weapons	- **Deterrence theory** states that countries are less likely to attack another country if that country has nuclear weapons it could use in response - It gives countries a reason to keep and maintain nuclear weapons with the hope they would not use them	
	Bentham's Act Utilitarianism - The Hedonic Calculus must be applied to each individual situation instead of forming rules - What kind of pleasure/pain can come from situations where nuclear weapons are involved? - Does deterrence theory avoid pain for others?	**Mill's Rule Utilitarianism** - The **Harm Principle** must be consulted, and rules created in order to work out if deterrence is ethical - Deterrence could lead to the greatest happiness if it avoids war - However, any use of nuclear weapons is seriously harmful to millions of people

5.   www.bit.ly/2Mmo8M6 – credit to A.J. Smith

The knowledge organiser distils key substantive knowledge to help students identify the foundational content for that unit. This particular example uses dual coding to categorise particular threads within the unit. This strategy can then be used at later points to connect aspects of knowledge together from one unit to the next, contextualising elements for students but also emphasising the longevity of such knowledge: the connections and the continuing narrative of the subject through these connections.

Students can be allocated a particular aspect to revise before then applying it within the lesson. The knowledge organiser, text and teacher are the lesson, as opposed to a hefty PowerPoint and a chunk-by-chunk approach to characters or ideas.

Alternatively, knowledge organisers can be used as an active part of self-quizzing for students as part of retrieval practice. Students can collect knowledge organisers to accumulate knowledge of units over the course of the year, but this also then acts as a way of laying out what needs to be known – which knowledge is central to learning?

Finally, if you can stand to part with it, ditch PowerPoint. It always raises a feisty debate, and PowerPoint can be a real point of contention amongst teachers. Jamie Thom refers to it in his blog as 'the curse', and I would be inclined to agree.

There are two arguments that I want to make regarding PowerPoint: what we think it does, and where it can fail to deliver. This is both in the classroom and in the preparation of medium-term planning itself – and above all, where it fails to deliver on time gained for you as a teacher that wants to reduce workload.

Speaking with numerous department leaders, there seems to be a genuine desire to support department staff in the resourcing of units of work. The less experienced the department members, the more inclined faculty heads were in wanting to provide extensive, step-by-step lesson plans to aid with workload. A unit document outlining what should happen each lesson would then be supported by one gigantic PowerPoint, along with the relevant extracts and worksheets etc. But does this really help or hinder?

We all know that teaching other people's lessons is a real challenge. Picking up a PowerPoint that someone else has created for their class or their context doesn't necessarily encourage or support someone's workload; where we are trying to provide a starting point for teachers, it can actually become more of an onerous task to make use of it.

PowerPoint has become a crutch which implies teachers can be teachers simply by putting an explanatory screen behind themselves. We may as well have the Microsoft Office paperclip by our side, cheering us on as we deliver our lesson. Teaching often feels like an intangible profession, difficult to measure your workload and successes, and so we cling to bulky, jam-packed presentations for schemes like badges of honour, concrete demonstrations of work completed that really hold little substance in relation to the time that they took away from us.

Dull and distracting in equal measure at times, a presentation can disguise itself as a helping hand, but be far from it. We justify the use of it by stating it is a prompt or an outline, when not only have PowerPoints stolen hours of teacher time in their creation, but they rarely have staying power – and in fact, hinder learning when used to excess. Need convincing? No problem.

To justify the inclusion of PowerPoint within teaching, you need to consider the following elements. What is the purpose? Who will it benefit? (The creation of the presentation may be justifiable if the answer is you rather than the student, but this may alter the construction of it.) If you are using it as a prompt for yourself, is it worth the time creating it?

Removing PowerPoint from my teaching (forcing myself to try without for a week, and not really looking back) is one of the biggest time savers in my career to date. If I can't convince you to discard it altogether, here are a few ways of making what you do more effective in the classroom (and should hopefully save you some time).

- **One key message:** Mary Myatt does this perfectly. 'One key message' streamlines your presentation so that you are being selective as a teacher with the information that you want to teach, but also ensures that the key thread of the lesson remains at the forefront. This lends itself nicely to 'big questions', or enquiry-led learning within the classroom. An episode of learning could then look like this:

- To what extent is Gerald honourable?
- Where is this evidenced?
- What are his motives?
- Do we find his behaviour authentic?
- What other aspects are relevant here?
- Why does Priestley manufacture such an ambiguous character?

These questions would occupy one slide, and perhaps be crossed off as they are discussed or explored. Nothing more; nothing else is required.

- **Avoid overload:** Cognitive load theory is also at play here, as Bartlett outlines: 'What is remembered is only partly dependent on the information itself. Newly presented information is altered so that it is congruent with knowledge of the subject matter.'[6] Dissected, our working memory holds information for less than a minute before it is lost or allocated to schemas in our long-term memory. Our working memory holds four items as a representative figure, and the less that exists here, along with its compatibility to schema in our long-term memory, the more chance that information has of being retained. Oli Caviglioli details this in visual perfection if you would like a whistle-stop tour of CLT in more detail. To see through the lens of a learner, let's take a PowerPoint slide (See footnote for illustration)[7]:

6. Bartlett F. C. (1932). Remembering: A Study in Experimental and Social Psychology. Cambridge: Cambridge University Press.
7. www.bit.ly/2QqxjN9

- Have a big question to drive learning – ongoing.
- Have new content to be elaborated upon by the teacher.
- Have a question to discuss.
- Have an instruction to write once it has been discussed.
- Have stem sentences to drive discussion.

Putting prior knowledge to one side for a moment, let us all assume we know something of the topic beforehand. The student needs to read the content, listen to the delivery, read the question set, anticipate the answer of their speaking partner, mentally rehearse their own ideas, and relate it to the task to be able to articulate their verbal ideas in writing. And listen to you talk, which, according to Mayer (2002),[8] will be impossible. We cannot do multiple things well. Put simply, it is incredibly challenging to read at the same time as listening to someone speak, and certainly impossible to process all the information. What is most important: listening to you, the expert; or reading information that you, the expert, has written? Either, perhaps – but it is preferable (and less work for you) to choose one and run with it.

Style is everything

Phillips argues that 70% of the time focus is spent on a PowerPoint headline,[9] although it is rarely the most important part. If you place your big question here, maybe; but then what is the rest of the space for, if your only purpose is to display a big question? Unsubstantiated Comic Sans font choice (Dr Holly Joseph's visual tracking work is fascinating here)[10] also makes it far more of a challenge for learners

8. Richard E. Mayer (2002) Rote Versus Meaningful Learning, Theory Into Practice, 41:4, 226-232, DOI: 10.1207/s15430421tip4104_4
9. How to Avoid Death By PowerPoint: David JP Phillips at TEDxStockholmSalon (Transcript) Education / By Pangambam S / March 8 2018
10. Understanding children's written language comprehension through eye movements, H Joseph, Grant reference: PTA-026-27-1912, details at www.bit.ly/37ltYpP

to do what is expected of them. By centralising your one key message, you enable learners not to be led by placement, but by what is encompassing the space. Couple this with our colour choice – not white (unsubstantiated by vast research but commented by enough students with reading difficulties to warrant that it won't do harm) but a soft enough shade that, as Philips demands, 'I'm the most contrast-rich object. I got your focus. Why is that important? It's important because I am, I always have been, and I always will be the presentation. That is my visual aid.' I say it again: you are the most important feature.

I know what you're going to say: 'It helps me remember!' Then you need a prompt, not a PowerPoint. You don't stick your shopping list up on the projector so you know what to pick up at Sainsbury's on the way home, so why display what you need to students who don't need to know what you need? 'It allows me to be creative!' That's OK, but that's not what it's for. And if you are looking to shave time to play piano, I know which creative outlet I would be picking. 'What about cover? Or moving classrooms?' If your workload means that, for the majority of the time, you are setting cover lessons, then this is a separate kettle of fish to the entire argument, and a different concern altogether. If you are a middle leader of curriculum, supporting your department with cover, there are resources that have longevity to them that don't call for PowerPoint. That would call for another chapter entirely. Standard generic cover lessons are a key time saver here, but planning lessons for when you may be off is not a great way to use time. 'We can't photocopy!' This one is tough, because we can only deal with what is within your control. I would argue – and will do so, further on in this section – that depending on what needs to be copied, modelled work for example, I might let you off with a bit of PowerPoint. Only if it's something that stands the test of time and that you can return to without amendment over and over again. Am I joking? No, not entirely. My overarching message here is not that PowerPoint is useless, but that if you are spending a long time on something, it has to be worth it. It has to enhance your practice. The value of your time must be justified. And if you are using PowerPoint as an effective tool for modelling, key messages, dual coding to support your delivery (and let's be clear, your delivery is the most important resource), then it is of value. If you are using it as a prompt, to indulge your inner creative muse, or to provide a range of cover to your departmental staff, then it is of some small value. Either way, however long you have spent on its creation should mean that you reap the rewards for it tenfold. I will put my personal feelings aside and simply ask you: **did the slide take longer to prepare than the students took to learn?**

To return to the misconception that we may convince ourselves that a 160-slide PowerPoint is supporting staff and aiding with workload, I would argue it does the opposite. If, however, your PowerPoint supports me as a teacher to identify the big question that my students should work to answer, the key vocabulary that I will teach them, the opportunity to embed routines and habits so that they are ingrained in my teaching and part of what we do every day, only then might I argue it would be useful.

What's the alternative? Here are two possible alternatives that could have longevity in comparison:

- **A streamline sequence that outlines non negotiables:** and I mean that choice of term in its most positive format, if it hasn't already been bastardised in your place of work. The medium plan outlines what needs to be covered – both knowledge and skills practice, a suggested teaching outline and the particular practice focus for that week (for English, the particular text and purpose – e.g. language, structure, exploring narrative voice), and a clear correlation as to how it feeds into the curriculum narrative. This one-page quick reference guide provides a blueprint alongside a knowledge organiser for the unit, and the relevant accompanying resources so that even a teacher new to a department or a less experienced teacher can focus on the content, the knowledge baseline – the key information that they need to teach the topic effectively – and less so on 'how to fill an hour'. This also focuses energy into placing an emphasis on the teacher as a resource and not the resource as resource. A one-page overview that gives the teacher an explicit outline of what students need to know by the completion of teaching that content.

• **Reflection spreadsheet:** a spreadsheet completed retrospectively that enables teachers to look back on what they covered within that topic. This is the more tech-savvy option for those of us who long ago discarded the planner and love paperless working. A reflection spreadsheet enables a medium-term plan to exist electronically, and also enables collaborative working in a much more coherent manner. Do you work in one of those departments that states, 'It's on the shared area', only to find yourself spending 45 minutes wading through outdated resources that don't have any common thread to the topic you are trying to teach? The spreadsheet offers a series of solutions to a traditional shared space.

In addition to providing a sequence of delivery, the spreadsheet can act as a point of access for all linked resources, modelled exemplars and assessments. Staff can collaboratively add to the spreadsheet as they teach to demonstrate the questions covered that enabled great discussion – big questions, vocabulary, content knowledge from KO, modelled responses, five-a-day roulette. The result is a one-page go-to with a series of links that offers a time-efficient way to access a vast amount of subject knowledge and resources vital to the teaching of that unit.[11]

Both options strip away the excessive, somewhat disjointed PowerPoints and provide teachers with an audit starting point of what they need to know; it's exposing, but in a liberating sense: it allows teachers to see their own gaps, and a really clear pathway to get ahead. Teachers within departments could even use the spreadsheet as a way of considering their subject knowledge gaps

11. www.bit.ly/376q97q

and where they could prioritise their own reading. The time no longer spent planning presentations can be redirected into subject knowledge revision or writing exemplar responses. How often is it that units in school, particularly key stage 3, have modelled responses sat against each unit, when we often teach the same units year after year? If resourcing was carried out with a refocus on what teachers will need along the way on a day-to-day basis, and not handing over a PowerPoint as a step-by-step substitution for an instruction guide, not only would teachers feel confident, but they might actually feel more prepared to tackle topics in their lessons with tenacity, as opposed to teaching someone else's lessons because time doesn't allow any other option, and losing their sense of identity a little in the process.

- Create a resource provision that prioritises knowledge.
- Have a 'time spent vs value gained' approach to resourcing.
- Create effectively so that time can be used to empower staff to teach with a sense of identity.

Resourcing should be collaborative and with context

Teachers need to share their teaching practice and learning experiences in order to stimulate a learning culture in schools.
– Haiyan, Q., Walker, A., & Xiaowei, Y. (2017).[12]

Litdrive was a collaborative creation that emerged as a result of feeling isolated in my new role as literacy coordinator six years ago. I found myself in a position where I wanted to make an impact, but didn't feel that the role came with the necessary network within school to map out exactly how to go about planning a strategy, as is

---

12. Haiyan, Q., Walker, A., & Xiaowei, Y. (2017). Building and leading a learning culture among teachers: A case study of a Shanghai primary school. *Educational Management Administration & Leadership, 45*(1), 101–122.

the nature of whole-school responsibilities where one person drives an agenda. A year later, with over 14,000 members, Litdrive provides English teachers with the platform they need to help one another, and I can honestly say that I would not be the teacher that I am today without the network of people that have supported me to refine and revise my resourcing and teaching strategy within the classroom. My entire career has been the product of collaboration and sharing ideas; I shared and learned from incredible English teachers in my early-career teaching, which helped me to craft and refine my own approach within the classroom. Following changes in specification and framework, I shared ideas with Diane Duncan, Kate McCabe, Clare Percy and Freya O'Dell using the #KS3LTP to work towards a thoughtful and nourishing journey through the subject of English for students.

Resourcing needs collaboration for it to be a success, and with time being such a precious commodity in schools, this is all the more of a priority. Movements and emerging communities – such as #TeamEnglish, #CogSciSci, #HistoryTeachers, #EdchatRes and #ResearchEd, to name a slither of the networks ready and willing to support and guide teachers on social media – have made sharing not only possible, but instantaneous and contextual. Stretching networks that exist beyond regional hubs, or local authority equivalents, and away from the multi-academy trusts (who may, of course, strategise in a similar way in keeping with their collective ethos), networks like the previously mentioned communities keep challenge and drive change within education, and are a breath of fresh air to teachers in settings that are perhaps slightly more on the stagnant side.

Collaborative resourcing is nothing new, but in places it has become far more challenging. Academisation and the loss of local education authorities mean that in many regions, collaboration has become competition; the educational landscape in some regions has become a marketplace rather than a cooperative. We are all doing the same thing, but in isolation; and whilst places like Twitter and Facebook provide a bounty of help (depending upon the way they are used), they can become small echo chambers and do not represent the teaching population that are struggling in schools to effectively resource under time constraints and without the essential support and sounding board that is needed to not only improve, but simply survive.

Every school that thrives will boast collaborative planning. It not only claws back time, but it means that strategy and sequence have been considered, contested, refined and discussed before the curation process even begins. The wealth of experience that this can bring to planning is invaluable; it's simply a no-brainer. So why is this proving a difficulty for schools? What stops us working as a collegiate community? Usually it's just time – and a reluctance to share that we don't know how.

The issue at the start of my teaching career was that I had no experience of planning, no support with planning and no lesson resources. Every lesson was created from scratch. Units of work were sometimes absent altogether or at best were designed for experienced teachers with their own lessons and resources from previous years of teaching. Ironically, the PowerPoints were designed for the people that needed them the least. I would work until the early hours every single morning, before beginning teaching at 8.25 a.m., to decipher other people's lessons in the isolation of my classroom.

At entrance level, we don't consider the planning process over a longer period of time as a priority for trainees – it's the sequencing of a lesson, how to assert yourself within a classroom, managing your time. I know teachers who are almost a decade in and have never had to think about the cognitive implications for mapping out or resourcing for medium- or short-term planning; everything has just been there, sitting on *Tes* or a bumper-size PowerPoint (don't start me off again). But at some point, gain time will come around after the flurry of exam season, units are revisited (usually key stage 3 because the exam specifications hand over a ready-made menu) and members of the department are expected to plan a unit to teach. So, at this point, why are we not collaboratively planning effectively?

Two reasons. The first is that some people hate to share. Teaching is such a personal task to the individual, and the way in which we plan lessons is such a part of the rehearsal to teaching that it can be impossible to just take a 'pick-up-and-run' approach with other people's resources to deliver our lessons. When you speak to teachers about sharing their work, they hold the belief that what they create would not be of any value to others. Beyond that, the one-size-fits-all is sneered at as simplistic and just not in keeping with the complexity of teaching – can what I share be useful to students beyond my classroom, with my teaching approach?

Time is the other factor here. It is straightforward for one person in isolation to find time to work on their terms; time for two people to meet, explore and discuss ideas before moving forward with a general consensus and an action plan is really quite a tall order and comes with logistical challenges. With the best of intentions, if we physically don't have the time available for all people required to be in the same place, collaboration isn't possible. However, this process and the reflection process as a collaborative effort are quite possibly among the most vital spaces to make a place for within schools.

Why is this? This review of collaborative partnership and planning research speaks frankly: Schwab Learning (2003) documented the impact of collaborative partnerships and co teaching in 16 California elementary, middle, and secondary schools. Results included decreased referrals to intensive special education services, increased overall student achievement, fewer disruptive problems, less paperwork, increased number of students qualifying for gifted and talented education services, and decreased referrals for behavioural problems. In addition, teachers reported being happier and not as isolated.

Collaborative planning leads to strengthened teacher ownership over work that they value and invest in, strengthened relationships within departments between employees that have a range of knowledge and experience to offer, and a much more cohesive approach as a subject. Now, we can consider how to implement this within departments.

Give ownership: when looking to monitor and evaluate units of learning, ask department staff where their strengths and areas of development that interest them lie (the audit is an ideal point of reference for this). Set aside time at the end of the year where reflection is possible but before people feel overwhelmed to demonstrate that you value the importance of giving staff the opportunity to refine knowledge. Wherever possible, allocate one member of staff to champion a unit that they have subject-specific experience of, and they can then work with another member of staff who may feel less confident with that unit to improve or adapt the unit together. The process acts as a mentoring process but in a non-judgemental setting. Concisely identify what will be required on a one-page format, so that there is a discourse around the key aspects of the unit:

Unit 1 Year 7 History of Language Streamline Sequence	
Content to be covered	Etymology- what it is and practical application History of oral storytelling and print Understanding of literature timeline Thematic correlations through time/ allusion
Vocabulary teaching	Etymology Origin Morpheme Suffix Prefix Allusion Mythology Moral
Skills practice	Annotation What-how-why Cornell notes Big question enquiry

Unit 1 Year 7 History of Language Streamline Sequence	
Suggested teaching	1: Pandora's box: origin storytelling 2: Beowulf: moral, oral storytelling 3: Sir Gawain and the Green Knight: protagonist 4: Richard III: flawed protagonist 5: Oliver Twist: Bill Sykes and Fagin: antagonist 6: Harry Potter: Modern protagonist
Assessment opportunities	
Opportunities for further challenge	Retold tales: Roald Dahl, Anthony Horowitz, Myths and Legends, Carol Ann Duffy, Grimm Tales Retold
Correlation to the Curriculum	A history of literature

(See footnote for downloadable table)[13]

Planning in process: allocate a unit to two individuals who will teach that unit over the forthcoming academic year. Those colleagues are then responsible for keeping a collaborative working log – this is where a Reflection spreadsheet comes in handy – to monitor the success and possible gaps of learning or resource needs for the unit over the course of the year. Create a quick review check-in email that as each term ends, staff take five minutes to review the knowledge and consider what has worked and what they have needed to add or source to improve it. Gain time can then be used as a reflection and review process to create what will be used for the following year, as opposed to what I would call 'cold-creations' – resources that get created as one-offs that may never end up getting used, or resources being created in anticipation of what might be useful, as opposed to tried and tested to ensure they are fit for purpose.

13.   www.bit.ly/35htq24

Create a quality assurance system: utilise the strengths of your department and request that the person with the most confidence and experience in effective planning create a template overview model for a unit of work. This unit model acts as a how-to that outlines to staff how to approach the planning process, with a clear focus on non-negotiables, content, vocabulary, assessment opportunities and suggested sequence. Return to the model and reference it during departmental time, resources sharing emails etc., so that it becomes a rulebook to follow for effective planning. See the example in this footnote as a point of reference.[14]

This can then be a process for teachers within the department to complete, giving ownership through a collective sense of purpose.

Drive teacher confidence by sharing: middle leaders have the luxury of seeing the standard of teaching inside classrooms within their department, but in what context and frequency does this information get shared? Positive sharing of resources is key to breaking down the barriers that stop people from sharing in the first place; in the same way that not sharing encourages less sharing, sharing more encourages more sharing: it is a perpetual cycle. In my experience whilst quality assuring Litdrive's resource bank, teachers are cautious to share because they are afraid of what 'good' is meant to look like, and that their standard simply doesn't measure up. This is rarely the case, but as a less experienced teacher, it can be incredibly frustrating to be in a position that you either use the resources of others, or battle on in

---

14.   www.bit.ly/35kJdx7

isolation, too scared to share what you have created because you have very little to compare it to or you hold the common misconception that everyone must be creating something that is of a higher standard. Department leads: share your department's successes frequently and publicly; it doesn't always have to be a name game, or a calling-out of public praise – teachers are like students: their attitude to praise is personal – but the sharing itself is what matters. It means that a team is repeatedly exposed to what the gold standard is, and what effective application of subject knowledge and teaching strategy looks like. Beyond that, it creates a culture where sharing is common practice and I will categorically guarantee, the more that good work is highlighted, the more people will share; this is the nature of the beast. 'But not everyone shares!' I hear you cry. Who cares? The right people will. And that's the place to start.

Embedding this culture leads not only to a resource-rich working environment, but to one where feedback is welcomed and utilised – where you share openly, request feedback and are prepared to learn as a result. Did people use your resource? How did they use it, and did they make any adaptations? Did they use it in a different context from the one that you had originally intended, and what kind of impact did it make? All these discussions and the quick emails of thanks are of astronomical value and help to remove protective, praise-seeking egos from the planning process so that it benefits all instead of the few.

- -

A moment for time-wasting lethal mutations from Claire Hill, Assistant Principal at the Turner Schools Trust:

66 People who work in schools are often idea rich but time poor. Which means even when ideas are good, their implementation suffers from a lack of time,

understanding, and training to ensure they are effective. At this point, they can suffer from what Dylan Wiliam and others have termed 'lethal mutations' and what Nick Rose explains can render 'good ideas – even when well-rooted in research – no longer effective, or even counter-productive'. If teachers are to implement ideas well, they need to understand very clearly the why, what and how of the approaches they are asked to use in the classroom and a one-off INSET or meeting simply will not cut it. Teachers need to know why they are being asked to adapt or change their practice, and why this particular approach is their 'best bet' for supporting their students. Take feedback for example and the popularity of the whole-group feedback sheet. If teachers are not very clear that the reason why this approach is effective is that it informs that teacher of what needs to be re-taught and to support the student in future learning, this becomes just as ineffective as any other form of feedback. Similarly, if teachers do not see why they are being asked to use knowledge organisers or why dual coding can be support learning, then they become little more than a one-page summary or an exercise in using clipart, which can hinder learning rather than support it. To avoid this, time needs to be spent by whomever is introducing new ideas to really get to grips with why this an important change or addition to a teacher's practice – what does the research say? How is this being used successfully in other schools? If the 'why' isn't clear, it becomes much more likely that 'lethal mutations' will occur. Teachers then need to see, in a concrete way, what this looks like in their subject. Training sessions that take examples solely from humanities subjects or from science are unlikely to be useful to teachers who need to see how they can use this in a different context.

We give our students relevant and concrete examples as this assists learning – the same goes for adults. Similarly, we model for our students – using worked examples or narrating processes. It makes sense that this would also be helpful for teachers. Watching others use these approaches in the classroom – whether within school or through videos online – can help teachers to visualise and emulate ideas for their teaching. In addition, talking through the planning process together and narrating to one other what this looks like in the classroom as they plan or make resources can help make abstract ideas more tangible as well as helping to help to identify possible pitfalls or misconceptions. Fortunately, many schools are beginning to see the value in timetabling collaborative planning opportunities for departments which can be instrumental in ensuring ideas are understood and implemented well, avoiding these 'lethal mutations'.

Feeling brave? Good! Share what's working across the school. Collaboration works on varying levels within the school system and this is impactful on wellbeing for many reasons; you are helping colleagues to improve their practice, sharing an insight of something that worked, and by telling other departments about a strategy you use, those students may now make it habitual in their work within other subjects. Becky Wood's What-How-Why model for analytical writing works fantastically across other subjects such as history or geography as well as English; the strategies outlined in this section also lend themselves to being models that can form habitual practice, which we will look at in a moment. Sharing doesn't just aid your confidence and professional development (which are the key factors in maintaining a sense of accomplishment at work) but also aids students' demonstration of what they have learnt, and plays a central part in developing whole-school routines that students recognise and can apply as second nature.

Lastly, collaborate to avoid making for making's sake. There is nothing more heartbreaking than creating a resource only to find out there are five versions already in circulation. Talk to people; find out what they are doing in their classes, in other subjects; find out where they are in the unit that you are teaching as well. Those discussions will prevent both of you knocking up the throwaway resources that are causing us all to haemorrhage time.

- Use collaborative practice as a standard approach to departmental planning: no one works in isolation.
- Create audit measures to drive up the standard of resourcing and enable teachers to empower one another through sharing knowledge.
- Share within and across faculties to break down common worries around sharing best practice, and common language of the subject.

Resourcing should stand the test of time

A text can inspire, and a text can make us think. A text can absorb and engage. It might disturb, challenge or delight. It might become a fresh lens through which to see a difficult idea. I have argued elsewhere that this gives a text a power greater than that of a teacher   – Counsell, 2004

Frivolous resourcing has had an impact upon wellbeing in an indirect and subtle way over previous years within teaching. Lessons mimic game shows or computer games because engagement will only be achieved if we get down with the kids; when actually, this undermines our very purpose – to ourselves, and to the students. By dressing up our subject in the form of *Minecraft*, or disguising literature by dumbing it down to a *Who Wants to Be a Millionaire?* PowerPoint, we are implying that the content of these texts alone cannot possibly be engaging enough to warrant our attention in their naked form. You were lured in by characters and themes of texts; is it really so outrageous that others would have the same experience without you having to hide the content in posters or leaflets?

I have been guilty of such. By encouraging the idea that English in its entity is inferior, or less than worthy, this perpetuates itself in the excessive creation of resources that don't stand the test of time; they lack longevity because they are trying, vainly, to insist that English is cool. We don't need gimmicks to demonstrate just how cool our subjects are – you didn't go to university for three years because you were the only person on the planet who bought into the concept that literature was something of merit and value.

Consequently, it needs to be clear to students that English is English; the resource is an essential addition to the text to enable them to grasp key ideas, characters or thematic links, rather than for the sake of having a resource. Teaching sometimes falls into a false sense of security by thinking that placing a semi-filled piece of paper in front of students will help and develop their knowledge, but the opposite is often the case. Moreover, in five years' time, will your *Love Island* tweet correction starters be the *Snog, Marry, Avoid* character task of the past?

Stop making throwaway resources, and create resources that you can use across topics, year groups or throughout units instead of just singular lessons. I approach resourcing in the same way I spend money: cost per use. Is it worth the time I have spent trawling through a shared area, or compiling this resource myself, for the amount of time that I will spend using it? If the answer is no, then I don't do it. One-time worksheets do not last because they are not tried and tested, they give you another copying job to do in your already busy week (eight minutes a lesson, remember), and they simply do not deliver in helping you as a teacher to instil routines for your learners.

Another way to instil habits through resourcing is by setting up regular weekly spots for a particular aspect of practice for your subject. For English, Chris Curtis's 200-Word Challenge not only considers teacher workload, but also instils really beneficial learning habits in students. Once a week, students collaboratively plan and independently write at least 200 words in response to a writing task. The task is 'cold': students have not seen it before, and the task will include some non-negotiables to use in the writing – particularly vocabulary or stylistic choices in keeping with the task. The challenge lesson develops a student's ability to work in timed conditions with material that they have not been able to revise or review and working in silence is something that all pupils come to value as they move towards more formal examinations. The word challenge can be peer assessed – again, this is all about training good learning and exemplifying what that means and looks like – which enables teachers to take the opportunity to write a modelled example, mark the class books or carry out intervention for students who have been absent or require support. The impact of supporting students with a regular task such as this means students have a weekly window to practise habits that will yield great return not only in the exam hall, but across subjects. The weekly challenges are now an embedded part of many departments as a way of regular, repeated practice that will reap rewards as a result of being a permanent fixture.

Another way that can help to form habits for expectations is using a challenging writing frame that demands high standards from students. What-How-Why (developed by Claire Hill and Becky Wood and adapted and revised by a number of people in the #TeamEnglish community) has thrown out other approaches to writing such as PEE as unfit for purpose, and provides students with a far more thorough way of responding analytically to the knowledge of the subject. The framework enables students to develop far more interdependence with ideas and interpretation, enables students to move around the components of the framework so that they feel it fits their personal style, and makes sense to them.

This process not only allows students to explore literature in far greater depth than its predecessor, but it can also be used across the curriculum to do the same. Music, RS, drama and history all make use of such a tool and this builds upon familiarity and embedding of routines. Imagine being a student and having to recall eight different writing structures across all of your subjects, not accounting for those subjects that try to outline a different structure for each exam question. It's problematic, not only for students' cognitive load and feeling that essence of 'starting from scratch' every time they walk into your classroom, but also because it makes the teachers' role incredibly difficult as skills practice can be disjointed if we have to repeatedly start again when applying such a framework.

Another ideal way to create longevity in resourcing is to think outside of the traditional provision. I recently visited a school where the teacher had compiled a series of previous exam questions on Google Forms, so that she could pull up one at random for students to complete for revision. Using departmental gained time from the previous year, this was a really simple and effective way of having a bank of resources stored that didn't require printing and could be set for homework within five minutes. It's a sensible way of having a stockpile resource that can be used in a variety of ways.

Resources like Cloud 9 Writing – a collection of exemplar responses pulled together by Paul Moss from a range of school settings – provide an ideal way to equip your students with several key examples of the finished result. Through practice, students are then able to see just how achievable that end result is, and the impact of practice revelation means it is clear to them, and you, that it is learning that takes priority over simply doing.

We have been mis-sold the idea of the outstanding lesson for too long and buying into the concept that a lesson is the limit of the plan. By looking ahead and viewing episodes of learning for what they really are, we can move away from the lesson-by-lesson approach and resource learning voyages as opposed to day trips. Resourcing effectively means that you get to lay out the blueprint of what you want to see as an outcome for students.

As Tom Sherrington states, 'We have spent so long chasing rainbows ... diving down rabbit holes; grasping at straws; playing whack-a-mole'[15] but in effect, we just need to teach everyone better. This means not reducing self-expectation through limiting resources. Ultimately, resourcing should provide a series of structures that can then be taken away. For you to operate an effective and manageable workload, you must provide a template of content.

Here are some other examples of resources that are fantastic for standing the test of time. This is with my English head on, but I have attempted to include working examples that demonstrate longevity and could be used across other subject specialisms:

Exploration of character

Tweeted out as a method that I use when teaching literature as a way of carrying out character dissection with a more academic and analytical tone, this was quickly transferred into a visual by Jennifer Webb that can be used time and again for exploring the layers of a

---

15.   Tom Sherrington, Teach Everyone Better, 2018 accessed at www.bit.ly/30es9Z0

character, and their motivations. Notice the embedded use of what, how, why within the structure of the framework. [16]

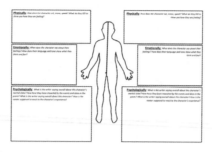

Thinking hard tasks

Inspired by Thinking Hard (@thinkinghard12 – the genius of Simon Hardwick and Martin Jones) and reignited by Alex Quigley within his book *Closing the Vocabulary Gap*, thinking hard tasks are high-challenge, maximum reward that focus on the impact of 'everyday interactions, routines and habits teachers use' to draw success from students. The tasks are quick to plan, transferable from unit to unit and channel analytical thinking to ensure that students can use such strategies for themselves once rehearsed. [17]

16. www.bit.ly/30ivKVU
17. www.bit.ly/2uFOliQ

Word wheels

Word wheels are an incredible way to drive the application of sophisticated vocabulary for a particular unit and are a key example of how the most straightforward ideas can often be the very best ones. The resource can be used year in, year out to drive students' discussion and debate. Shared by Hannah Antonio, with permission. [18]

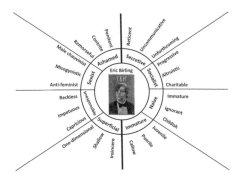

Poetry challenge grids

Created for GCSE poetry, the challenge grids explore different aspects of the poem but move between the how and why of critical analysis, rather than simple retrieval and selection tasks. Reusable and with very little planning required, these stand the test of time when consolidating content. The questions do not just retrieve knowledge, but also act as a springboard for discussion. These could be very easily adapted for any subject content. [19]

---

18.   www.bit.ly/2ZKwZgr
19.   www.bit.ly/2uFOliQ

A thought on booklets, books and glue sticks

Booklets are rapidly becoming the alternative resource in the room to hefty PowerPoints and mountains of worksheets, and they are the logical next step to accompany a successful, knowledge-driven curriculum, but I feel that they require a caveat. Whilst they save a department time on resourcing (so that teachers don't have to then go home to their respective dimly lit lounges to plot away planning different lessons for the evening), they do come with a warning sticker: they need time to ensure that they meet the required standard to deliver. To resource a department so the team are enriched and empowered by high-quality resources, senior leadership must support giving the time away to enable staff to produce work of a good quality. That's nothing new; just joined-up thinking.

The other simple (yet incredibly effective) strategy is to hole-punch booklets or books so that all resources and additional worksheets can be kept in a structured order, without the despair of resourcing your classroom with 32 glue sticks, only to find in two weeks that half of them have gone, and the other half are looking very sorry for themselves. By keeping everything together with hole-punched books and a nifty treasury tag, student books are easily accessible, and you never need to worry about a child eating a glue stick ever again.

Booklets (and the absence of glue sticks and reams of worksheets) refine not only the process of learning but imply high expectations: here is the very best of our subject for you, because you should hold it in the highest regard. If we create rushed work, it brings us little fulfilment, and we don't look to expect appreciation of the topic from our students. It does not value time.

Raise the bar for all

Aim Higher booklets were provided as an accompaniment to units of work as a way to encourage students to read around the unit and develop a deeper understanding of the themes or ideas being held up for observation by the writer. They also enabled students to appreciate and contextualise what they were studying, to understand that imagined texts with imagined characters were being deliberately manipulated by authors as a way to challenge the ideas and perceptions of the world around them. Using Doug Lemov's principles around effective hinge questions and drawing the key ideas of the text that would then feed into class discussion, I provide students with a copy of the booklet at the start of the unit, but do not instruct what section needs to be completed at what point, or in any particular order. Students became experts in different aspects of the text, which can then be used to feed into class discussion. It was an ideal way to empower students to become experts in their field, and to recognise the value of knowledge. Those that read the texts presented demonstrate their understanding during lessons, and it was repeatedly made explicit that it was the habitual practice of reading around the text that paid off.

It is also the perfect resource for reusing time and again. The issue with exam-focused booklets and resourcing is that they are only as good as the lifetime of the exam specification itself; how many times have we seen this in practice, with teachers complaining at changes in specification, and resourcing companies throwing out 'new and improved' provision, cashing in on exam changes? Once you look beyond this noise, it must be noted that the content never changes. In English, literature is literature is literature. Literature is the world. The world changes, but in a cumulative state; this is not *Nineteen Eighty-Four*. Words are not erased. Ideas do not disappear. We only add to what we already have.

Section summary
- Avoid over creation – if you find yourself creating to procrastinate, solve a problem or a quick fix, is there a more effective way that can be more ingrained in your practice? Remember, 20 minutes on a worksheet a week is over ten hours an academic year better spent elsewhere.

- Strip back your teaching and teach with the long-term gain at the forefront of what you do.
- Create resources that have longevity and can be used across subjects, year groups or topics.

- -

Litdrive was developed as an enhancement of #TeamEnglish, a subject specialism community for English teachers where teachers could network, share strategy and support one another to develop their practice. Founded by Becky Wood and Nikki Carlin, the @Team_ English1 account of Twitter now boasts an incredible 27,000 followers and counting and continues to provide a place for teachers to connect. Nikki, a director of English in a school in North Manchester, spoke to me about the value of collaborative resourcing across education, and how we need to ensure there is a value to what we do if we are to take care of ourselves as a profession.

To what extent do you see resourcing as integral to teaching? Surely teachers are paid to resource their lessons so they should accept it as part of their role in school? Teachers are a resilient bunch of people and we all know that resourcing is a major part of our job. However, it is the way in which we provide/create resources for our pupils that is causing the problem. I am one of those teachers who used to love making shiny, flashy new resources for my classes and I spent hours of my time making PowerPoints and card sorts in my first few years of teaching. Unfortunately, this just isn't sustainable so I can see why people pay huge sums of money to access resource provision sites. The Twitter teaching community didn't really exist when I first started out so I, like many others, was trying to reinvent the wheel every time I started a new text or unit of work. Sharing within departments is great, but sometimes you need a fresh angle or find that something simply doesn't work for your class so you're back to square one.

Nowadays the main resources I take into my classroom are a pen, the text, and a lot of background subject knowledge so I can teach with confidence and clarity. But I have only had time to do all that extra reading and research because I no longer spend hours on resources. Finding the Team English community saved me a great deal of time at a point in my career when the workload could have become overwhelming.

Do you see wellbeing and resourcing as intrinsically linked, in your experience?
Absolutely, simply because of the time and skill it takes to create a good resource. Some people are really good at zoning in on what a resource needs to do and they can make whole units of work that make sense and follow a clear idea but, and this is not a criticism at all, for some teachers resourcing is not their main strength and they can find it stressful and incredibly difficult. I enjoy making resources but as my responsibilities have increased over the course of my career, I have found less and less time to make them. NQTs pressed for time also find this really challenging and should be able to rely on their departments to support them in this.

What led you to set up #TeamEnglish?
I was already using Twitter a lot as I had found the brilliant teaching community on there to be really helpful in answering questions and sharing resources. As we approached the first term of teaching the new GCSE specification, there were more and more resources being shared and requested, born of our collective anxiety about the new texts and unseen elements. I started a 'list' called #TeamEnglish as I thought it would be useful for people to easily find fellow English teachers. I asked people to contact me if they wanted adding and to use the hashtag if they wanted to ask questions. The response was overwhelming, and I soon realised that a list wasn't going to be sufficient. I contacted Becky Wood, who I had always found to be completely lovely and selfless in her willingness to help and share and asked if she would be interested in running a Team English account with me. Luckily, she said yes and so @Team_English1 was born! It took off immediately, and since the first day we have always been busy retweeting people's resources, requests for help, and responding to questions.

What are the key messages behind Team English?
Our key messages have to be support and collaboration. Team English is a community and it wouldn't work if it wasn't for all of our followers and

supporters. Becky and I have always made our intentions clear; we share anything and everything that people are willing to put out there. It takes some courage to share a resource publicly and we don't judge anything. There is no room for egos in Team English! We do our best to help everyone who gets in touch with us; we receive lots of DMs from people who are really struggling with their workload and with anxiety or stress. We can't always answer their questions ourselves, but we always put them in touch with someone who can. I really love that people see us as a place to turn to for support and help; it's what separates us from resourcing corporations and profit-making groups.

Do you think Team English has had a fundamental impact on wellbeing? How would you measure that?

I underestimated how much Team English helped people until we received some testimonials from our followers. A small group of us decided one year to apply for a Tes award for best English department (we figured we were a virtual department at least!) and as part of the process we had to collect testimonials from people to support us. Becky took charge of this and one day sent me a document with hundreds of responses; it made me cry! There were countless messages from English teachers who said they were close to quitting but didn't because they found Team English. They said we had helped them through periods of anxiety, stress, and depression; we had restored their enthusiasm for the subject and helped them reduce their workload. And when I say 'we' I mean the entire community, not just me and Becky. I don't know if we can measure the impact we have had on wellbeing in a quantitative way, but I do know we have helped people and that feels pretty good!

From managing the account, what indicators have you seen that wellbeing and resourcing is an issue for English teachers?

The very large majority of tweets we receive at Team English are requests for resources or ideas to help teach a text. That is followed by tweets from people sharing said resources and the number of likes and retweets is always huge; the whole team love to share and help people out because we know how time-consuming planning and resourcing can be.

The DMs we receive are often from people who feel they are drowning and really need some help and advice. Those messages make me so sad because they are almost always down to one thing: school leadership teams panicking about progress, data, and Ofsted. Their panic and knee-jerk reactions lead to huge workloads falling on teachers who are already under pressure. I feel fairly confident in saying that English teachers have the heaviest workload of any department in a secondary school – the sheer amount of writing produced in a week's worth of lessons (alongside the pressure of being a core subject) can lead to a toxic environment if support is lacking. Resourcing is a huge part of this. For many the new specification felt more like a threat than an opportunity; I like to think that the wealth of resources shared on Team English have helped change people's views in that regard.

Do you think this is just English? What other stress points are at play here? Is this actually measurable, and is the impact of supporting resourcing provisions measurable?

I don't think the workload and stress of resourcing is a uniquely English problem, but I do think we have it worse than other subjects! I'm not being self-pitying – I love my job and I genuinely don't want to do anything else; but schools can and should do a lot more to help ease the burden of our workload. Introducing periods for shared planning, using department meeting time for subject specific CPD, allowing whole-class feedback (and of course a Litdrive membership!) – these would all help.

Is this measurable? Through staff voice and survey feedback, yes, I think it is. You need to take the temperature every now and again to see what the wellbeing is like in your department and school but more important than that is to respond to that feedback in a meaningful way.

What do you feel would aid teachers in effective, quality resourcing?

Time and subject knowledge as well as a willingness to share more, especially for those not on Twitter. That's why Litdrive is such a great idea; it's bringing the best of Team English to a wider audience. In my English department we use our meeting time for subject-specific CPD. We analyse texts, write creatively as a group and work through past papers together. The feedback from my team is overwhelmingly positive; just because we're teachers doesn't mean we have stopped learning. All of this contributes to greater confidence in creating resources – especially model answers, which are the most useful tool you can have as an English teacher. It saves time too as we are not all creating resources in isolation but really collaborating.

What are we already doing to combat this, and what more could be done?
Well, Litdrive is a start, as is Team English. However, this is only useful for English teachers and I think all subjects could do with a community that is as active and widely known about. The growth of initiatives like whole-class feedback is really helping but that relies on school leadership teams supporting the idea. In English and maths I am seeing a growing number of teachers using visualisers and delivering lessons which consist entirely of annotating texts or tasks, questioning pupils, and modelling responses; I am fully on board with this as it reduces the need for extensive resources and relies on the teacher being the resource.

There is a lot we have done already, but still a great deal more to do. We need all subjects to have a resource community they can rely on for quality material and help, as well as school leaders to understand that their teachers are their most valuable resource and as such, they should be supported in perfecting their craft, not given meaningless and burdensome tasks to complete.

Finally, to what do you attribute the success of #TeamEnglish?
Every single person that has ever shared a resource, answered a question, or offered support and kindness to a fellow teacher. If others didn't join in, then it would just be me and Becky shouting into the void.

Matt Lynch is an English teacher in North Manchester, and has previously held several roles within schools, including an extended time as a head of department. Here, he shares his thoughts around the changing climate of resourcing in education.

Tell us a little bit about your journey so far as a teacher.
This academic year will be my 24th as a teacher of English. Having completed my training in inner-city schools in Birmingham, I worked for four years in a

comprehensive school in Manchester teaching key stages 3 to 5. I then moved to Brighton, where, again, I worked for four years on a split-site comprehensive with responsibility for coordinating key stage 4. In 2005 I became a head of faculty in the Manchester school where I had begun my career, and I served in that role for ten years, relinquishing it in 2015 due to chronic health issues. I'm now working as a main-scale English teacher on a part-time basis in a local secondary school.

Why do you think there's such a mass market for resourcing? Why are we not using the things we used last year, or the year before? What can you do as a novice teacher to make informed choices when there's too much of something?

In my experience, teachers typically wait around 12 to 18 months for textbook-style publications and exam-board-approved 'study support guides' to become available to the market following the implementation, for example, of new GCSE specifications. Consequently, they have no choice but to design and produce their own resources. While this affords teachers the opportunity to think flexibly and creatively about the delivery of their curriculum – the 'how' – it invariably leads to a diverse range of approaches and accompanying resources.

Teachers typically revisit and 'tweak' their resources for different reasons, too: having trialled a resource in the classroom, one evaluates its impact on students' learning – essentially, did it serve its intended purpose? We're constantly making minor adjustments and refinements as we reflect on the effectiveness of a resource. Those refinements also sometimes occur as a result of a quick chat with colleagues over a brew at break in the staffroom about how they are tackling X, Y or Z in their classrooms, or via access to – and reflection upon – resources shared by teachers beyond one's own school setting on platforms such as Twitter or resource sharing websites such as Litdrive, Tes or Teachit (which is now owned by the exam board AQA).

How does a novice make choices with so much variety on offer? I'd argue that the most effective resource is the teacher's own subject knowledge. There is no substitute for knowledge – whizzy, interactive resources might keep your students occupied and 'engaged' for a short time but what are they learning, really? Departments can help by ensuring both long-term and medium-term plans are in place, providing a clear teaching and learning 'journey', alongside readily accessible, centrally stored units of work.

What has happened to resourcing during your time as a teacher and a head of department?

There has always been a mass market for resources. As a trainee in 1995, I recall being furnished by my PGCE tutor with photocopied 'packs' – produced by ILEA (and sponsored by Esso) – to support the teaching of various SoW, along with A4 ring binder folders listing possible activities or tasks while studying a novel or a Shakespeare play. These were numbered tasks – like 'Write Macbeth's diary entry after meeting the witches' – which focused mainly on character and theme or plot, but matters of form and generic or stylistic conventions were largely immaterial. Tasks like this were not expected to invite or encourage discussion by teachers or students of the likelihood of Macbeth being able to write or his seeming ready access to paper and ink on a battlefield. As long as students wrote in the first person, it was a diary and teachers had 'covered' one of the range of forms stipulated by the national curriculum. At its worst, it was tick-box teaching.

In my first post, I was issued with a long-term plan and some helpful colleagues generously shared their own resources: often lever arch folders containing notes, reading lists, a 'menu' of activities or tasks and some differentiated worksheets for mixed-ability classes. There wasn't much collaboration, the quality of resources was very variable and there was much duplication of workload, which seemed to me to be a lot of wasted time. As an NQT, I kept my head down and said nothing. Main scale teachers were not involved in decisions around curriculum planning and our opinions were not sought.

Later, as a head of department, curriculum reviews were initially mapped by a team of three post-holders and me. Provisional curriculum design was then taken to a faculty development meeting where the rationale was explained, ideas were discussed, and suggestions were reviewed. It was very important to me that there was a sense of ownership, that there was 'buy-in' across the team, a shared understanding of what we were doing, why we were doing it and what we were hoping to achieve.

With medium-term planning outlining what was expected to be taught, staff worked in trios to produce units of learning (the number of four-part lesson plans which were written!). These resources were stored centrally and electronically for ease of access, with an expectation that staff would adapt them as part of their planning to suit the needs of their classes.

How has the culture around resourcing changed to have an impact on teacher wellbeing, detrimental or otherwise?

It is a culture which is shaped by whole-school policy and often by an SLT's perception (and arguably, their experience) of the government's inspectorate which impacts on teacher wellbeing, adversely or otherwise.

Sean Harford's presence on Twitter (sorely missed!) did much to demystify Ofsted, reminded us they are human and debunked lots of the myths which were impacting negatively on teachers, often through unnecessary workload produced in response to the demands of a misguided or ill-advised SLT about 'what Ofsted expects to see'.

Unnecessary 'resources' like seating plans colour coded by pupil sub-group profile and lesson plans for an Ofsted inspector (which – by the time you had recorded how many students in a given class were PP, SEND, EAL, G&T, LAC, objectives, outcomes, and listed what resources you would be using and other similarly pointless details which no one looked at – invariably took longer to fill out than the 60-minute lesson took to teach!) are happily a thing of the past for many, thanks to social media. Conversely, social media also reveals the extent to which colleagues across the nation are still expected by SLT to dance to a tune no one has been playing for several years now!

What's standing in our way to better wellbeing through effective resourcing?

Teaching and learning policies often dictate how a teacher can work and are, therefore, integral determiners of a teacher's wellbeing.

I once worked in a school where all students' written work had to be marked within a fortnight of its production. The feedback had to be dated, teachers had to provide each pupil with a detailed written comment, always beginning with WWW ('what went well'), identifying the strengths of the response in relation to the learning objectives. This then had to be followed by an EBI ('even better if'), identifying (again in relation to the learning objectives or success criteria) how a pupil could improve their work. I think that this was fairly standard 'feedback' practice across schools in the UK over the last ten years and, unfortunately, it remains so in many. I want to say this: it was a complete and utter waste of my time. It sucked the joy out of my job and left me feeling exhausted. Having taken about two and a quarter hours to feed back one set of 30 year 10 responses, I had very little energy and even less enthusiasm to plan that year 8 lesson for the following day (which I hadn't been able to prepare any earlier having taught back-to-back lessons for two and half school days). It's all too familiar, sadly.

If you are a member of SLT and this is how you operate policy in your school, please stop. Any impact on pupil progress you imagine this practice might cultivate will be outweighed by the harm it is causing to your teachers' wellbeing, robbing them of time that might be better spent planning lessons, being a mum, a husband, caring for an elderly parent, cooking dinner, reading their kids a bedtime story or catching up on their favourite TV show – things that all contribute positively to a person's wellbeing.

How can we resource effectively by teaching in a way that will sustain us? As a classroom teacher, is this something that's within our control?
In recent years, the ways in which teachers think about pedagogy and the kinds of resources they produce has shifted, partly in response to the latest research findings and partly due to an ideological shift towards a knowledge-rich – or knowledge-led – curriculum. Arguably, cognitive science and other educational research findings are influencing and even transforming how teachers resource their curriculum in ways that are more sustainable. Rosenshine's 'Principles', by way of illustration, emphasise the importance of thoughtfully sequencing concepts; providing models; questioning to check for understanding; spaced review and retrieval practice; and stages of practice from scaffolds to independence. In terms of my own classroom practice, retrieval practice, questioning to check for understanding, and 'I do – We do – You do' modelling – followed by stages of guided practice – are now routine. As the years roll on, I have essentially replaced a rigid four-part

lesson structure with one which typically contains the aforementioned four elements, the difference being that the latter is evidence-informed and has had a more visible, notable impact on my pupils' knowledge and skills – and on my wellbeing.

In response to the question 'Is this something that's within our control?', I would suggest that the degree to which a teacher has autonomy in her classroom is – and always has been – determined by the level of professional trust and expertise on a school's leadership team. I'm very fortunate to now work in a school which prizes professional development, managed by a leadership team who are keen to explore cognitive science research findings and their implications for teaching and learning in our classrooms. It has an SLT who have created a whole-school professional learning programme which invites teachers to trial different pedagogical approaches, evaluating the impact on pupils' learning and their own professional practice.

REFLECT

- What was the last resource that you created? How long did it take you and how does this compare with how many times you envisage that you or others will use it? How would you measure the time taken against the value of the resource?

- Keep an accurate time account of the resourcing you have carried out this week, including time spent planning lessons: how much does this contribute to your overall working time? Is it sustainable?

- Dissect this time account further, or do the same for the following week, but measure the amount of time that you spend collaborating with others within the department to plan or resource. Where is there scope to accommodate for this? Is this something that could become a feature in department time or meetings?

- Share one thing with your department each week: it could be an article, someone's blog to enrich subject knowledge, a news article relevant to your topic with a suggestion as to how you plan to use it. Request feedback from what you share, so that you can learn and refine what may be useful to others. Record how you feel when sharing, but also what you learn as a result of sharing. Do you share a particular type of resource, depending upon how you feel about sharing it? Think about how you could share resources that prompt discussion with others as well as helping them – an opinion piece, perhaps, or a critical theory. How can you make sharing resources a more habitual part of your practice?

- In comparison to the time spent resourcing, what time did you invest in your other areas of professional development, or subject knowledge reading?

- What local networks do you have access to and how could you include your department to reach out to other local networks to build on this further?

- What subject associations or further reading take place within your department that drive forward subject knowledge for all?

- What two changes could you make to your resourcing approach that will benefit students and you?

Conversation and connection

'Good Morning!' said Bilbo, and he meant it. The sun was shining, and the grass was very green. But Gandalf looked at him from under long bushy eyebrows that stick out further than the brim of his shady hat.
'What do you mean?' he said. 'Do you wish me a good morning, or mean that it is a good morning whether I want it or not; or that you feel good this morning; or that it is a morning to be good on?'
'All of them at once,' said Bilbo. 'And a very fine morning for a pipe of tobacco out of doors, into the bargain. — **J.R.R. Tolkien, The Hobbit**

In a world where I sometimes get distracted by the thought that my children may draw me with a rectangular iPhone as a facial feature, we all know the facts that a) we spend far too much time on our phones, particularly during a heavy work week; and b) this can sometimes be a poor substitute for real-life conversations. Indeed, in my early years of teaching, and as a single parent, I would sometimes go for extended periods of time without speaking in person to an actual grown-up. Talking with and utilising the teams to which we belong to is one of the most powerful ways for us to keep our heads above water, to learn from one another. However, all too often in and outside of teaching, our discussions take a different shape now, as we work harder, for longer, and often in isolation or in our roles as performers. Email has replaced the conversation, and to what gain?

Email: the kiss of death for the conversation

Emails. The communication masterstroke of the corporate world, email came prancing along as a mainstream business response to speed up communication. Shoving fax aside, email originally took the form of an electronic letter in both format and formality. Emails have become, in some contexts, an alternative to a casual text exchange, and a far more definitive alternative to speaking. On paper (or not), they appear to be a teacher's favourite form of communication: unable to leave a room for extended periods of time due to teaching classes, and often with timetables that can sometimes take weeks to align for meeting? Send an email! Right?

Not so much. Email is a key bugbear in schools, due to frequency, volume, person-environment fit and above all, the huge discrepancy from one school to the next on setting an agenda for all of these things. Stress sourced from emails is meta-present; there is a vast sense of unfulfillment in any text-based conversation and this can stem from either the way in which email is used or just the desire for fewer emails. Our biggest source of stress originates from factors outside of our control, so email definitely qualifies here. But is this really something that we need to consider? Are a few emails really that bad? (Spoiler alert: yes)

Cardinal sins of email:
- **Reply all:** You've been included on a group email that is arranging the best time for a meeting of 12 people, but you don't need to attend. But one person has replied all, instigating a back-and-forth exchange about whether the time proposed is actually the best time because year 10 revision is that day and the London trip is due back at 4 p.m., not to mention it's the same week as parents' evening. None of that has any impact on your life, because you don't need to attend; yet 14 email chimes later, and here you are, having to delete as you go.
- **Middle of the night:** just to ensure that everyone knows David is still working on that spreadsheet, an email arrives at 23.42 p.m.

to clarify exactly how hard David has been working. He goes to bed at 23.43 p.m., thrilled that his email will be the first one you see in the morning. How exciting.

- **Every font variation to spice it up a bit:** Peter has to send a great deal of dry, data-driven information that clarifies exactly how everyone isn't adhering to the three-step programme quality assurance for key stage 3 analysis. Peter remedies this by using a plethora of colours, underlined subtitles, extensive bullet points and eight sub sections, outlined with bold words for emphasis. Staff have started trying to work out the solution to the cryptic language by connecting the buzzwords, but the game wanes by the third paragraph.
- **Caps lock:** Just caps lock. IN the subject heading. NO email body.
- **Collective punishment:** Usually about dirty mugs. Often accompanied with a photo in case you didn't believe them.
- **Delayed telling offs:** 'Can you pop and see me in my room at the end of the day before you go home? Thanks.' Just so you can mull over the content of said meeting for the entire day, with absolutely no indication as to whether it's good, bad or requires tissues and/or a P45.
- **Emails that are sent to everyone but not everyone needs them:** 'Just for the teachers of Nathan Harris.' Look up the teachers of Nathan Harris, for the love of all that is holy.
- **Emails to confirm what has been said:** Emails to confirm meetings, in a cover-your-back approach to the workplace. Not minutes, just a confirmation of a chat. So, just to be clear, we had a chat. Like handing over a receipt to every verbal exchange you ever had, just in case that person claims in a month's time that you didn't chat. Because you definitely did have a chat.

It would appear that this is quite the epidemic. An overlooked aspect of the workplace is the physiological impact of email: a study carried out by the University of Loughborough found that effects included increased blood pressure, heart rate, cortisol rates and candidates' perceived stress.[1] This was accompanied by additional wider implications of email abuse, with examples of management via email as opposed to face-to-face meetings, social detachment of staff (which is hardly surprising if you're not actually interacting with anyone outside the realm of a keyboard) and lots of emails to confirm discussions or meetings had taken place in a 'cover-your back' approach to duties.[2] In addition, email interruption took a greater-than-expected amount of time, which impacted work productivity, an aspect somewhat overlooked by research study: if you are checking emails during lessons, because you feel there isn't a choice, how is your teaching impacted as a result? If you are reading over a deadline-enforcing email at home, how might this affect your mood, or your ability to focus on other things as a consequence? A study carried out by the Future Work Centre found that 'there was a 'strong relationship' between use of the 'push' feature that automatically updates emails on devices as soon as they arrive and perceived email pressure: 'People feel compelled to check emails as they arrive, even if they know they aren't required to do so.'

The study identified that implemented strategies that didn't actually address the core issues behind how email left colleagues feeling generated quick fixes but were not sustainable within a matter of months. More significantly, 'email-free time' did not provide a remedy to the stressor levels. If anything, in the most toxic of schools with a high email count (a recent Twitter poll showed that emails in some schools were in excess of 40 a day), email-free time would just be putting off all the fleeting ideas or messages sat drafted in outboxes.

The corporate world sometimes boasts up to 100 emails a day; my partner who is in a senior management position feels that around a third of the ones he receives daily are information only – although to what degree that information is essential, he couldn't say. It is

1. Marulanda-Carter, Laura (2019): Email stress and its management in public sector organisations. figshare. Thesis.
2. Email stress and desired email use, Stich, Jean-François, Lancaster University, 2016

the ultimate in 'fear of missing out': if someone didn't send it to you, would you have needed to know it? More importantly, are they sending it to you to reinforce the 'cover your back' mantra that using email has adopted? Emails always come with a fierce argument on both sides: those who send say, 'If you don't want to know, don't check'; and those that oppose say, 'Don't send to begin with.' Telling someone simply to be less anxious about the 40 emails that they know are waiting for them at the end of a day of teaching just doesn't cut the mustard for me.

- Can we assume that staff know how to email appropriately and use strategies that will support workload, and subsequently, stress reduction?
- What examples do we have of this in the workplace, if senior leadership use email so poorly?

Sam Strickland said during a recent ResearchED session, 'If it's more than two lines, I will come and find you, because the email warrants a conversation.' How can we ensure that we use email in a way that helps and doesn't hinder, and what can we do when it's being abused in full defiance of the email etiquette?

Senior leaders: set the tone for your school and be explicit in your boundaries. What is your whole-school approach to email? If you want to make a valid and profound increase in productivity and colleague relationships, and a decrease in work-related stress, consider the guidelines you collectively adhere to as a school. Some examples:

- Are there specified no-email points for staff once they leave work?
- Do you have reasonable expectations or an allocated time so that staff can check their emails in good time for deadlines set? For example, if a member of staff teaches all day and only reads their email every 24 hours at 3 p.m., is this sufficient for them

to act on everything sent in a timely manner? If not, what needs to change?

- Are emails in your school concise, clear and as short as possible?
- Are emails polite and positive in language?
- Is email reserved for particular messages, and are other options available to communicate key messages, such as a staff noticeboard, T&L blog, student communications for tutors, calendared meetings, shared drives for minutes or updates (the possibilities are endless)?
- Do you speak directly with staff that misuse the guidelines, without resorting to blanket emails that chastise?
- Are staff reminded of these key messages regarding email, so that you are regularly endorsing a really healthy email culture?

Daring to send an email?

Some questions to ask yourself: Is this sent to the right person, at the right time, giving the right timescale for the right reason? How would it feel to be the recipient of this email?

- **Remember you are a human:** if we start to distance ourselves from email as the sole method of communicating with other human beings, and remember our working body parts, the mouth, things start to become slightly fuller of humanity and simple human kindness. Not sound like anywhere you work? If your senior leadership team haven't set boundaries for email, propose it! If you're not quite there, then there are some measures you can take to ensure that as a serial recipient, your guidelines are clear to others:
- **Set an auto response to explain:** you teach and so are able to check email sporadically but aim to respond within two business days. I have found that this often resulted in follow-up emails to the first to say things had been resolved, or emails recalled where clearly the sender had reconsidered the fact that I wouldn't be in a position to meet a two-hour deadline after all.

- **Call off the tennis match:** Once the groundwork of an auto response has been laid, don't fall into the trap of short back-and-forth emails to attempt to resolve something quickly. The quickfire exchange is scientifically proven to result in nothing except more confusion at best, and the need for a meeting at worst. These are what I like to call conversation replacements, and you tend to find that the face-to-face version is far less hostile, curt and usually more effective at moving towards a resolution.
- **Full attention:** Avoid engaging in email responses when you are doing something else at the same time. Give someone's concerns or queries your full attention, or schedule for a time that you are able to do so. If the reply will be any more than a couple of lines, give two options for a chat at a time that suits you. That way, you still control the demands of your working week.

WhatsApp: the department you can never leave

In the last eight years alone, there appears to have been a blurring of boundaries between school and home, and now we are able to reach people in a way that previously wasn't available to us. Work can transcend boundaries of the physical workplace; but often, workplace policy has not played catch-up to support this, and we are left to our own judgement to lay out our own personal boundaries, relying instead on the pull of 'fear of missing out' and self-expectation that we place upon ourselves.

As an alternative to checking emails outside of 'working hours' (whatever they may be!), WhatsApp groups are the new slinky sidekick to email, the hero of the hour. The discussion sways from work to books to work again, means that teachers often feel obligated to contribute or respond or feel that they're not 'keeping up' with all the replies, essentially as though they're stood on the outskirts of a really animated conversation, without having much to say.

The impact of this on mental health is concerning: in a case study of 80 candidates, 'the results supported a negative indirect effect of daily workplace tele pressure during off-job hours on daily psychological detachment, mediated via daily work-related smartphone use during off-job hours'.[3] There are two elements to consider here: first, that this is the time dedicated to work that we can attempt to justify as 'fun'; and second, that creating this channel of communication outside of work leaves employees open to discussing work in an entirely different context to a meeting, face to face, with a select number of people present – a channel that makes you readily available at any given hour. Instead of a system that can be governed with compassion for staff, we have something else entirely.

You may read this as saying, 'What's the harm? It's just WhatsApp!' and to those who can successfully self-regulate, indeed it is. But for a more vulnerable member of staff, it can be the place they double-guess the words of others; or for the NQT new to the school, it can be the place that everyone seems to know everyone except them; or for the one member of staff that never says no to anything, it can be the place that they take on new projects at 11 p.m. on a Friday evening.

Rhys, a Head of Faculty in South Warwickshire, shares his insights:

❝ As mobiles are now so prominent in people's lives it is easy to see those lines become blurred. The only link to my professional job on my phone is Twitter as I only have a professional Twitter account. I don't have my work emails connected on here (though may check through Safari) and I don't have any work groups on WhatsApp. Therefore, by keeping it to Twitter I can keep it in its box. I know notifications that pop up on this app will be work related. I don't want WhatsApp, which is my social/fun app, to then start being populated with work discussions. WhatsApp can cause minefields when it comes to miscommunication (especially tone) and I prefer to talk work face to face – it is easier to read voice and facial expressions than words on a screen. I've seen other departmental work groups (shown when at a pub with members of the

---

3.   Santuzzi, Alecia & Barber, Larissa. (2018). *Workplace Telepressure and Worker Well-Being: The Intervening Role of Psychological Detachment*. Occupational Health Science. 10.1007/s41542-018-0022-8.

department) and been shocked by the way some members were speaking to others. So, for that reason I keep my teaching career away from WhatsApp.

In terms of checking out-of-hours emails, I limit myself to the following times: Sunday evenings when planning and then sometimes in the morning during my wake-up routine. Both of them are to give myself a heads-up if something has happened – I have a nice car drive to plan how to respond/what to do if that's the case. I'm much better (aren't we all!) at responding once I've had a think. This also ties into my problem with WhatsApp as well – it's too instant. People can say/do things on there without thinking, especially in heat-of-the-moment discussions.

- -

One head of department adores her team WhatsApp group, claiming it has helped her to bond with them over the last year.

- -

Tanya shares her perspective on how to set boundaries with her WhatsApp rules:

We have clear rules for our WhatsApp group; I wrote them up and took a photo of them, which is our WhatsApp picture. They're really straightforward!

- NO work chat. Ever. No students, colleagues, queries, nothing.
- Use to share or organise: we share pictures far more than messages, which is then far easier to catch up on. Food, pets, babies, books, films, wine to try! We even use it to organise department meals. This also makes it easier to follow the next rule, which is…
- Reply direct. By replying directly to a picture or message, the discussion follows a thread.
- No excuses, no apologies: leave at any time. You can always come back but if you've got a lot on, you haven't got time to look at what Greg had in his burger.
- Be kind. The group is a place to share things in a positive space, and life's too short for grumbling.

- -

We have a responsibility to ourselves to put boundaries in place, and we should not feel apologetic for this self-care and consideration for ourselves. You won't miss anything; you won't be odd; you won't feel heartbroken about not seeing what Kelly eat at that new Chinese restaurant on Thursday night. If you don't want in on late-night department chat, don't get involved. It's that straightforward. And until someone concocts a policy to outline that it is part of your role in school, you don't need to feel bad about it.

Praise and thank-yous

We need to get better at praising in schools. I've sat through my fair share of cringeworthy 'thank-yous' that lack any sense of authenticity and often lose meaning after a prolonged period of time.

Why? Well, we're British: we hate positive praise as it doesn't align with our sardonic nature and isn't about the weather. However, the issue lies a little deeper than that, and this applies to children and adults: 'Praise for successful performance on an easy task can be interpreted by a student as evidence that the teacher has a low perception of his or her ability.'[4] We are as students: if we get even the slightest indication that we don't deserve the praise, we are unconvinced. If we don't believe that our achievement warrants praise, we find the praise ingenuine and dismiss it as valued or useful. It becomes trite, and not a compliment that we carry with us. We want praise, but because we have been noticed as an, 'individual who made that contribution ... This must come from a deep place.'[5]

In such busy places, this is difficult to do on an individual level, but it must be done in such a way, because blanket praise is as useful as a chocolate teapot. It serves no one and warms nothing. Taking the time to praise on an individual level, in a way that it can be accepted as a gift, is the most powerful praise of all, and (not that we praise for this reason) it's the type of work that repays itself, because people feel important and empowered. Less praise in the right way is so much more enriching to the soul than scattered, misdirected praise at people that are possibly less deserving but did that one good thing. How do we give less praise, better?

---

4. www.bit.ly/2ShEhq8
5. Myatt, M. (2016) High challenge, low threat. Woodbridge: John Catt Educational.

- **Value the intrinsic:** thank colleagues at the end of a half term, term, year. Select precise moments that they have supported you and the impact they made. 'Thank you for your support with year 10 this year; your help with how to approach tackling little Johnny was what has helped me to become a better teacher.' However, take moments to value the finer details, the consistently selfless – the person who asks how you are; the person who was in school for an hour because Molly in year 10 missed a lesson last week and feels anxious about being behind; the person who brings milk in every Monday; the person who left two packets of biscuits in the staffroom and not just because it was their birthday; the person that's been used for cover for the last three weeks on the trot and doesn't ask for the time back (give it to them anyway, with a thank-you); the person who took the time to phone the parents of the child that never gets a great phone call home. Look out for the small acts that keep the school afloat.

- **Give full words:** by that, I mean make sure your thank-yous are full of authenticity. Thank only when you have something genuine to give thanks for, and when it is something that you have seen first-hand and has directly impacted you in some way. If you oversee a large team, keep a log of who you thank, for what and when, to make sure you don't miss anyone, and you actively look for ways to thank people. Use this at the end of the year to assist people with their performance management system. Support people with your thanks.

- **Do not shy away from being open:** vulnerability is necessary to connection with others (for more on this, I strongly recommend that you look up Brene Brown). Authenticity is when you are willing to let go of who you think you should be to be who you are. The more you say the positive things in your head, the easier it becomes – which is fantastic – but the more real it feels to all parties. Be humble in your thanks and share when your accomplishments are a result of the contribution of a team. I don't mean go into the world and splatter it with compliments

– the postman doesn't care if you like his new haircut – but connect with the people around you as people.

• **Appreciate that different people like different forms of praise:** Jamie Thom observes this in our students, but this has an equal importance to adults in schools: 'There is certainly no one-size-fits-all mechanism for praising young people.'[6] Those extroverted amongst us like the recognition, the publicity of praise, as it helps us to feel as though others will recognise this expertise; if we are praised for our approach in the classroom, others may find it useful – we like to help.

In the same vein, introverted colleagues will die a little inside if you call upon them publicly. The idea of having to perform a thank-you mini speech on the spot makes them feel a little nauseous at best. We all have a preferred form of being noticed for hard work, and it really is key to understanding how to respond accordingly to the people around you. This could take the form of saying whatever you want to say face to face, leaving a note, sharing the work of one person with a group or team, or using meeting time to mention how someone has made an impact on your own workload. All of these are only possible by getting to know colleagues as individuals, and not simply as people that work alongside you.

The best side effect of giving praise? It's great for your health: as Winston Churchill once said, 'We make a living by what we get. We make a life by what we give.' For more information on altruism and its connection to wellbeing, the Mental Health Foundation wrote a fantastic report in 2012 entitled *Doing Good? Altruism and wellbeing in an age of austerity*[7] that explored a range of research to support the simple act of looking after others. Letting others notice that you value their work is probably one of the easiest and yet

6. Thom, J. (2018) *Slow teaching: on finding calm, clarity and impact in the classroom.* Woodbridge: John Catt Educational.
7. Accessible at www.bit.ly/2MnVSsy

discarded gestures in the workplace, but finding a balance between the personal and strong, systematic ways that place emphasis on the great work that people are doing every day is – and I mean this with complete gravity – life-changing stuff.

Being human
Effective relationships

Education is much more complex than that. It is about the trust and bond betweenateacherandyoungperson(andparents)thatcreatestheenvironment where learning can occur and grow.   – **Pamela Wright, *The Guardian*, June 2013**[1]

The eye cannot say to the hand, 'I have no need of you,' nor again the head to the feet, 'I have no need of you.' On the contrary, the parts of the body that seem to be weaker are indispensable, and on those parts of the body that we think less honourable we bestow the greater honour, and our unpresentable parts are treated with greater modesty, which our more presentable parts do not require.   – **1 Corinthians 12:21–24**

*When the road looks rough ahead
And you're miles and miles from your nice warm bed
You just remember what your old pal said
Boy, you've got a friend in me*
     – **Randy Newman, 'You've Got a Friend in Me' (1996)**

What is it?
Relationships are among the most important foundations that successful teaching is based upon. Healthy relationships lead to healthy lives, both physically and mentally. An 80-year study into

1.   Accessed at www.bit.ly/2tmV1Sx

happiness carried out by Harvard University found that people who are socially connected to family, friends and community are physically healthier, and live longer than people who are less well connected with others. The ongoing research project – one of the longest of its kind – has been studying the extent of happiness since the Great Depression, and found that healthy relationships with others, both professionally and personally, had a bigger indicator of good health than genetic correlation, social background and even cholesterol levels.[2] Relationships are central to self-fulfilment, which is something of a perpetual state, as we work towards finding a balance between self-assurance and feeding our innate desire as human beings to belong to something.

In the community of a school, relationships are everyone's responsibility. They are the difference between a sense of collective vision and fragmentation; they define success or failure; they build or crumble both the reputation of a school and the reputation of the people who operate within it. When staff share a vision towards building the type of school that they aspire to work in, or the people that they want to work for, this can be incredibly powerful in orchestrating change – and, I would argue, the catalyst for such a shift.

In addition to school success, humanity for one another is essential – not just in school but in our everyday lives if we are to experience personal success as well as the professional definition of it. Irrespective of your position or experience within a school, we have a collective responsibility to look out for one another in what can be an incredibly challenging setting. Due to the nature of the school 'year', we condense a year of our lives into what is a matter of 39 weeks, and schools can at times act as a pressure-cooked microcosm of the wider world. We are attempting to place high, aspirational targets for ourselves and students in a period of time

2.   Waldinger, R. J. and Schulz, M. S. (2010) 'What's love got to do with it? Social functioning, perceived health, and daily happiness in married octogenarians', *Psychology and Aging* 25 (2) pp. 422–431.

that is compressed, and to do so, we operate in hourly slots, often spending hours in isolation from other adults. Subsequently, we need to work that little bit harder to maintain relationships outside of hasty corridor exchanges and brief emails: we need to work to look out for one another in a setting that makes it more difficult to do just that in comparison to other professions. In a sector where 'conversations are the relationship' means more than ever, ironically so, it's a challenge for us to get off the starting block.

Just being aware of that makes for a fantastic starting point. Mary Myatt describes such places as 'big hearted' as she observes organisations such as McDonald's that embrace connections: 'Most of them (the staff) will look at you. This is a sign that one organisation understands the importance of this element of big-heartedness.'[3] We need to look at and out for one another. Andy Sammons states, 'Being compassionate isn't an isolated thing: it's about recognising the difficulties of others in every situation.'[4] It is with this approach that I want to consider the impact of relationships in school, because in the most successful, workload-light schools, people are persevering because they know that others are with them in the journey forwards.

This chapter will explore what relationships mean, and how they can contribute to an improvement in teacher purpose. Positive student-teacher relationships are central to job satisfaction. At their most successful, the student-teacher relationships that work will be the motivation behind not only academic success, but success in ways that cannot be measured. Students achieve at a higher level when taught by those that they have been in a position to build meaningful relationships with, over a sustained period of time and ultimately, why retention is so key to student outcomes. In fact, there are significant studies that examine teacher turnover, and indeed, they outline the difficulty in pinpointing the lack of attainment as a factor related to teacher retention, or teacher quality – or more so, that one actually

3.   Myatt, Mary, Big Heartedness settings, 2016, accessed at www.bit.ly/2FgbqdX
4.   Sammons, A. (2019) *The compassionate teacher*. Woodbridge: John Catt Educational.

leads to the other.[5] However, there is far more than measurement and research to be considered here: if students trust in the teacher, they trust that the teacher is in a position to ensure that they can succeed. If someone has faith in what you are doing, that faith will ultimately lead to your ability to develop self-efficacy and self-regulation. If the relationship is valuable, and supports your achievement in a successful way, you will in turn believe that you will succeed. Very rarely are there tales of student success with a complete lack of educational support. Support and mutual trust build foundations with far more longevity than a determination to prove someone wrong. When we start to address teacher wellbeing, student-teacher relationships are pivotal to whether we walk out of work feeling accomplished or burdened. The relationship is the work in all cases.

As relationships are at the heart of any thriving enterprise, they are also the most challenging aspect to build, develop and maintain. The pressures and differing agendas that can come with the nature of a school system – with some staff in positions of leadership responsible for very different key messages and with very different agendas – can result in a struggle of balance as these parties must collectively come together to form a collaborative vision. It is vital that relationships are maintained not only to fuel a school culture, but also to fuel the staff body: if staff do not feel that they are helping to steer the ship, it is this disengagement that can feed into deeper discontentment. Will Smith, of Greenshaw Learning Trust, states that in the best schools within the trust, staff feel 'like they're a part of what is happening in the school and that they have as much of a stake in it as anybody else.'[6] Providing ownership to staff is key to taking everyone on the same journey to success and true job fulfilment.

If we are to get the very best from people, relationships are our starting point; we can safely make the assumption that nobody comes to work to do a bad job. People want to give their best, and there's

5. How Teacher Turnover Harms Student Achievement Matthew Ronfeldt, Susanna Loeb, and Jim Wyckoff CALDER Working Paper No. 70 January 2012
6. We Are In Beta podcast, 9th April 2019, transcript accessed at www.bit.ly/34Qd2qg

always a reason when people feel unable to do so. It is the conversations between people that will determine how easy it is within a school for staff to achieve their measure – not the measure set by others – of what it feels like to do their very best. The way in which we form, sustain and make time for conversations with people is the driving factor behind a meaningful sense of collective shared vision.

Why does it aid wellbeing?

Toxic workplaces are not exclusive to teaching: workplace bullying and misuse of power and hierarchy are prevalent within all industries. However, an exacerbating feature within schools is the pressure from various external agencies, which increases feelings of unrest and victimisation. School staff are placed under immense pressure from external parties, regulatory bodies, trustees and stakeholders, parents, children, and leadership teams (not to mention themselves). Multiple motivations are set against one another and this makes for an incredibly difficult setting in which to feel a sense of acting as a collegiate. As demands and agendas are set, humanity can sometimes be lost. A mixed agenda of values or poor communication can have a devastating effect upon your sense of accomplishment and the feeling that you are part of something that matters. No one feels that they are feeding into something if they come to work and repeatedly experience futility.

To go to work and feel wary, anxious or hindered by poor relationships means that you are unable to carry out the work that is expected of you and that you expect of yourself. It disables your ability to feel a sense of professional self-worth, but also personal self-worth because often, the relationships that have broken down are the ones that we need in order to feel supported. We feel the impact of toxicity within school not only through poor relationships, but also in the way that it can then warp our perception of ourselves. As a result, job self-alienation can occur, a psychological separation where we no longer engage with our key values as individuals, because to us, they have lost significance. We need a sense of authenticity to feel that we want to keep doing what we are doing, and so if we start to lose our sense of identity, this crumbles our *why*. It acts as a distraction to the real work, the real focus of our importance.

I have been at the receiving end of workplace bullying, in several contexts, with several variations, from several layers of management. I have been ridiculed and undermined in front of adults and students; I have been micromanaged to the extent that I struggled to have any confidence in my own opinion of which direction my work should take. Bullying is an institution so deep-rooted within human relationships that bullies will claim they have good intent and the bullied will subsequently come to doubt that they are even being bullied. Founding Litdrive has opened my inbox to reams of bullying stories, from data manipulation to oppressive management of teaching; from using pay progression as a rare gift to withhold as opposed to something that someone simply earns for doing the work required of them. Teachers whisper tales of enforcement of power as an inherent entity throughout their everyday experience of management. Teaching is not the only place that workplace bullying is rife, but predictably, the higher the stress levels the pressures within a sector, the more likely that workplace bullying will take an established presence amongst staff. Put simply: the bullies bully because they feel bullied. Pressure filters down as those in leadership project their own concerns or anxieties onto others. The result? Complete fragmentation of a hierarchical system.

For the sake of clarity, workplace bullying is defined as

> any inappropriate behaviour, direct or indirect, whether verbal, physical or otherwise, conducted by one or more persons against another or others, at the place of work or in the course of employment, which could reasonably be regarded as undermining the individual's right to dignity at work. (p. 5)[7]

---

7.   Warszewska-Makuch, M. (2019) 'Coping with stress caused by workplace bullying: an umbrella review', *Medycyna Pracy* 70 (2) pp. 249–257.

The microcosmic nature of schools means that support systems can vary incredibly in the amount of face-to-face contact time that people have to actually liaise with those aligned to support them. The bubble-esque nature of teaching, where the capacity for those meaningful conversations is limited, results in having to navigate your way through the differing dynamics of relationships but with a limited time to do so. The multiple hats that we wear as teachers with students, parents, our own family, become quite the expansive collection as we move through the different roles in the eight hours of a typical school day. Instances of bullying arise when the lines are blurred as to what is or is not acceptable. Insults become minimised as banter and demands placed upon you become just the tasks that you should complete as part of the remit of your role. The role is never-ending, and so we rely upon the relationships with those who have control over workload to determine the limit of our workload, or when we start to say no – whichever happens first.

I asked teachers on Twitter what the most unreasonable demand placed upon them in the name of teaching had been:

66 **@DrMBoyd:** Asked to fill in paperwork for school when I was off recovering from my second cancer surgery.

66 **@dutaut:** To come back from my grandmother's funeral early because Ofsted has called. (I hadn't even been to the funeral yet.)

66 **@cherylcwebb:** To miss my baby nephew's funeral. Entitlement is really for 'immediate family'. I politely told my school where to stick it. Needless to say, I don't work there anymore.

66 **@MissLLewis:** Saturday school. A colleague said she no longer wanted to do it as she was missing out on taking her child to karate. She was told it was denying her mum the chance of spending time with her grandson and could she Skype a session instead?

66 **@Lit_Liverbird:** Being told not to wear trousers because I am a woman... in 1994... by a male head and female deputy.

66 **@HughesHaili:** To continue to teach a child who constantly threatened to physically assault me and screamed obscenities in my face.

❝ **@emmray:** To go into work when I was signed off with depression and anxiety – I was accused of letting the team down.

❝ **@MrHtheTeacher:** I used to get the first bus to town then a bus from there to work and a half hour walk to arrive at half past seven. Head said I was far too late to work so had to taxi to his so he could drive me in for 6:45. Not nice! Plus 12-13-hour days were expected he advised me.

❝ **@missymusician81:** I had an emergency appendectomy after my appendix burst and I ended up with peritonitis. I popped into school during recovery once I was able to move to collect stuff before the end of term. was asked to spend 2hrs completing reports as I had 'missed' them whilst in surgery!!!!

❝ **Anon:** Making up spurious grades for ks3 students – well done – you went up from a made-up 0.3 to a made-up 0.6!

❝ **@OneAboutSue:** Having a lesson observation as part of an informal capability procedure on the first day back after a period of sick leave…

These were the people that were happy to share in a public forum. There were over a hundred that shared privately, and the stories that they shared with me told a collective narrative lacking in humanity.

Workplace bullying doesn't announce itself with neon signs and a rendition of the Imperial March (although I could think of a few prior colleagues who could do a pretty impressive stride in time to it). It can take its presence in a far quieter form. As mentioned in my first chapter, bullying is most eloquent and cataclysmic when you question your ability to make a judgement; your confidence ebbs so that it becomes more difficult for you to ascertain if what is happening is bullying – not to add the somewhat childish connotations that we attach to the word, so that we find a great discomfort to say we are being bullied, as we are professional adults, and not children in a playground. Ultimately, it impacts our capacity to carry out a job well.

When people are unable to speak their truth, free from the constraint of power and in a place of emotional safety, the unsaid words present themselves elsewhere in schools. They are the whispered words outside classrooms, or the climate of a staffroom; they are the impatience and anxiety that comes home with you to your children, or the email checks that distract you in the evening during dinner. They are the unsaid conversations that you instead have with your partner, or even yourself, mulling over how to have difficult conversations that you anticipate will feature the following day. The words we don't say stay with us because we feel that they hold little value to anyone, and because no one has sought to hear them. They stay, and instead we look for indications or glimmers that they might have a place in the words of others; but actually, this doesn't bring us the same satisfaction that saying our own words would. We wait to see if others feel the same in the hope they may speak, but this isn't as satisfying as the conversation would have been. Just because other people say what we have thought, doesn't mean this holds the same value as someone hearing our voices using our words.

Subsequently, these words shift our energies into feelings of unresolved conflict or clarity – energy that we could have put to much better use. The misconstrued emails to clipped replies, the to-do lists from management that seem to speak without listening to the people that they impact, the small resentments resulting in lessening efforts to do good work. When value is lost through our disconnections in others, this has wider implications for the school as a whole.

Positive relationships in school must be at the forefront if we are to make demonstrative change in teaching. If we refocus for a clear vision in schools, leading with a value in positive relationships, this has a visible outcome: improved staff retention, reduction in staff absence rates, valued staff feedback and an increase in productivity in schools, where time is being married with common sense and a purposeful, collective drive to be better. Shared visions through the art of conversation are the starting point that will enable us to make tangible change. Ginott stated, 'I have come to the frightening conclusion that I am the decisive element,[8] and this resonates when we explore how powerful effective relationships can be in driving towards a common goal.

In this section, I have tried to cover the vast range of relationships in schools, and how we can work to ensure these relationships are effective and beneficial to our professional contentment. Working in schools with incredibly poor or disconnected relationships with children, these unsaid or unfinished conversations will eat away at teacher purpose, as we start drift further from our roles as teachers to fight our own corner, time and again, against behaviour without a policy to endorse our actions. As Katharine Birbalsingh, head of Michaela School in Wembley, stated in a recent interview with influential EduTwitter figure Tom Rogers, 'Teachers don't leave teaching because of Michael Gove; they leave teaching because of workload or behaviour.'[9] It really is that straightforward.

And so, whilst I explore the key components of what great people do to form healthy relationships in schools, I also want to broach the ugly stuff. When you manage to do the grubby work of repairing relationships from what appeared to be a point of no return, or you manage to build a deep sense of self-preservation in the midst of toxicity, that deserves credit. Some of the most virulent relationships that occur in schools can be the ones that prompt teachers to walk out of jobs, have their confidence shattered and, in some scenarios, never return to teaching again. Teachers are leaving teaching – not just specific schools – as a result of their experiences, and it is simply not good enough. We have a responsibility to ourselves to elevate standards in schools so that the schools where staff operate in such a pernicious way are left standing without the staff needed to drive them, whilst we vote with our feet to other schools, instead of other careers.

8.   Teacher and Child: A Book for Parents and Teachers: Haim G. Ginott: 9780020139744: Amazon.com: Books.
9.   Interview with Katharine Birbalsingh and Tom Rogers, 1st October 2019, accessed at www.bit.ly/2SPLVbq

Symbiosis: colleagues and collective change

'How we spend our days is, of course, how we spend our lives.'
                                                    – Annie Dillard[10]

'A guy needs somebody – to be near him. A guy goes nuts if he ain't got nobody. Don't make no difference who the guy is, long's he's with you. I tell ya, I tell ya a guy gets too lonely an' he gets sick.'
                              – John Steinbeck, *Of Mice and Men*[11]

Strong, trusting professional relationships make you feel valued and respected within the wider school community, and we spend more time with some of the staff body than we do with our own families, so it is vital that we participate in healthy exchange, and support one another to be better. The people that we surround ourselves with are often the people that grow to know us best. We can only hope that the people that grow to know us best stick around because they like what they know! As secondary teachers clock up an average of 48 hours a week working, and primary teachers an even more substantial 52 hours,[12] over a third of our lives is spent at work, so it would be rather nice to get along. Teaching works at supersonic speed, at high intensity in regard to tasks set and emotional investment in those tasks: relationships with our colleagues adopt the same pattern with the same velocity. I would argue that teacher friends are some of the strongest relationships you will forge, because in the same way that *Big Brother* contestants build bonds for life, built through a collective experience of being kept under both constraint and scrutiny, teachers find common purpose in both the wonderful and the woeful of the school workplace. (Replace with a slightly less imprisoned, culturally poor

---

10. Dillard, Annie. The Writing Life. New York: Harper & Row, 1989. Print.
11. Steinbeck, John. Of Mice and Men. New York, N.Y., U.S.A.: Penguin Books, 1994.
12. www.bit.ly/2tuhNrm

metaphor if you will.) Aside from those that lead us, our colleagues are the ones that we go to in confidence with professional and personal issues; when we want to celebrate something, we are proud of; when we need to admit our mistakes; when we need to vent, and only teachers will understand us. All of this raises the question then: why does negativity within a workforce even exist in schools in that case? Surely, we lean upon each other too much and too often for tensions to arise?

Multiple reasons are at play here, but accountability or individual pressures are a contributory factor. The pressures of a to-do list that doesn't feel comparable to that of others, or that is unreasonable, then leads to a hefty dose of resentment. In workplaces where treatment of staff is neither fair nor consistent (and this often results if leadership agendas change frequently), it becomes a matter of concern when staff can fall in or out of favour pretty easily. If we feel that matters other than the work are receiving recognition, they don't feel valuable in the same way. The difference between a collective workforce and a fragmented one can be in the way that professionals see leaders building trust, giving praise or developing a sense of inclusion amongst staff. Staff notice this more when it is done to others than when it is done to them: our sense of social justice is incredibly strong when someone is treated in a specific way and we take our position as bystander. If leaders begin to treat groups of people differently, it is often not the leaders that people grow resentful of, but the groups of people receiving the preferential treatment to begin with. When we move away from shared purposes and collective vision, it is the people amongst you rather than above you that suffer, because the points of contention evolve into multicellular forms: reduction in goodwill, unwillingness to support; a *Hunger Games*-esque approach to others, if you will.

Another key contributor is time. The tighter the time is to connect with other professionals, the less time there is to build a sense of community within a school. Where schools have lost time to take lunches, or time to get to a staff room, or time to speak with the other adults in the building, sometimes just to decompress, what is known as self-alienation begins to occur. Job 'self-alienation is a psychological separation that can be found in everyday life and social communication both inside and outside the environment' (Sharfi et al., 2013): we start to distance ourselves from the professional self that we had hoped to create. Our sense of self can only exist outside our own perception if we share it with others, and so if there isn't an outlet to do so, we start to question the parts of ourselves that truly exist. Are we proficient? Are we professionally empathetic? How do we know, without the chance to practice such things?

Power is the final determinant of negative relationships between colleagues. Leadership and the way a whole-school culture is fostered sets the pace and tone for the interactions in the wider body: the influence of power as a social construct doesn't just exemplify itself through the people within it, but the systems there to support the people. Foucault outlines power as a 'fluid concept' and power relations as 'mobile, reversible and unstable'.[13] Bullying exists as a power microcosm: it uses power as a tool of instruction, and is present at all levels, irrespective of professional authority and a formal position of power. Power in schools does not sit behind a select number of doors or email signatures, but shifts and circulates until it creates 'a swarm of points of resistance'.[14] This implies that perhaps the power in schools lies with those that perceive they have power, as opposed to those that actually have it. The structure of a school with differing agendas and a range of TLRs that form micro-physics of power like the waves of an ocean (each with their own professionally set direction but their own personal-professional agenda sitting discreetly behind that) results in what I term 'the *Matrix* effect': there are so many agendas and motives at play that it

13. The Impact of Workplace Bullying on Primary School Teachers and Principals, Declan Fahie and Dympna Devine School of Education, University College Dublin, *Scandinavian Journal of Educational Research*, 2014 Vol. 58, No. 2, 235–252, http://dx.doi.org/10.1080/00313831.2012.725099
14. Mona Lilja (2018) The politics of time and temporality in Foucault's theorisation of resistance: ruptures, time-lags and decelerations, *Journal of Political Power*, 11:3, 419-432.

starts to become a layered conversation with so much sub-text to it. Power should originate from a place of respect and support, but this is often not the case.

- What impacts poor working relationships?
- Does power come with a job title, or a personality type?
- What should a position of authority mean for those that you direct?

Sadly, it is the external elements of the workplace that take a negative influence; according to Herzberg, internal factors increase job satisfaction, whereas external factors affect job satisfaction negatively.[15] That means that we are capable of building our own recognition of a job well done, but any negative impact usually comes from the feedback of others. That doesn't, however, mean we cannot change the narrative.

In a study of over 200 employees, it was found that whilst workplace relationships could have a position impact upon self-perception of job satisfaction, there was a darker, more complex side to these friendships; friendships often dissolved as a result of a breakdown in trust, usually when a promotion or opportunity arose and both parties were interested, or the third-party rule: when another colleague or person in a position of management was involved and one of the two parties of the friendship behaved differently.[16] I feel that this is unavoidable, and part of human nature: we compete as part of our instinct. With the introduction of larger roles as a result of academisation, the collaborative nature of the work is present, but the rules to govern this work are higher stakes, and fewer. If we are to continue, collaboration needs to be at the heart of what we do, but does that mean that we need to fight our inner gladiator to manage it?

15. Papin, L. M. (2005). Teacher retention and satisfaction among inner-city educators. Unpublished doctoral dissertation. Arizona State University

16. Hogrefe Verlag. Having Workplace Friends Is Not Always Fun – A Critical Incident Study Sabine Hommelhoff Related information Chair of Work and Organizational Psychology, Friedrich-Alexander University Erlangen-Nürnberg, 2019.

I hope not. But the unhealthiest schools are the do-or-die ones: the schools that reward those who work longest and hardest, which is no basis for a collectively driven, healthy work mindset. The broader implications of negative workplace interactions for schools and schooling are the ones that we should concern ourselves with, because whilst regulatory gradings will continue to be rubber stamped onto banners outside schools, unhealthy schools cannot operate at an 'outstanding' level for very long without the collaboration of a united staff body who are interested in the work. What can we do to create healthy relationships that we build in school? How do we make great choices for ourselves both professionally and personally?

Choose your crowd

Your mood can be determined by the people that you surround yourself with. Every new teacher has been told the old radiators or drains analogy, but it's not really as straightforward as only choosing positive people to spend your time with at work. 'Work is frequently punctuated with acts of friendship',[17] but if the structures of a school system are poor, these people are often in short supply. Moreover, when you want to discuss a situation that has been particularly challenging, or you just want to talk about how horrendous your weekend was, the positive crowd are not actually who you need. It isn't positivity that we seek out, but authenticity. Andy Sammons outlines this need to seek out a non-judgemental crowd with preferential qualities, in that 'judgements are often fused with emotions and feelings, whereas preferences are less bound, less intrinsic and more easily reconciled with personal values'.[18] It is with this preference-led approach that we should try to build our own networks; in a workplace where we have to work that little bit harder to ensure we have meaningful, human connections, there needs to be a conscious effort to do exactly that. Different people serve different purposes to form a secure support

---

17. Friendships in the Workplace. In: Derlega V.J., Winstead B.A. (eds) Friendship and Social Interaction. Springer Series in Social Psychology. Springer, New York, NY, 1986.
18. Sammons, A. (2019) *The compassionate teacher.* Woodbridge: John Catt Educational.

network, but consider what the colleagues that you spend the most time with bring to the proverbial table:

- **The one who inspires us:** it may be that this isn't a person that you spend a great deal of time with, and perhaps you just admire their work or ethos from afar, but this person is one of the most vital people in your circle. The most valuable thing we can do for ourselves is to have people around us that drive us to be a better version of ourselves. This could be due to the position they hold, the way in which they maintain a level of professionalism at even the most challenging of times, or even how they treat others, but I learn the most from someone who demonstrates elements of the person that I want to become. Resilience is not a characteristic trait that we can learn in isolation from others, and this person can enable you to see that in action.
- **The one we simultaneously learn from:** this is the person that exchanges knowledge with me. They value my perspective on learning, or how to tackle particular situations, but they bring an equal value to our friendship with their approach and opinion. They are constructive with their words, form a civilised debate if we disagree and are amiable to explore ideas with. This person pushes me intellectually to reconsider my ethos and values.
- **The one who provides us with honesty:** this person is positively brutal. At the times when I need to hear it the most, and want to hear it the least, this person will present the truth to me, raw and bloody on a far-from-silver platter. Never one to feel that they need to choose their words carefully, and never one to consider what I may do with their feedback or how it will be received, this person is the one I go to if I already know the answers to my issue, but just wasn't quite ready to admit it yet.
- **The one who provides positivity:** Jon has never said a negative word about anyone. If you mention that the spoons in the sink are starting to grow mould on them, Jon will take a diplomatic approach and stock the kitchen with cleaning equipment for

everyone. Responsible for the random gifts of chocolate on people's desks, he keeps plants in his classroom and gives them to people if they're fed up, or fancy trying to keep something alive for a half a term. He is optimistic without rainbows, and kind without over-sugaring. He fully comprehends how demanding this job is, because he's one of us, and yet he relentlessly continues to remain an advocate for teachers looking after teachers.

Your professional circle should shy away from those with whom you share common purpose, those that simply agree with you, because that isn't what you will always need in times of difficulty. In the same vein, none of these people would be healthy in isolation, but that is what makes them such an incredible group collectively; they provide a resource pool to draw from when you need them the most. Use the action plan to consider your own crowd, but also how you fulfil elements of other people's crowds. Do you find that you play the same role irrespective of whose crowd it is? Or do you bring different values to different people?

Negative pockets of staff only breed negative pockets. Do not confuse letting off a little steam with deep-rooted negativity: the difference is stark, and the latter is significantly more damaging. Those that tell the trainee teachers that it's the worst job in the world, or watch the clock at well-meant, thoughtfully considered meetings; those that argue with children using personal language and who refuse to speak to parents because they believe it's simply not in their job remit. It's those people that I urge to read this book, because they have become jaded as a result of broken systems and broken relationships. Have conversations that drive solutions, as opposed to festering problems.

Changing hats

In most positions within a profession, the multitude of roles is not as prevalent as in teaching, where there are so many that we may not pay full attention to some of the lesser used ones. We are advocates for children, service providers to parents, employees, colleagues, managers of people. However, aside from a hierarchical system of management, we still bring several different agendas to different people. Take this example:

A science teacher with a teaching and learning responsibility for STEM

- delivers a teaching and learning group with information to present back to the department.
- attends STEM club and oversees technician in assisting role.
- attends peer coaching with colleague in English.
  attends whole-school meeting with actions for their own CPD.

In the space of one working day, the teacher has become transient of power of hierarchy, because they have been utilised in a way that fuels their confidence, which means they have to re-evolve according to context and conversation. In the best of schools, this teacher won't have encountered an issue around hierarchical power in all scenarios, and that is what we should expect of our staff if we want them to effectively switch between one role and the next over the course of the day, every day. According to Kosar and Yalcinkaya, 'as the level of confidence of the teachers in the institutions and the colleagues they work with increases, the citizenship behaviour increases'.[19] A culture where colleagues are simultaneously learning from and imparting knowledge to other colleagues 'creates a virtual circle of goodwill, of safe space, where it is neither cheesy nor corny to say what you value about another person'.[20] The most effective organisations are ones where the people feel a sense of ownership. This is a dual-layered process, crafted by leadership but taken by teachers; if we want to work in an organisation where colleagues share knowledge, work collaboratively and make a consistent,

---

19. Kosar, D. & Yalcinkaya, M. (2013). Organizational culture and organizational trust as predictors of teachers' organizational citizenship behaviors. Educational Administration: Theory and Practice, 19(4), 603-627.
20. Myatt, M. (2016) *High challenge, low threat*. Woodbridge: John Catt Educational.

considered effort to collectively improve, we have to be honest and think about how we contribute to that. Does the culture of the school encourage conversations that transcend the historical constraints of hierarchy? Is staff voice encouraged and welcomed as part of the orchestration of what are fundamental micro-transformations? By strategically creating spaces for staff voice that aren't perhaps part of a formal structure, but simply enabling people to speak through various channels about how to improve, this makes for an incredibly healthy workspace.

Resolution and compassion

The higher the pressure in a school, the less cooperative relationships are. This may sound like a straightforward consequence to what happens when we place ourselves under stress, but it is worth considering the fundamental impact we could make, simply from allowing others some breathing room. How do we achieve this in positions of non-leadership? By holding the importance of resolution and compassion in high regard. We teach teachers how to teach, we sometimes teach teachers effective behaviour management, but we do not begin to take steps to train teachers in how to work with other adults, and there are wider implications if we do not manage to do this successfully. We do not teach the prestige of emotional intelligence.

A concurrent thread that runs through teachers' narratives of broken relationships, both between colleagues and between students, is the motion of unresolved conflict. The discontentment of not being able to resolve disagreement burdens both parties in any relationship, but the position is particularly contentious if it is a professional one; the workplace is not an ideal setting to behave as we may want to in the heat of the moment, and we need to be able to temper our temper. When we are unable to say how we truly feel, it becomes a matter of stalemate before we learn how to move forward through discussion and problem-solving negotiation. Easier said than done! Pruitt and Rubin describe this social conflict as being when, 'parties believe that both sides' aspirations cannot be satisfied at the same time'.[21] Anyone that spends more than five minutes a day on Twitter knows the polar opposites that teacher opinion can escalate to – and with incredible speed; it is only a matter of consequence that this carries into our school buildings. Pruitt and Rubin outline the fallout of such conflicts as the dual concern model: concern for one's own outcome, and concern for the other side's outcome. It becomes a case in our minds of choosing one over the other, and the *Hunger Games* in us always chooses our own, because on the whole, it seems that it is the better bet. How do we fight against our innate desire to fight?

Theorists offer five key strategies when moving towards a resolution; but perhaps in some cases, the feeling of resolution is all that we need: not going to bed on an argument; not walking out of school on one either. This is not the only key to building strong relationships, but an essential part of positive outcomes for change. Resolving conflicts means challenging normal processes and procedures to improve individual productivity or introduce innovative systems.[22] By challenging ideas, we can adapt them as more workable ideas in future. It is argued that conflict is necessary for change.

The five basic conflict strategies are as follows. **Contending** is an attempt to resolve the conflict on one's own terms without regard for the other side's interests. **Contentious tactics** include threats, punishments, and pre-emptive actions. **Problem-solving** strategies attempt to find mutually appealing solutions. Problem-solving tactics include making concessions and discussing underlying interests. **Yielding** is an attempt to reduce conflict by lowering one's aspirations. Parties may choose to withdraw from a conflict. Finally, they may choose to remain in the conflict but be **inactive**, waiting for the other side to make a move.

21. Social Conflict: Escalation, Stalemate and Settlement, Dean G. Pruitt and Jeffrey Z. Rubin, (New York: Random House, 1986).This Book Summary written by: Conflict Research Consortium Staff
22. Robbins, S.P, et al, (2003). Management Forest NSW: Pearson Education, Pp 385-421.

To apply this five-strong strategy to educational setting, let's consider some examples:

- You have put an idea forward in a department meeting and a colleague says it is awful without explanation or constructive criticism.
- You have volunteered for a task within the department and so has someone else. Your head of department has left it for you to decide between yourselves.
- Your colleague visited your lesson and spoke to you in a way that you felt undermined you in front of the students. The class laughed at your expense.
- You created a piece of work to share with the department, and in your absence, a colleague has taken full credit for the work.
- A member of the pastoral team removed a student from your lesson. The policy is that they can be relocated but the member of staff returns to ask if the student can be returned to you if they apologise.

It is not for me to outline how you should respond as a professional, but perhaps take a moment of reflection and consider which of the five strategies would be most effective and why. My general rules are:

- Go out of your way to speak face to face with someone
- Remain objective in reference to opinions or conduct, interrogating the reality of the other party so that you understand how it may differ from your own.
- Provide an alternative scenario that you feel would have been more pleasing for both parties. Consider the third option when resolving conflict as opposed to falling into a 'me versus them' stalemate situation that no one truly benefits from.
- Be time mindful: will you still mean what you want to say in an hour's time? A day? When will what you want to say be best received: first thing in the morning, or just before home time? Are you the best person to deliver this message?
- Tackle the most difficult conversation today: the most precarious conversations are the ones that warrant our attention the most.

Have them as a matter of priority; the more we take ourselves through the process of a tough talk, the more apparent it is that they are never as horrendous as we might have anticipated, but we get better at having them.

It takes energy to be gracious and maintain professionalism, and we cannot claim to master it at all times, because we are human, after all. However, it takes far more energy to carry around unresolved conflict – it's exhausting – and when mulling over the five strategies, a good starting point may be to consider what is greater: the reward of your stake of interest or the reward of being the person that resolved the situation. Being an agent of change means driving towards better solutions for more people, which doesn't run concurrent with being right or 'winning'.

- Choose your crowd.
- Transcend systems for conversations that develop people.
- Lead conversations with compassion.

Not standing for banter

I have experienced my fair share of close-to-the-bone 'banter' in the workplace and this becomes another layer of unresolved conflict. Affecting twice as many women as men (one in five versus one in ten),[23] passing off inappropriate or lewd comments as humour has become as rife in school staff rooms as in other sectors, with 4% of women leaving their role as a result of supposed 'banter'. The cited report shared the types of topics used to ridicule, with the more severe about mental health, sexual orientation or ethnicity. What may appear to be just a light-hearted jibe at a colleague can actually have a lasting impact upon their mental health, as the lines between acceptable humour and offensive comments are blurred. I once stood behind two men in a queue in a coffee shop who were presumably there for a work meeting. I, along with my then 6-year-old son, endured a back-and-forth commentary as

---

23. Institute of Leadership and Management article, Kate Cooper, accessed at www.bit.ly/37Boffh

they systematically critiqued each female member of staff in their office, in a discourse that could only be likened to an episode of Snog, Marry, Avoid. When I called them out, they looked at me with a heady hybrid of embarrassment and confusion: why would I be offended by a conversation that didn't refer directly to me? And this is the conundrum that banter creates: it normalises language used to describe others and attempts to reduce it to a gag, a wind-up, a preoccupied thought that has little meaning.

- Have you finished having kids now? You're pretty much permanently pregnant.
- She must struggle to get around the tables on a good day.
- You wouldn't want to meet her in a dark alleyway – or a light one come to that!
- Did you put that badge on your boobs on purpose?
- Red lippy for school is a bit much, isn't it?
- Why aren't you making dinner when you get home?
- Didn't leave any of your pants floating about, did you?

It means exactly what it sets out to say. Matt Pinkett and Mark Roberts outline their concerns over the concept of piss-taking as acceptable humour, stating that 'when complaints were made to senior leadership team, they were largely downplayed or hushed up'.[24] Certainly, when a comment is minimised to a joke, it shifts the blame from the participant to recipient. Even more concerning is when a colleague doesn't appear to know the difference between teasing and insults and isn't called out for it. That is directly detrimental not only to the individual affected, but the school community; the more that such comments are deemed acceptable, the deeper rooted the issue. Here are some strategies in calling out banter for exactly what it is:

If you are comfortable doing so, call the individual out immediately. Banter can be rife as a result of the individual not being previously informed that what they're doing is rude, or hurtful: they may not even realise that what they are saying is upsetting or offensive. Not to say that this excuses such behaviour, but they may never have had a discussion about the fact that some people find it unacceptable to have their weight/gender/sexual orientation as the topic of jest (I know, right?).

24. *Boys Don't Try*, Matt Pinkett and Mark Roberts, David Fulton, 2018

Find your resolution, but you must have one when it comes to banter. If you have been at the centre of a joke, this will sit as unresolved conflict, and will potentially niggle away at you. It will also shape the professional relationship that you have with the individual, and warp future, unrelated conversations because you are still (rightly) hurt or upset by the way they dismissed such comments as light hearted or well meaning. Offence is subjective; UNISON have policies in place to outline if you are indirectly offended (in an overheard conversation, for example) by someone's comments to another person, and no one is in a position to tell you the extent to which you should or should not be affected by comments that you view as offensive. You feel how you feel, and it is not to others to determine whether you should be upset by something or not; but in the same breath, on the whole, people don't set out to infuriate other people.

Be firm in your report to leadership, and do not shy away from the fact that you are entitled to do so. If such events are left un-dealt with, as Pinkett and Roberts advise, 'such attitudes are normalised and cascaded down to your pupils', particularly if such instances are in open view of students. We have a duty to look after ourselves first and foremost, but also to exemplify positive professional relationships for children. In some instances, such comments are made in front of children, which not only impacts your working relationship, but also undermines your position in front of students, which then takes further work to remedy. Request the support that is necessary to correct misconceptions that this is acceptable and treat it as a re-education of sorts.

Professional safety nets

We have our crowd, but not a clique. We are having fierce, productive conversations in school; we are holding those to account who don't consider our reasonable boundaries, and we navigate towards positive, nurturing relationships over negative unproductivity. Now what? How can we start to build on these foundations so that the relationships we have mobilise what we do? How can we use discourse to steer ourselves and others towards harmonious working relationships?

Create something to belong to

As human beings, we have an inherent desire to belong. Belonging fuels our sense of identity, how able we are to validate ourselves, and ultimately, our contentment depends upon our collective ownership. 'Human beings have a pervasive drive to form and maintain at least a minimum quantity of lasting, positive, and significant interpersonal relationships'[25] through interactions with others and in the context of a stable and constant framework where others show a genuine and earnest care for us. Essentially, we need to have conversations that leave us satisfied, and in a setting where it feels as though people care. Create something in your workplace that enables you the opportunity to have these conversations, away from the subject of the day. It could be a reading club, it could be helping out with the school allotment. It could simply be starting a Friday cake club. Kick-box together every Thursday for 20 minutes; start a breakfast club (I mean, everyone likes breakfast, for crying out loud). How many staff have you only known by their first name and never their face, due to the fact that they have only been at the end of an email for a year or more? We have looked around us at INSET, and wondered who the new faces are, and sometimes sadly never had the opportunity to find out before the next INSET when they are no longer present. Don't be in that school! There is great value to disconnecting from teaching with other teachers who understand the pressures of the role. This is paramount to building a culture of care; if we want to build relationships with the people we work with, we have to present more and more ways to see each other as human beings rather than as names on the end of emails. It doesn't need to be gigantic, or structured, it just needs to provide a way of saying hi to people. That's it.

- Build systems that prioritise and utilise professional relationships.
- Create systematic ways for people to belong.

25. Pillow DR, Malone GP, Hale WJ. The need to belong and its association with fully satisfying relationships: A tale of two measures. *Pers Individ Dif.* 2015 Feb;74:259-264. doi: 10.1016/j.paid.2014.10.031. PMID: 27134325; PMCID: PMC4848456.

Leaders and liability

The way in which leaders shape relationships in schools makes the difference between attracting and retaining good people and repelling them. I don't need more than a few words to convince you that the best people in leadership are the ones running the schools that people want to work within. If humanity is innate, what excuse do we have?

- -

Can you share an example of poor leadership in a school?

66 **Katie Smith:** Saturday school. A colleague said she no longer wanted to do it as she was missing out on taking her child to karate. She was told it was denying her mum the chance of spending time with her grandson if she did that.

66 **Maisey Laurels:** I had an emergency appendectomy after my appendix burst and I ended up with peritonitis. I popped into school during recovery once I was able to move to collect stuff before the end of term and was asked to spend 2hrs completing reports as I had 'missed' them whilst in surgery!

66 **Tim Lees:** My Head would regularly visit our department meetings and when I spoke, would tap impatiently on the table if I started to take longer than she deemed necessary to deliver something, or interrupt and speak for me.

66 **Anon:** One of my year 11s didn't complete the writing task on language paper 1 because she ran out of time in the real exam so I was told I needed to give up two of my free lessons to ensure she got top marks on paper 2 to make up for it

66 **Sarah Brown:** Asked 1st 'how long will it take?' And then just told to get back to school from my grandad's deathbed, because the Head needed a form from me. Grandad died while I was on the M1 heading back.

66 **Simone Shepherd:** My Deputy Head announced that due to my pregnancy, I would be 'useless' for break and lunch duties in front of the whole staff body in an INSET session. I was also excluded from CPD coaching discussion that day because I wouldn't be able to contribute anything of any substance and made to sit on a table on my own during the discussion sessions.'

❝ **Lisa Adams:** 'In my first job I was Head of Dance, but also taught some English to make a full timetable. I was expected to change from dance clothes to formal clothes (which could have been 2/3 changes a day) which did it for 2 weeks then refused...I felt like Superman in the phone box!'

Leaders shape a school vision and set the purpose. One person cannot steer a ship, but they do have to narrate the story of a school in order for the staff to know which direction to take with their everyday decisions and choices. This craft and curation is not loud or fleeting; effective school leaders use the quieter parts of professional humanity to build a team in this way. It starts with 'a sense of belonging ... they will work hard to ensure everyone is included ... No special treatment of one person or one group over another ... They understand that belonging goes beyond words.'[26] When I asked teachers about their experience of conflict in the workplace, for every ten anecdotes shared, nine involved a line manager or member of their senior leadership team. One teacher stated that 'it's never the children, but always the adults that make going into work difficult.' This isn't an issue solely amongst teaching; poor management has been evident in aspects of every job I have ever had. One area that I found of great interest when I first started to work in schools was the role of human resources. In banking, our HR department was the voice of reason, indicating to leaders exactly how we could manager effectively, operate in a timely manner, ensure that we were using language and carrying out actions in a way that prioritised the person. In schools, some of the treatment that individuals have encountered would have resulted in incredibly severe disciplinary action, or at least, crisis meetings, whilst colleagues discussed how that employee had been treated in such a manner. In contrast, I found that the fault or blame never lay at a leader's feet, but at a teacher's. Where are we going wrong?

If you become a manager within an organisation, it is usually as a result of carrying out the role within your team at an exceptional

---

26. Myatt, M. (2016) *High challenge, low threat*. Woodbridge: John Catt Educational.

level. You are expected to lead by example, having lived out the roles of the individuals that you will now manage. Teaching, even more so: you are expected to earn your stripes at every level of the school system in order to then manage the people that come after you. However, we do not train educational leaders in what is meant by effective leadership; we train them in teaching, or a specialism (data, curriculum), but public relations, human resources, financial planning – all of these skill sets are meant to either come naturally or holistically through experience. Many private sector positions train their staff at the start of a job as part of recruitment policy; the process is anticipatory, and staff are skilled for the role that they will undertake in advance of the role itself. As a senior leader within the finance sector, I underwent HR training, had a professional coach who I met with regularly and who was employed by the business but whose priorities were adhered to my development as opposed to my development within the company. I had a network of leaders within the same role in different areas of the North West who I met with weekly to discuss common issues, but who were additionally on the end of a phone call, should I need advice or support. These were all fastidious, methodological processes to provide me with the safety net that I needed for the multiple times that I would fail – and for knowing what to do about it. I was being trained to develop a sense of resilience.

In education, we seem to fill in the gaps as we go along, and not always the right gaps. Tom Rees explores the concept of transformational leadership in his article for Ambition First, where he toys with the language used for leadership advertisements in education, and how the focus becomes driving a vision, perhaps more than the reflection and pragmatism that is also required for sustainable change. He highlights that job advertisements for leaders in education place adjectives such as, 'dynamic', 'strong' and 'inspirational'[27] as key skills for credible leadership, all of which are

27. Tom Rees, Help Leaders Keep Getting Better, March 2019, accessed at www.bit. ly/2sEDKUV

predominantly masculine, but also, lacking in the micro skill set required to manage people, as opposed to processes.

I believe that many of the questions that we have around leadership in schools root back to our diverse definition of what it is to be a leader. Connolly, James and Fertig consider the difference between educational management and leadership, posing the idea that 'educational management entails carrying the responsibility for the proper functioning of a system',[28] as opposed to people. Being new to leadership, particularly when the position is secured internally, brings its own challenges to the dynamics of a school: 'Teacher leadership introduces new structures of interactions in schools that [make] teacher leaders find themselves continuously juggling between two different agendas of professional interests.'[29] Leaders find themselves in a different point of the school hierarchy and have to very rapidly work out how to successfully navigate that. It may involve leading people that were previously colleagues within the same department, who they will have had an entirely different relationship with before, and some don't know how to start paving the way to reformat those relationships. We also cannot ignore that we are in a recruitment and retention crisis, and this will inevitably (whether we feel comfortable enough to admit it or not) result in poor leadership, where leaders are placed in positions of huge responsibility without either the training, experience or support network to help them voyage through it. It becomes a perpetual state: inexperienced leadership is more likely to result in poor leadership in any place of work. If we want to look at improving retention in schools, avoiding schools scrabbling around for long-term supply, we must improve our capacity as effective leaders, but also leadership's ability to build and sustain relationships with staff so that schools keep brilliant teachers.

28. Michael Connolly, Chris James, Michael Fertig, The difference between educational management and educational leadership and the importance of educational responsibility, Published in Educational Management Administration & Leadership, 2017
29. Charlotte Struyve • Chloe´ Meredith • Sarah Gielen, Who am I and where do I belong? The perception and evaluation of teacher leaders concerning teacher leadership practices and micropolitics in schools, February 2014

STOP TALKING ABOUT WELLBEING

Leaders discard authority for trust

The best leaders are those that start with the clear, explicit assumption that no one is setting out to do a bad job, and if further support is needed, it is their responsibility to fulfil that duty. Evelyn Forde outlines the idea that the senior leadership team at Copthall School are there 'to serve' the staff,[30] and it is this act of looking inwards, and with thoughtful reflection before moving forward that makes leadership effective. These leaders recognise the importance of goodwill loading, and the difference between appreciation and expectation; they understand that goodwill is essential to running a school, where the pressures of workload differ dramatically from one month to the next, according to the demands of the calendar. They pre-emptively thank those going the extra mile, and don't see it as just part and parcel of teaching. They thank with gifts of time and recognition. They know that just by using the correct language with individuals, and being genuinely thankful in advance (as opposed to enforcing and operating with assumption and authority), better work will take place. Trust is gained through an explicit use of agenda, and agenda setting with trust of staff capability is the preference over micromanagement. Effective leaders understand the need for time and space to complete good work, so will use accountability as a conversation to understand the issues at hand, rather than as a weapon of blame. They hold people to deadlines because they have faith in the work that these people do, but are receptive to discourse and narrative over binary processes and ultimatums that threaten the withdrawal of autonomy. They follow a few key mantras, and work to simplify – not overfill – workload for their staff. Here are a few ways that senior leaders work with staff to keep purpose paramount.

Bring the best to the table
When I have worked for really effective leaders, I've always felt like I had a voice. Their door was always open, or they made time to

30. www.bit.ly/37X06zU

listen, and it was a conversation on a level playing field: my opinion was as valued as a senior member of staff, as was the caretaker's, the technician's, and those of the staff in reprographics. Every member of staff was thanked at the end of the school year, in no particular order, because hierarchy did not play a role in the system. It was there as a support mechanism, but never as a method to enforce, oversee, scrutinise or silence.

In our finest schools, this is key to forging relationships that last between leadership and staff. Keeping to commitments, remembering that the primary role of a position in management is to support, and recognising the promises being made to people are the three most valuable elements of empowering others, and ultimately keeping them in a school. Being listened to, provided with responsibility and trust to run projects, and engagement in leadership activities all lead to a stronger sense of empowerment within your own role in school. Our fulfilment comes from self-belief in our capabilities, which can only start with someone believing in us to begin with.

Gratitude and humility

Effective leaders are vulnerable in their thanks and show their vulnerability by demonstrating that they don't know everything. Leaders lead through vision, not knowing it all, and regularly expose themselves to those that they lead by showing that the value of their work lies with those that help them to achieve it. They're leaders because they look at the landscape and consider who the best people are to join with them to make change. They understand that this is impossible as a solitary exercise, and explicitly share this with their staff. Whilst silently confident, they hold the work as a testament to the people that surround them. They take every opportunity to share that with outsiders: their praise is relentless, they are observant and not always to celebrate the end result, but instead, the journey. They understand the humanity of good leadership, and that not all success can provide a measurement outcome. The wider implications of what Mary

Myatt calls 'feeding the well' repay a school system tenfold; treating people like human beings first and employees second will always reap rewards. Schools providing staff with free tea and coffee, time to see their children in school plays or sports days, food to celebrate the end of the year – these can be really small-cost ways in which staff feel valued.

Finally, effective leaders comprehend that they are in a position of great responsibility when it comes to inspiring others. Leaders in schools are role models both with what they do say and with what they choose not to say. Brilliant leaders understand the gravity of timing and the giving of time to attend to the important conversations. They are also exemplary when outlining what to work towards; they provide the template to future leaders for how to lead. Expressing humility ensures that leadership is accessible, achievable and not an end point to a career, but an empowering stop-off that enables you to look at the map, the bigger picture, before taking everyone along with you in the right direction. The best leaders will inspire the leaders of the future as a blueprint of not what a leader is, or what their staff should emulate, but the underpinning principles that will help them to deliberate over the sort of leader they could become.

- Trust your staff and share that you have complete faith that they will achieve great things as a result of their expertise.
- Remove hierarchical structures that threaten to break down honest exchanges between staff and leaders.
- Recognise humility as a key strength for shaping future leaders.

Connections in the classroom: student systems

The relationships that we forge with students can be lifelong as a teacher. We don't walk out and leave the connections at the school gates: they follow us to later life, or even just sometimes to that family summer holiday 1400 miles away in Kefalonia, or if you're anything like me, every time you pop to the shops, go for a run, or sit in the doctor's waiting room. As a teacher, you stand as a representative of your community, and with students, you remain in that role irrespective of how much time passes. The connection that you develop over that time can determine whether they stop to say hello or carry on walking. Beyond that, the connection is what brings us to the role and what holds us to stay. Some may call it guilt, but the term doesn't quite match the emotion: we feel bound by our sense of purpose – duty, even. And to achieve it, we must interact with students. That may imply that it is a requirement and not enjoyable, but quite the opposite – we rely upon healthy student-teacher relationships for us to feel as though we are moving forwards with what we want to accomplish. They are necessary.

Without the relationships that we build with children in our classroom, it is hard to find a sense of purpose; look back at your 'why', and I would bet that children were at its core. Some of our fondest and funniest stories are from lessons (and some children stay with us our entire career) because of these memories – bonds built through support and nurture; but we also have memories of the 'not quite' children – the ones you feel you didn't manage to reach or support, or keep in the classroom long enough to make a difference. Irrespective of our rationality, we hold ourselves to account for these children, even though we know there are more factors at play and at stake. We feel responsible – and that is why 'It's for the kids' works every single time.

Play nicely, please

If we are to teach – and there is an ounce of truth in those 'Get into Teaching' adverts, as the teacher gets an 'ooooh' of awe and wonder at the knowledge they've sprinkled like fairy dust about the room, before a cackle of laughter explodes as they drop a gag, or (in the instance of the age-old science gimmick) blow up a bit of magnesium for the craic – then we all know we need to nail behaviour.

We also know that in some schools, it's the toughest nut to crack. Behaviour isn't an issue for a teacher, but an issue for a school. In the schools that work collectively as a staff body, teachers are there to teach, and the senior leadership team use those systems to deal with behaviour that threatens the teachers' ability to do so. Broken support systems that prevent children from learning and teachers from teaching leave us all with more than a sour taste; they erode the reason that teachers signed up in the first place. The more time that is taken away from your core purpose – to teach children – the more you feel disconnected from that purpose. Poor behavioural support eradicates being able to carry out your role and this disappointment and resentment results in teachers leaving, because they do not feel they have a choice – and they do so reluctantly. They have become negotiators, jailors, or prisoners themselves, held by policy which doesn't quite correlate with the image that initial advert quite promised.

All schools have behaviour systems, but the reality is that there are schools in all contexts, and all pockets of the country that have concerning levels, narratives and consequences of poor behaviour. It is not just low-level disruption, or barely a percentage of pupils, or only a particular margin of a cohort. The 'justs', 'barelys' and 'onlys' are excuses for letting teachers down. It is not as a result of SEN requirements, or because teachers are too strict, or because teachers are too easy going, or because it's just not 'the good old days' anymore. It is because of the systems in which teachers cannot teach, so they leave.

> *Whole school structures have the biggest impact ... The resistance to this comes mainly from people who rarely see or deal with difficult classrooms and schools. In such circumstances, errors can multiply, untouched by reality: beautiful fantasies about the way life and children should be ... Fictions like: children will behave if lessons are more fun or relevant; directing children's behaviour is oppressive; all misbehaviour can be*

amended by conversational or therapeutic approaches etc. These would be comical if they didn't have such a devastating effect.' — **Tom Bennett**[31]

There is little evidence that directly links teacher turnover to student outcomes, but studies explore the potential damage caused by poor relationships in schools, and surmise that teacher turnover reduces when teachers are able to teach to a good standard. 'When teachers leave schools, previously held relationships and relational patterns are altered. To the degree that turnover disrupts the formation and maintenance of staff cohesion and community, it may also affect student achievement.'[32] This leads me to conclude that we teach better if we can remain in a role longer, and as a result, we have the time to forge meaningful relationships with students. It would be simplistic to draw correlations between turnover and outcomes, because there are too many variables attached to student success; but I do make the assumption here that teacher consistency will never be harmful for students, if the teaching is of a good standard. Beyond outcomes and grades, relationships are where we build schools, and it is unjust to talk about the importance of relationships in relation to attainment.

Similarly, we need to be realistic when we talk about the impact of teacher retention and turnover; we are in the middle of a recruitment crisis, and replacement of staff is difficult, particularly in specific regions of the UK. Schools cannot be in a position to choose what we perceive to be a teacher of poor quality over no one at all, and so it simply isn't realistic to state that the most effective way to measure or govern teacher quality is to strip our profession of the poor ones to make way for the better, as Dylan Wiliam once wryly implied.[33]

31. www.bit.ly/35u5n0e
32. Ronfeldt, Matthew, Hamilton Lankford, Susanna Loeb, James Wycko. 2011. 'How Teacher Turnover Harms Student Achievement', NBER Working Paper No. 17176.
33. Wiliam, D., Teacher Quality, accessed at www.bit.ly/39KRmhS

Student relationships are built of many things, but student behaviour in regard to wellbeing and workload in this case of argument can be simplified to three overarching factors: relationships, expectations and external factors. The final element is one of the most important to note, and I want to emphasise this: *you cannot control student behaviour.* You cannot determine all of the contributing factors that feed into how a child feels that day, just as they cannot control the argument you had with your spouse that morning, or the car that cut you up on the motorway. No more 'He's good for me' or 'The better planned your lesson, the better the behaviour.' Stop making teachers feel like they have jurisdiction over children's reactions.

Broken systems and unresolved conflict

Children misbehave for a variety of reasons. I'm not an expert on child behaviour – I don't feel that my experience of parenting a raucous toddler and an almost impeccably behaved ten-year-old warrant me expressing my opinion on this. But I do know that in the absence of a decent behaviour system that works, the lack of boundaries can be dangerous and detrimental on many levels and to both teachers and students alike. Here is an example that you may be able to draw parallels with:

A teacher has what they refer to as the 'challenging year 9' class four times a week. The first two weeks of the year were calm enough: expectations were set, the course outlined, and then behaviour begins to obstruct learning. Students will talk over the teacher, repeatedly. He had it ingrained in him from training: 'Don't speak until they stop – no matter what.' So, he tries to do that. It doesn't work. He singles a couple of kids out as an example, because it gets to the point that more children are speaking than not, and those children challenge him for victimisation. He sends the students to the head of department, as per policy. The students say the right things and are relocated back in his room for their next lesson, without any contact made with home. Some may apologise to him in front of the head of department; some do not. He tries a new seating plan; it makes no difference. By this stage, the class has started to feel a little as though it's formed part of an uprising – let's call it a mutiny of the classroom. He feels literally outnumbered.

He emails the head of year and form tutors; they are surprised at the names mentioned and say they will have a word. A word makes a difference for some, for the short term. The teacher starts to worry about the progress he is making through the unit content in comparison to the other classes. He tries to pinpoint the two most disruptive students and attempts to have a discussion with the head of year. He is informed that both students he has identified as a key issue have 'a lot going on outside the classroom' right now and that he should treat them with care. He's advised to go and see them in maths with Mr Y, because 'they are good for him', but struggles with his 22/25-hour teaching timetable to find the time to pop along to someone else's lesson. He dreads the four days of five that he teaches the class and starts to focus all of his energy into fixing the problem, thinking over it on his commute to and from work, and discussing it when he gets home. He tries a variety of suggested 'strategies' but doesn't allow them very long to see an impact, because he feels as though it simply means more time is being wasted in comparison to the other classes. He refocuses on a different four to six children each lesson and contacts home about their 'low-level disruption', and is told by parents that they already know, the children have informed them and they are concerned that this is just a result of being bored as a result of the lack of challenge in his classroom.

The 'good kids' have joined the previous 'high-profile' students and what should take 15 minutes to teach now takes an hour. The teacher starts to feel that if it were not for those two children, his classroom would be a bit more manageable – when they are absent, he feels that things are slightly more productive. He goes to see his head of department, who tells him that the two students he feels are the issue cannot be moved due to class sizes. The head of department has every faith that the teacher is capable of turning things around by 'seeing things through' and continuing to contact home as per the policy, and he will just have to 'make the best of it'.

The use of an inadequate behaviour policy which lacks clarity and consistency is like throwing a rock into a river as a way of stemming a flood; it doesn't even begin to solve the problem, because the river is too big, and your rock is too small.

The policy may be present – in that there is one – but it isn't a policy that draws lines for students and places learning at the core of a teacher's role.

The teacher feels unsupported and tries to compensate with what is within his control in the absence of a system; he liaises with the relevant teams, speaks with his line manager, contacts parents and reviews what he could do within the classroom. Without consequences for the students, or senior support from outside the classroom to convey the message that *as a teacher, he should simply be able to teach*, his role becomes clouded to both him and the students. His unresolved conflict becomes directed at a select few, and without a consistent message to all students, they believe that he is singling them out, and he believes that they are the issue as ringleaders. The behaviour management system becomes localised without wider support of holding models of the right behaviour or the right consequences of an absence of that behaviour. It becomes a stalemate between the child and the teacher, and the relationship approaches a point of irreparability: the student will view all consequences as a direct action from the teacher and not the school. It becomes personal.

For a child, unresolved conflict becomes a systemic issue as well. If we do not distance teachers with the assistance of a decent behaviour system, students go through their educational journey with the ingrained impression that some teachers are more accepting than others, some teachers are prepared to let things slide, and some teachers care less about the progress that they make. None of that is true, but the lack of structure creates a level of resentment on both sides: the teacher with the system, and perhaps even the child; and the student with the teacher, because the system doesn't exist to them.

We're not meant to discuss resentment towards children – it makes us seem unprofessional and unkind towards children –

but it is one of the many sad outcomes of when we don't have effective systems to support teachers or even worse, we blame teachers for behaviour that isn't their own. Jackson (2002) argues that: 'Teachers frequently experience a whole range of unpleasant feelings towards pupils ... Intense feeling of resentment can also be felt towards the head teacher or members of the senior management team, especially if teachers feel their suffering is not being taken seriously enough or that they are not being sufficiently supported.'[34] Teachers will feel failure, or guilt that they have not managed to do anything other than fail this child or that class. Left unprocessed, Jackson suggests that teachers may then 'react' rather than 'reflect' when tackling the problem at hand – which is what we see from the teacher's actions. They become fixated on solving the problem because they are not being provided with the space and time to rebuild the relationships necessary for learning to take place. Ultimately, an emotionally demanding and stressful job coupled with a lack of reflective space can lead to teachers losing touch with the very ideals that may have initially motivated their entry to the profession in the first place.[35]

As an even wider implication, a teacher forced into this position will then struggle to practise social and emotional competence that wouldn't be difficult under usual circumstances. If you want to see why teachers shout in classrooms or see behaviour as a personal flaw ('David is just an idiot') as opposed to highlighting its intrinsic link to learning ('David doesn't listen when I explain a task'), remove a behaviour policy. We – adults, humans – will act in unrecognisable ways when we feel vulnerable, cornered and without options.[36]

---

34. Jackson, E. (2002). Mental health in schools – what about the staff? Thinking about the impact of work discussion groups in school settings. Journal of Child Psychotherapy, 28(2), 129–146

35. Halit M. Hulusi & Peter Maggs, Containing the containers:Work Discussion Group supervision for teachers – a psychodynamic approach, Educational & Child Psychology Vol. 32 No. 3 © The British Psychological Society, 2015

36. Bandura, A. 1998. 'Personal and Collective Efficacy in Human Adaptation and Change.' In Advances in Psychological Sciences. Vol. 1: Social, Personal and Cultural Aspects, edited by J. G. Adair, D. Belanger, and K. L. Dion, 51–71. Hove: Psychology Press.

What does an ideal behaviour management system look like for a teacher then? It should fit the needs of the teachers, students, and community of the school. It should draw lines for what is completely intolerable within society and prepare children adequately for the consequences that await them. It should place emphasis on the work, and how valuable both time and work are to success. When I talk through behaviour choices with students, I always return to that notion of time: it is their choice to waste time that others in hundreds of schools around the country will now have as an advantage. Above all, it should place trust in the teacher. It should take the teacher's voice as central to understanding what is required for that work to take place.

- -

Things you may have been told about behaviour – and why they are wrong:

- **'He's good for me.'** If a teacher declares such a thing, it is because the system hasn't worked, and the child is choosing who they behave for. Children may behave differently for different adults, but this is based upon a whole range of factors that don't distil down to 'He's good for me'.

- **'Fun will keep a class engaged enough to stop bad behaviour.'** This can be fulfilled by allowing them to run around every 30 minutes to let off some steam, bribing them with sweets, or relating your subject to a famous rapper/game show/reality TV programme/*Avengers* task/cartoon/poster. If you bribe children, you are implicitly letting them know that you don't value your subject enough to regard it as interesting enough in its own right.

- **'Go and see little Johnny in maths; he's good there.'** Going to see little Johnny in a different setting may give you an insight into the subjects that little Johnny likes, but won't help you to strategise behaviour. If you want to get behaviour right in your classroom, go see a teacher making good use of your pastoral team. That person is using the system to ensure that they are a teacher in the classroom and those that are in school to manage behaviour manage behaviour.

- **'If you use the system, you're a poor teacher.'** All schools have behaviour issues in some context and some level and some capacity. You are not a bad teacher for dealing with behaviour issues; you are simply a teacher dealing with behaviour issues. Remember that there is only so much that is within your control, and other colleagues are paid to deal with what is beyond your scope as a teacher. Your job is to teach. Don't feel bad for returning to this message.

As a teacher, you are not the only one dealing with unresolved conflict in multiple scenarios throughout the day. What we need to do as adults is recognise and model the fact that we can know how to compartmentalise, leave our personal concerns (sometimes) at the door and model a professional understanding of how to do so for students. I often describe teaching as 'a series of unfinished arguments, and then you go home'. This lack of resolution can be the difficulty that we have in moving on or feeling as though we have succeeded in whatever it was that we set out to do that day. Dealing with students will sometimes fail to provide a sense of resolution – they're children, not robots, after all – but what we can do instead is create a microcosm of systems in our classrooms that demonstrate:

- I'm invested in you – sometimes more than you are yourself.
- I place all value in the work, and I reward your efforts in relation to the work.
- My lines are clear, and I remind you of them frequently.

Warm-strict: no guessing
Warm-strict shows unconditional care for students through clear boundaries and a recognition for hard work. Classrooms should not be places of fear, and kind-strict is often perceived as such that fear is the denominating driver. But what warm-strict promises is a really clear, manageable, accessible way for students to understand what it is that you want from them. In the most successful classrooms, 'the teacher and students laugh together ... There is ... room to express interests and passions and veer off into new corners of the subject from time to time'[37] with a clear respect for the subject itself from the

---

37. Sherrington, T. (2017) *The learning rainforest*. Woodbridge: John Catt Educational.

student, because it is exemplified by the teacher. The teacher refuses to let the student down by allowing them to waste time.

My classes know that my sole wish is for them to work hard and reap the reward of that. They know because I tell them. Repeatedly. I open with a short introduction at the start of the year about how I have high expectations of them because they are all capable and I refuse to do anything other than support them to learn. I return to this and link all of my praise to specific examples of working hard and getting it right. Be explicit in your hopes and dreams for the students that you teach; reinforce these ideas and show that your faith in the student is constant and recognised by hard work. This praise doesn't come generously or often; I will only praise when that child has achieved something that we all collectively deem a remarkable comment, input or behaviour. I thank children a lot for their behaviour. I recognise when they are respectful, or spontaneous in being helpful. My praise is distributed in a range of ways, starting off by setting up a class to learn at the start of a lesson: 'Thank you for being quiet to listen, David; thank you for helping with books, Molly; thank you for being ready to learn with your equipment, Sarah; thank you for reminding us of the page number, Chris; thank you for having your knowledge organiser out for us to refer to, Lawrence.' I smile; I make jokes (albeit appalling ones); I bring my TA into the conversation about the work; we learn as a collective. The work does not have to be serious to be taken seriously. I throw adjectives to distribute praise for insightful ideas or challenging the ideas of others: I repeatedly hold them up as 'fantastic', 'excellent', 'spectacular', 'mature', 'incredible' – because without them, the work would not take place. I don't shout anymore; I used to, but I realised that it was an indication that I had lost control (usually with something else completely unrelated to shouting at the topic itself) and that I hadn't started from a warm, clear starting point.

I demand silence to speak. Nonverbally; I wait and smile at those who wait with me, ready to listen. I demand behaviour that will enable us to learn and be mutually respectful of one another: standing quietly at the end of a lesson; saying goodbye to each individual as they leave; having any discussions at the end of the class, away from an audience. These things are what build relationships.

I often write any required emails home during student independent work, outlining my disappointment, so that students can read my words and understand how they have let themselves down. They also know that I refuse to let them do so repeatedly. I find power in other ways than words or battles, because I make it clear that I don't want it; I want to relinquish the power in the form of them feeling empowered by learning, not because I have screamed that they should do so. There are no other options but to learn, and I reinforce that over and over: we learn or there's a problem, because learning is what makes the world go around.

I take my position as expert incredibly seriously – and explicitly outline this to the class; I spend my time ensuring I know my subject and my texts well. There is 'a statistically significant difference in student motivation when students perceived that a) strong student-teacher relationships were present, b) high content knowledge of a teacher was exhibited, and c) exemplary teaching ability was displayed'.[38] If I am to place such a high value on the work, and expect them to follow, then I must show that it is important to me. I cannot demand reading and not read; I cannot demand that they not be scared to fail, and then cover up my lack of knowledge on a particular aspect of a text. I am ten steps ahead with an English degree and more years of experience than any self-respecting old lady wants to get into, but I still acknowledge that knowledge is wonderful, because it is endless, and I do not have all of it.

Warm-strict is not ruling through iron law, to take your road or the highroad. It's not punishment with smiles, or brainwashed manipulation to get kids to do what you want them to do. It is simply showing children that you put a value on them and the work, and the

---

38. Farmer, A. The impact of student-teacher relationships, content knowledge, and teaching ability on students with diverse motivation levels. Language Teaching and Educational Research, 2018.

students' self-belief that they can do the work is your ultimate goal. It isn't completion of work or attainment of knowledge that fulfils our purpose as teachers, but the students' realisation that the learning is the reward. The learning is what they are aiming for, and that this is both a prizeless and prize-fuelled plight, because it never ends.

How do we demonstrate that we want nothing more than children to believe they can achieve? We demonstrate it in all that we do and all that we say. That sounds small and grand all at once, but if you tie all conversations to our actions, and not us as people, it becomes clear that we have faith that children can make good choices when it comes to their own learning.

In a previous school, where behaviour was not followed up with consistency, and where removal of children from your classroom was just a relocation that passed the burden to another member of the team, a lot of my actions were driven by guilt and shame. Guilt that I would be placing pressure on others if I chose to have a child removed from my class, and shame at the implication that this was as a result of not being able to cope. Consequently, with a year 11 group that saw period 5 on a Friday as a free weekly party, and with a pastoral team that would only take two students maximum (sometimes walking them around the school for a lap before returning them 'because they want to say sorry'), I had to create my own binary system, my own line. My expectations are high, and clear: **I will not make a judgement based on hearsay and previous records with teachers. I will give you two weeks to make a brilliant first impression with equipment, note taking, listening and contributing in class discussion.**

After two weeks, I emailed home for all students. The emails were positive comments or concerns about behaviour. No grand speeches about where you want to go in life, no blanket collective punishment. After that, I would send a weekly email home or make a phone call for at least five students in every class that worked consistently hard over the week, including Friday period 5. To qualify for such a return, my guidelines were:

- Produce all work to the highest possible standard – no bare minimum attempts.
- Contribute at least once to class discussion to an extent that I am satisfied with, every lesson.
- Do not hold up the learning of anyone, including yourself.

If one of these areas was a concern, an email or phone call was made on Friday evening, so that parents/carers had the weekend to have the necessary discussions. If one or more of these aspects was a concern, the student was removed and sent to the head of department, or pastoral, depending on availability. It was implied that I needed to keep children in lessons, and I shared the same line that I was not prepared to have them in my lessons if they did not value what they were doing. My dialogue was, 'If I care more than they do, there's something wrong here.' Parents heard from me frequently, and I repeatedly escalated to the relevant heads of year, or my head of department, with objection rebellion. It wasn't personal (it can often seem that way when the system doesn't make it explicit as to what is or isn't acceptable behaviour) and by connecting behaviour to progress at every stage of the required dialogue, I distanced myself. 'You've chosen to...; You leave me with no alternative...; I would be a poor teacher if I didn't....' I'm a teacher. I'm teaching. I cannot teach because these children's behaviour stops the possibility of me doing so. This has happened six, seven, eight times in as many weeks. I will email home and CC you in to discuss an action plan with parents. I will **hold that line**.

Compliance to conformism

The three stages of conformism outlined by Kelman[39] are compliance, identification and internalisation. We cannot operate schools on compliance alone: our classrooms would be quiet, but not productive. Relationships aid our mental health because we

---

39. Kelman HC. Compliance, identification, and internalization: Three processes of attitude change. Journal of Conflict Resolution. 1958;2 (1) :51-60.

know the familiarity of the lines that we have drawn in the sand. Most times, it's not the relationship itself that creates anxiety, but the uncertainty and unpredictability of that relationship. No one knows how things will pan out, because no one has set out their stall of 'This is what I would like from you. This is how I expect people to behave with me, not for me.' For this context, students need to view the lines, identify where they sit within them and if it is reasonable and manageable to sit on the right side of the line, but then understand (and this can only come with time; time is fundamental here) where that line sits and aligns with their own values and belief systems.

You wouldn't storm into a restaurant, demanding at the top of your lungs that people bend to your will, or stipulate the same to a group of your peers in training. The common mistake that we sometimes make with teacher-student relationships is assuming that hierarchy is a feature here. Using hierarchy as a method of building relationships is futile – we know this from the restaurant experience! We model mutual respect, particularly in the scenario where students have yet to see what this means and what it should look like. If you have been taught that the way to interact with someone is through insults, belittlement, or exertion of power, how would you know what positive relationships should look like?

Two things happened as a result of my approach. I got a reputation for being strict, so ended up with 'the naughty ones'; and I got through loads of content in my lessons. That makes it sound like it was a seamless process (it wasn't) but the conversations I was having with students, staff and parents were all the same: 'They can do better than this, I believe this to be true'; 'This is what I am not prepared to accept from them.' I don't believe that a teacher can successfully perform their role to the best of their ability without an effective behaviour system; let me be clear on that. I don't expect teachers to march into schools and feel a newfound sense of enlightenment because I wrote a few pages about conforming. However, while the conversations you have and the line you hold may start out as exhausting, by half term, we all know where we stand and what will fly in your classroom (nothing – except learning).

By making my classroom a microcosm, and using the systems in the way that they have been theorised to me, I haven't had to vote with my feet as a result of behaviour. Ultimately, stress will impact learning, and so if the behaviour isn't there, as we all know, learning simply won't exist in our classrooms. The element of certainty through what they can expect from you will inadvertently lead to an improved sense of calm for students because there is a level of predictability. It also means that when the learning does get a little unpredictable – tangents that we can go off on as we teach content – then it feels safe to do so.

Whilst I am reluctant to add to your workload in a book about reducing workload, some things are worth spending the time on. Drop in on an after-school club for five minutes on your way out of school. Chat to the drama club kids or watch the play rehearsals. Watch the football team play or ask the food tech teacher if you can judge the final treats in the next practical lesson. Ask your line manager or the trips coordinator if you can shadow someone running a trip and attend it (preferably not in your department so that the trip would not be in your subject specialism). Be curious about seeing the students that you teach in different contexts, away from your relationship in the classroom. See students doing something that they love or will love to talk to you about; not only is this good for the soul, but it can help to humanise relationships again, if the focus has been on the work.

Honestly? I cannot write a paragraph or two about how to battle day in, day out against a behaviour process that fails children – because that is exactly what it does, and it's wrong. And in this scenario, which is a reality for all too many teachers, we then have to work with parents in a methodical way to ensure we can be teachers – and teach.

- You are not responsible for the behaviour of others.
- Working without a strong behaviour system will always be a challenge because you are a teacher, not a structure.
- Compliance and conformism are not the same thing.
- Make pockets of time to see students outside of lessons.

The cheerleaders: productive relationships with parents

Parents are our most untapped resource in schools, and one of the most fantastically beneficial to us. The EEF recently outlined the benefits of parental engagement, highlighting the direct correlation between achievement and parent support:

> The association between parental engagement and a child's academic success is well established and there is a long history of research into parental engagement programmes. However, there is surprisingly little robust evidence about the impact of approaches designed to improve learning through increased parental engagement.[40]

Whilst the majority of research foci were carried out at primary level, with more structured engagement programmes with parents, there are a multitude of ways to build relationships on a less formalised level that will aid the relationships that you build in the classroom. Epstein identified six different types of parental involvement clustered around parenting, communicating, volunteering, learning at home, decision making, and community collaboration:[41] building

---

40. EEF Parental Engagement evidence summary, accessed at www.bit.ly/2rY0ZJ0 12th August 2019.
41. Epstein, J. (1995). School/family/community partnerships: Caring for the children we share. Phi Delta Kappan, 701-712.

a network between school and the community can be powerful not only to the attainment of students, but to the staff that work within it. Parent governance is a fundamental way in which parents ensure that the key vision and messages of the school are upheld, and so it is only logical that as classroom teachers, we try to incorporate the role of parents within our own driving purpose of providing an education for their children. To do so will not only enrich the school and its place within the community but also enrich the teacher and their place within the local setting.

Parents enjoy the personable nature of a teacher because they can see that this person is genuinely invested in their child, in all children, being successful. Indeed, in a meta-study of research into parental engagement, a study showed that parents who described their children's schools as welcoming and empowering reported being more involved than parents who did not describe a positive school climate.[42] We are right to hold the role of parents in high regard in school, and ultimately, it is these small touches between school and home that build the reputation of a school, not the grand gestures or promises made by a banner or a mission statement. If we want children to succeed, and recognise the value in doing so, we have to gather our best cheerleaders to assist in reinforcing messages.

Contact home

Whilst several different types of software have recently become available to schools to improve parent contact, it is perhaps not the contact that we wish to make when it comes to development, effort and attainment. Texting software can serve as a beneficial tool for administration purposes, but the EEF research outcome indicates that keeping parents informed of key dates and current learning had very little impact on student attainment, with only a small decrease in absenteeism.[43]

---

42. Griffith, J. (1996). Relation of parental involvement, empowerment, and schools traits to student academic performance, The Journal of Educational Research, 91 (1), 33-41.
43. www.bit.ly/2sTP7Z6

Contacting home has long been the threat to wield over students as a method of promoting behaviour, as though the fear of having to have a conversation is reason alone to behave. There are multiple issues with such an approach: as a teacher, you are relinquishing control of your own authority (the old 'Wait until your father gets home' routine, and Mum is completely undermined as a result); and then there's the desensitisation of repeatedly contacting home. Imagine that you are a parent, and by 4 p.m., you have had three calls from the school regarding negative behaviour that you need to discuss with your child. Even more perturbing, if two phone calls are to discuss negative behaviour and one to discuss positive behaviour, it implies that as we might expect, their child is perhaps behaving in a particular way for particular teachers. It also implies several misleading messages to the parent, but fundamentally, the message is mixed. The parent then needs to discuss each incident in turn, establish what action to take moving forward, and contact the teacher to agree a plan of action.

How can we work with parents to establish an approach for behaviour that means it doesn't become a case of managing several phone calls at the end of the day, conversations that take place in kitchens, not schools, reaching a resolution where you feel a sense of ownership as the teacher, without it having a massive impact on your workload? The limited time that we have in our working day to resolve such issues means that inevitably, it is not always done well, and we rely on parents to essentially do the job for us. It's not a collective dialogue between the three parties required to make it a successful outcome for all involved, and this needs improvement.

In some contexts, parents' evenings are no longer fit for purpose; in many households, both parents work full time and navigating childcare of other dependants is difficult, and as a result, it may be that some parents only see attendance as a priority if there is something to be concerned about. If we are going to build and develop relationships with home that develop relationships in turn with our students, we have to create opportunities for this to happen, perhaps outside the realms of the traditional formality of sitting opposite one another at a desk, akin to an interview, with undertones of a court case prosecution, as we bring the evidence of work (or lack thereof), and the family form their defence. The conditions for such a meeting are hardly in line with the nurturing, supportive conversations that we hope to take place. What other lines of communication are available to us in schools?

My proposal would be to put practices into place that open up the lines of conversation before something goes wrong, or something needs to be put right. Sometimes, we may pick up a class in year 8 or 9, and have never spoken to any of the parents of that class before. Their parents' evening could be set in the spring term; where have we made the effort to speak to parents – all parents – before that point?

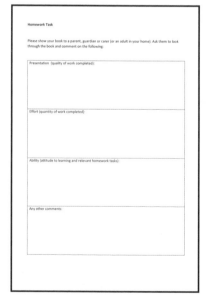

Fiona Ritson created a fantastic tool[44] for ensuring that all parents are given an insight into her classroom by utilising this method (which is really prevalent through primary schools but drops off when we get to secondary) for a secondary setting. Keeping a firm fix on praise interconnected with effort, the feedback sheet gives parents the opportunity to have open discussions with their child around the connection between effort and achievement. It places an emphasis on the importance of the work, and valuing time in the

---

44.   www.bit.ly/2uIrenL – with permission from Fiona Ritson, who advises that you 'send this out two weeks prior to parents' evening. This way you will know of any concerns in advance and will be better prepared on the night.'

classroom.

The parent-student-teacher dialogue then acts as a really explicit way to link effort with progress made and helps parents that may be working with time pressures to feel as though they have a way to support their child. Word of warning: this needs to be addressed as a strategic measure for fear that parents may end up with ten bits of 'homework' to do! Nevertheless, the impact that these have made to my own teaching practice – as a time-efficient, meaningful way to build relationships as a support system for students – has been invaluable.

Another practical tool for communicating with home via books is to include cover unit sheets. Cover unit sheets provide parents with information about what their children are studying, how it feeds into the bigger picture with their acquisition of the subject, base knowledge that they need to know and how to support them with their learning, but also areas of exploration that the topic may direct them towards: further reading, cross-curricular knowledge or projects that they may like to explore. The information places the emphasis on knowledge and enables parents to see the journey of that term, or unit, so that they can then play an active role in forming dialogue at home. It avoids the monosyllabic responses to 'Had a good day?' but it also ensures that you have opened a line of communication at parents' evenings.

It's good to talk

There's a great deal of power in a phone call, but when talking to teachers about the things that trigger anxiety in schools, calling home features frequently as a task that causes unnecessary stress, particularly (and understandably) phone calls where we need to share concerns around behaviour. We have to remember that the conversation will always run the risk of becoming emotionally loaded, and as an inexperienced teacher, at the start of my career, simple semantics would have made the difference between a damaging conversation and a productive one. Parents' evenings and phone calls are key times for the need to choose language and be productive with time spent. Phone calls like this are vital to maintaining relationships, but without a structure and mindful language, they can also be the biggest suckers of time. What is also interesting to note – and which came up during a discussion about this on Twitter – is that for some more introverted teachers, having to make phone calls is actually quite a daunting prospect:

66 I hate the whole thing about having to make a phone call home every evening to build positive relationships with parents. So time consuming. Also, phone calls give me mad anxiety.

66 So pleased to read this & realise I'm not the only one who gets anxious at the thought of making a phone-call. We have to call home for parking a student and I really struggle with it. It also takes up my lunchtime or makes me late to collect my own children.

66 Completely agree here. Also, the fact that sometimes conversations go sideways, or can't reach a solution, spend 10 mins of the call drifting in and out of irrelevant topics, exhausted after a full day teaching, colleagues ear-wigging conversations in the staff room. The worst.

66 As a parent I don't think I would like or want to be called every day. Not even once a week. Nor emailed often. Does that make me a bad parent?

The key concerns highlighted seemed to be a hatred of picking up the phone, the time that phone calls took to make because of digression or a sluggish move to a resolution, and (particularly with more negative matters) the way that the discussion might go because the teacher was not going to be the bearer of good news. Coming back to the guideline of value versus time, the value gained as a result of contacting home must justify the time we spend on it. We want to feel a sense of resolution, and that we are moving forward, so our conversations must be structured in such a way that they will set the tone for such an outcome. To do this successfully, you need to be able to anticipate what may be said, and plan the language you will use with your response to ensure buy-in from the parent or carer.

- Don't shy away from the reason for your call: open with it.
- Outline the concern.
- Provide a solution.
- Make a measurable action for the child to support their own learning.

Link all behaviour to progress; stress that attainment is not fixed: 'Success is not dependent on a predetermined scale of ability but is dependent on students and educators expecting that learning capacity can be transformed, grown and enhanced through external intervention.'[45] Calling home has to be concise and honest. As an NQT, I would worry about the impact of being critical of someone's child or concerned that they hadn't been poorly behaved frequently enough to justify my call; the same at parents' evenings. The truth is that if behaviour has stopped you teaching and that child learning, it is time lost that they will never regain and it warrants your time and their parents' time. The structure of such calls needs to be concise, not only for you, but so the parent is clear as to what the call is about and what you are asking of them. Using the structure, outline what has happened, why it concerned you, what the consequence is, and an action moving forward. You'll find that discussions are shorter but also leave you feeling far more confident in your ability to move forward with that student.

When we discuss student behaviour with parents, we must make it explicitly clear the impact upon their progress as a result. The language that we use to frame such discussions may need to shift to look like this:

The issue	What we go to say	What we should say
Repeatedly forgetting equipment	Ben needs to remember his pen	Without equipment, Ben is struggling to complete work to the best of his ability
Distracting other students	Ben has been whistling/ shouting/ making noises like a cat	Ben's behaviour has held up his own progress and the progress of others, which I cannot allow to happen

45. www.bit.ly/2QvrNK7

Not completing work in lessons	Ben barely writes anything	I know that Ben is capable of fantastic ideas, but I'm unable to give him credit for them if he doesn't demonstrate this in his written work.
Not completing homework or handing in homework on time	Ben never hands in homework	I'd really like to work with Ben to organise his workload, so he can develop his ability to complete independent work at home.
Attendance / late to your lessons	Ben is never on time to lessons	Ben isn't making the progress I would hope because he often misses the important instructions provided at the start of the lesson
Ben is behaving in an undermining way that you are struggling to articulate, such as undermining your knowledge by disagreeing with you, or dismissing what you say as nonsense, or when sanctioned, arguing that he did not do anything to begin with	Ben's attitude is poor	It appears as though Ben is struggling to agree with the basic knowledge of the subject, and often chooses a public forum to express this, which holds up the learning of others. Can I suggest he writes down questions he may have, and use his lesson notes to clear up any misconceptions as a first point of support?
Ben looks bored in your lessons and repeatedly refuses to engage. He often tries to answer questions directed at him with 'Dunno' when you know he is far more capable than the effort he demonstrates	Ben doesn't try	Ben often doesn't seem challenged in lessons, but he frequently doesn't attempt the more challenging work set when I know that he is potentially capable. However, if he doesn't evidence this through regular practice in classwork, he will fail to meet that potential, which is really concerning.

The language outlines the concern with a specific link to the work, because that is where we place our values. The concern is deep rooted, and this makes it incredibly hard to argue with. It has heart at the centre, with a view to support and drive success through achievement.

Of course, this won't make all phone calls easy; parents are stakeholders in the school business, and school systems owe it to them to listen when there is a sense of concern or dissatisfaction. However, when concerns reach that point, they should usually be passed to other hands. **You are the teacher: your job is to teach.** To do so, it is in your interest to build conversations in a way that feels productive and conclusive to both you and parents. Showing you care far before parents' evening results in the workload being a manageable task, and ensures that parents' evenings are not among the stressful pressure points, as they often can be. (This is something we discuss later.)

- Create systematic solutions for reaching out to parents.
- Use tools to highlight the learning journey to parents and carers.
- Structure phone conversations so they are solution driven.

Sam Strickland, head at The Duston School, Northampton, has invested time and resources to build a school built upon the foundations of strong relationships. In the two years since his appointment, he has made an instrumental impact in improving behaviour systems and workload culture following a period of deep-rooted toxicity within the school. I discussed the vision and key messages behind his approach with him, and he provided an insight into the steps that he has taken to ensure that this remains at the forefront of the school's ethos and whole-school culture.

Why are relationships within schools a key factor when it comes to looking after teacher wellbeing?

I strongly believe that emotional intelligence plays a major role here. If you know your colleagues and have taken time to invest in them then you will know (ideally) when someone is struggling, needs help, needs support. I firmly advocate creating a supportive, open and collaborative working environment within a school. Negative/poor relationships can lead to so many issues between staff. I would also argue that the overall climate of a school is set and dictated by the mood, approach and persona of the head.

Isn't this an effect rather than a cause? Are relationships something a school leader should be aware of when planning strategic change and putting systems in place?

I think relationships can be both a cause and an effect. Much is down to the actual institution itself and where it is in its own journey.

Relationships are a factor that needs to be considered when thinking about strategic change. I would advocate forming and forging a clear relationship as a leader with your staff so that they buy into you and your vision for a school.

What are the challenges facing staff-student relationships and how does that have a fundamental impact upon wellbeing?

Inconsistency is a huge issue, as is a lack of support, a poorly communicated vision and a poorly thought out approach to student care. If the student care model is imbalanced then this can also seriously impact negatively on relationships. Where student-staff relationships are poor, with a poor climate for learning and approach to behaviour, staff can develop extreme mental health, self-esteem and wellbeing issues. Staff can, potentially, leave a school in their droves or, worse still, leave the profession.

How would you describe the status and emphasis upon positive relationships when you first arrived at Duston?

Prior to my arrival, there had been an incredibly toxic head, and as a result, relationships and trust from staff were understandably really poor. The senior leadership team were newly appointed, had all been in their roles for 6–12 months and so were finding their feet in what I viewed as quite traditional roles: a data lead, a curriculum lead, and no one person to oversee student care. Student-staff relationships were incredibly weak; it was like the Wild West. There were 60 to 90 students walking the corridors, a convoluted behaviour system that showed up so many inconsistencies and there had not been any exclusions for the last two years. Only 40% of detentions set were actually sat, and there was no regard for the system because it didn't work. Pastoral were in an office at the furthest point from the students, and student care wasn't supported.

How did you start to tackle such challenges?

My thoughts here are clear:

- A really clear mission statement and set of aims
- A really clear, systematic and strict approach to behaviour
- A clear set of non-negotiables
- A clear approach to student care
- High visibility of senior leaders and pastoral staff
- Key support for the most disaffected and vulnerable
- Clear opportunities for staff to discuss issues

- Not blaming staff for poor behaviour
- Not taking the view that good relationships solely come from well-planned lessons
- Prioritising the teacher as the expert and being explicit about this with everyone
- Communicate, communicate, communicate – and communicate some more

Can we just explore this emphasis on communication? What does this look like at a practical level for students and staff, and how does this contribute to pragmatic preservation of staff wellbeing?

We have a clear meeting structure that supports the precious commodity of time in school but also focuses and revisits key messages to affirm what we at Duston are working to achieve. The previous meeting structure led to key teams only having meetings once a half term and these were so long that the time would be used ineffectively: we needed a system that allowed leaders to meet with teams – both senior and middle leaders – to deliver key messages and revisit those frequently. There are daily meetings of some kind, but on the whole, these are 10–15 minutes (particularly in the morning) and reinforce our teaching and learning priorities around routines for learning. Middle leaders are not directed in what they have to communicate or cover with their teams, and they have the freedom to direct the agenda, and a fortnightly time to do so. This takes place every other week, and then the alternate week is given as lieu time for the frequent, brief morning meeting time.

We are incredibly proud to share with staff that we operate at 1105 hours of directed time; but this isn't used as a stick or a demand for gratitude. It is to emphasise that we understand that the job is hard, and we are not trying to work people to the very limit of themselves.

On the note of time, Thursdays are our after-school commitment day for parents' evenings etc. It could of course be any day, but if you set Tuesday as parents' evening, that is a really long week for your staff.

What systems do you have in place to ensure that staff can develop relationships with students that can enable them to succeed, or drive forward key messages around the whole-school ethos?

All of the points to my previous answer are valid here, plus:

- Centralised detentions
- A systematic approach to sanctions
- A house system that rewards pupil successes
- A clear approach to the role of the tutor, which assists in building relationships
- Prioritising the teacher as the expert
- Clear routines for learning

What work still needs to be done in schools to improve student-staff relationships, in your opinion?

I would argue that we need to be able to say who the adults actually are in all of our schools. Some do this incredibly well and some do this very badly. I think some approaches to behaviour in some schools need considering or reconsidering, as does the idea that the teacher is the expert. We cannot say that behaviour is down to well-planned lessons, because it just isn't true.

Let's explore staff relationships. What do you feel are common obstacles to successful, productive relationships between teachers, or between teachers and those in a position of leadership?

It is the age-old issue of time but it remains a major issue. We try to do far too much, without any real thought or consideration – except of the fact we have to do it. We rarely stop to process and consider why we're doing it, who it's for, what impact it will have or the opportunity cost. If there were fewer priorities and staff were given more time to work collaboratively, this would promote relationships. Reducing the volume of emails so staff communicate face-to-face is another key issue.

The Duston workload charter[46] ensures that relationships remain central to all we do.

Could you explain the thought process behind the Duston workload charter? What led you to formulate such a document for your school? How have you seen an impact?

We have done a lot to support staff workload since I joined the school. My view is that a happy school is a successful school. Happy staff are likely to be

---

46. www.bit.ly/2sYElRd

effective teachers and they are also far more likely to feel valued and stay. The idea behind the document was to formalise fully into one neat area all of the measures that we have enacted to support staff. This serves as a clear overview for existing staff and forms part of our marketing material to recruit new staff. Whilst the document itself is in its infancy, the measures are not. We have seen a real slow-down in staff turnover, with retention now strong. There has also been a real interest externally in the work that we do as a school and the support that we give to staff. We still have work to do. I want to continue to focus on time and invite union representatives locally to provide feedback so we can constantly look to improve. I also think it is a fantastic tool for recruitment, as it lays out the kind of culture that exists in your school.

We asked all staff to contribute to the completion of the document. Swathes of staff have contributed to and discussed the supportive measures that are in place. Our action research group, which is over 20 members of staff, consulted the entire staff body and we tweaked and amended the final document as a result. A copy will be provided to every member of staff and I want to use it as an aid to remind staff that this is just a job: there is an endpoint to their workload.

What can school leaders do to develop positive relationships in their schools? What advice would you offer?

Leaders can actively listen more, reflect more and engage more with their staff. Meeting one to one with colleagues in an informal manner to discuss them, their role, their professional needs and their views on school X all help. The benefits are huge. People (staff) will recognise that you are human, that you are doing the same job, that you have the same motivation and that, fundamentally, you care about them. If you meet with staff and take a genuine interest in them, you are likely to create an army of advocates for where you are taking a school. Ultimately, whilst the impact is huge, it is impossible to measure. I also feel that leaders need to trust staff. And they need to be more flexible with time off requests. Allowing colleague X two hours to watch their child's Christmas play may seem questionable but in reality this is incredibly important to your colleague: it is something that they will never get the chance to do again and allowing them to see it will create, in most cases, a real sense of loyalty.

Don't be afraid to tackle workload and discuss it – it needs to be addressed in all schools. Don't take the view or set the precedent that teaching is meant to hurt, because it's not. It is a hard job but that doesn't mean it should break staff in the process.

It is about being brave enough to make judgement calls that may be taboo or may be unusual but being able to explain your why is really powerful here. Many of the key messages here are simple and although changing mindsets can be challenging, as long as you are able to explain your why the process can be really empowering. More work is not better work.

Section summary:
- Prioritise human connections within the workplace at all levels.
- Choose your crowd.
- Do not tolerate behaviour that you wouldn't tolerate of yourself.
- View leadership as a support system.
- Do not ignore the conversations that need your attention the most.
- Hold the line and link to pupil progress.
- Make language choices with parents to drive student success.

REFLECT

Yourself
- Where do you make time for human connections?
- Who creates your crowd? Are these nurturing, positive relationships?
- How do you have opportunities to collaborate with others?

Your sense of agency within the school
- Are there outlets for you to discuss reasons behind decisions, or be part of driving change where these decisions require further thought?
- How are staff supported at your workplace?
- Where are you given the opportunity to be human first, employee second?
- Which relationships at work are most difficult? Can you pinpoint why?
- How might you suggest small ways to ensure there is a staff voice at particular discussions?
- Are you having the conversations that you anticipate will be the most difficult?

Student relationships
- How do you make your expectations clear?
- Where do your systems support you to teach?
- What could you suggest as a small improvement to the current system?
- Do you actively seek out ways to demonstrate the value of the work?

Parents and carers
- Do you regularly utilise parent relationships to help drive up standards of behaviour?
- How much time do you spend managing behaviour vs making concise phone calls to eradicate it?
- Is there an opportunity for you to explore different outlets to build strong teacher-parent relationships outside of the traditional praise/sanction approach?
- Consider the language that you use the next time you make a phone call, and time the call. Was the discussion explicitly linked to progress made? How could you avoid digression in future so that you have ownership of the outcome?

Objective rebellion

'Reject your sense of injury and the injury itself disappears.'
– Marcus Aurelius, *Meditations*

When we discuss change in schools, it often feels like wishful thinking. We are victims of our own cognitive bias; processes have always been carried out in this way, or we have always had to like it and lump it. Often, we view teaching as a rite of passage; there are certain elements that we seem to believe are just part and parcel of what it means to teach, but I feel that this is such a dangerous approach and one that has perhaps led us to our current destination – burnout and exit rate. It's just not good enough to say, 'That's just teaching; it's meant to be hard' anymore – it never was, but then I think we already know that. So now we have started to explore what it is that needs to change, what's standing in our way and how do we go about the task of overcoming it?

Complaint without conclusion; problems without progress

We are all familiar with who the biggest martyrs are within our staff body. The ones who complain openly: they have too much planning, too much marking, an inbox spilling over the sides, to-do lists longer than both arms, they came in at 6.30 a.m., they're not leaving until 7 p.m., their kids don't recognise them anymore, they've lost the ability to eat with such a miniscule lunch break, they refuse to run any extracurricular clubs, they haven't run a trip for their entire career and pride themselves on it; no one thanks you for it, after all. They're the ones that sigh at an alarming volume and impeccable regularity during directed meetings, one eye on the clock and one foot tapping out impatiently on the floor as they pretend to listen to whatever's being shared; but let's be honest – and they will – they've heard it a million times over anyway. They refuse all offers of help, temporary or otherwise – no, they will do their own copying because there's so much of it, and planning has become a monumental task but you couldn't possibly understand, because you don't have the composition of the workload that they have.

Martyrs are dangerous to us all for the following reasons:

- They sell a poor version of what teaching really is, particularly to early-career teachers.
- Their complaining is loud but not productive.
- They do not want to hear your solutions.
- They hide behind the problem because they're worried that not having the problem to complain about could be exposed to them (they're worried they're not doing a good job).
- They genuinely make us wonder what it is that they are doing which we are not, especially at 7 p.m. as we switch on the television.

Martyrs are necessary to change; their voices usually build in force to demonstrate when an issue is an issue, and because of the volume they select to complain, it's hard to ignore. However, martyrdom is not a productive or evolutionary state of being; it eats at you, because it is not a state that seeks to eradicate itself. It doesn't pass. It doesn't fix. The only person that is damaged as a result of martyrdom is you. Whilst sharing concerns can be productive and conducive to the process of seeking solutions, putting all of our energy into a negative space is really quite damaging to us individually. Research carried out at the University of Warwick explored the amplification of panic, and the alarming rate in which bad news can fuel hysteria when passed from person to person.[1] We can see this in action within our schools: news of a change that will impact workload leaps from one conversation to the next, and the discussions become focused upon the negative aspect of the news, as opposed to digesting and considering it in its full complexity. In addition, the study revealed that even when presented with neutral, fact-based information afterwards, this would not reduce the panic induced as a result of the original news. Again, to apply this to a school setting, once we are infuriated by a change in process or addition to our workload, if it is not delivered in such a way that we understand its value and why we are doing it, there is absolutely no convincing us.

However, this process is necessary for change; in fact, the most effective schools provide channels and forums for staff to challenge, question or make suggestions to improve processes, so that any evolution within the school is as a result of a collective transition, refined and adapted by all along the way. It is a representation of a school leadership team and staff body, along with the students working in a symbiotic way, with the same intentions, dismissive of the idea or process as something that one person owns. When a crisis occurs, one person did not drop the ball – when the ball drops, we, all staff, run to pick it up.

Of course, this is not always the case, and where change is instructed as opposed to shared, or driven with a singular voice and not the voice of many, there tends to be a distinct lack of channels for the staff to discuss or question new ideas or even existing processes that don't seem to deliver. In the absence of such an ideal, we revert to complaining without conclusions; our complaints are not heard by the people who wish to drive change and would appreciate us helping to do so.

So we have all of this knowledge, we know that our time in school is not being used in the most productive way, we want to ask

---

1.   Jagiello, R. D. and Hills, T. T. (2018), Bad News Has Wings: Dread Risk Mediates Social Amplification in Risk Communication. *Risk Analysis*, 38: 2193-2207.

to trial that marking approach, re-consider our assessment models, evaluate the way in which we use meetings – but we don't have an outlet to be able to have these discussions, or we may be concerned that they won't be met with receptive responses. How do we have conversations in a way that will help us individually to feel as though we have a sense of autonomy and control over our own workload, but at the same time, sets a tone that as a profession, the way in which we are working is no longer fit for purpose?

Objective rebellion

Objective rebellion is disrupting the discourse but in a way that causes question and not criticism. It is to ask for the justification or value behind the decision, in a professional way, delivered so that the focus is the task, and not the individual. It is to hold an idea up for scrutiny and remove any semblance of ego, or attachment to the idea itself. The conversation is about the idea, and not who created it and how. Objective rebellion aims to leap straight to the probing inquiry of why we are doing something in this way, and why not a different way, a more effective way, a more compassionate way.

A great deal of discontentment within schools, and in fact many workplaces, is that staff don't understand the reason behind the action. It is not always that a procedure seems illogical, but just that we don't understand the technicalities in order to embrace it.

If we lead in a traditionally hierarchical sense, with top-down direction, leaders will argue that not all information needs to be communicated to all staff: some policies are there simply to follow. I would contest this, because when a decision to change the way in which you operate as a school directly impacts the staff body, they are entitled to understand how and why this decision has been made; equally, if you want your staff body to move together to achieve the vision that you drive, it is paramount that they understand and unpack the purpose behind the process, so that they feel a sense of duty to what it is that you are trying to achieve. Craig Bonny-Meekings, a director of English in a school in Nuneaton, states that he is pleased and proud to work somewhere where challenge is a positive word:

> *Our head encourages all staff – support, teaching, canteen staff – to go straight to her with any issues or suggestions for ways to do things. We have staff voice boxes in all buildings for anonymous contact, which are then addressed and answered directly during whole-staff briefings. Line management meetings tend to be two-sided conversations as opposed to a presentation of evidence. It's a very healthy feeling school where you feel your voice is heard and important.*

The various levels that can be applied can enable a school to move away from dogma and direction and move towards a collection of staff that understand the underpinning values of the school journey, and how they can contribute towards it. I would like to return to the mantra that **no one sets out to do a bad job.**

Complaining is seen as an intrusion set to disrupt plans, but actually, if we listen hard and create the correct climate to do so, these 'complaints' become critical, insightful feedback for our schools.

How do we objectively rebel?

Rebellion has become a tainted word, but in this context, it is simply to question a process to understand it better. Here are a series of scenarios and strategies that objectively question in a way that is critically compassionate:

Try to look at the situation in an objective way; remember, it is incredibly rare that someone is deliberately out to upset you. It isn't personal – work with that assumption. People honestly just don't think beyond their own workload sometimes, particularly in reference to tasks where accountability of time pressure features heavily.

If you want to have a meeting to discuss something that is bothering you, which will play on your mind, outline a specific timeline for when you would like to discuss it, and give a brief, objective overview as to what you want to discuss.

> *I am unhappy with my appraisal outcome and need an urgent meeting.*

Becomes:

> *Do you have ten minutes for a short meeting about my appraisal outcome between now and Thursday? I would like to query the wording around my data, and how it links to the decision that was made. I'm free either period 4 Tuesday, or after school Wednesday. I will bring along all the relevant documentation for year 9 student outcomes to make the conversation productive.*

The request provides a timescale, agenda, enough detail for preparation and you are bringing along the relevant tools required for an efficient discussion. You have given two options for meeting times that suit you, and mentally, this aids your ability to know that it will be dealt with promptly for you; you regain a sense of ownership over the concern, which helps to alleviate the possible anxiety you may be suffering as a result. The email isn't accusatory or emotionally invested ('I'm annoyed about my appraisal and don't think it's fair' might be true in the heat of the moment but isn't helpful!) and moves towards working with someone, not against them.

We often confuse assertion with confrontation, but most in a position of line management will be happy to explain the thought process or reasons behind a decision, to the extent that they are able. If a timetable has been altered several times and has a detrimental impact on the classroom teacher's workload as a result, then that deserves a conversation. If the behaviour of a student has been escalated and the classroom teacher cannot see explicitly as to what the next steps are within the framework of the policy, but it is impacting upon their capacity to teach, then that deserves a conversation. Structures are there to support you, and if they do not do so, then they're not fit for purpose – and you guessed it: that deserves a conversation.

Other examples of some common points of frustration:

What you want to say	What you ought to say
My timetable has changed four times this year without notice and I'm sick of it.	Can I ask why the timetables have changed again so soon? And if there are future changes to be made, could there be some notice, and possibly some time to discuss the new classes or collaboratively plan with the existing teacher? It would really help me to make a great start with them.
I've been put on bus duty *again* this year and it's the only day I teach all day – why does this keep happening?	Am I able to swap this bus duty? I find it really difficult to get there on time as it is my only full teaching day – I could do a Monday or Thursday?
We have mock exams for our classes in two weeks and haven't had the time to teach the content for the exam!	Can I ask why we are using this content for the mock exam? I've found a great alternative that uses content taught last term; could I show you the paper? I'd really value your input.
I've been told not to leave school during the working day but needed to pop out for lunch and got a telling off at reception because I might be needed. Why can't I go to get a sandwich?	Can I ask what the policy is for leaving the premises at lunchtime, so that I can understand this further? I like to pop out at lunchtimes and want to make sure that this doesn't impact if I am needed somewhere in school.
I've been used for cover for every week of the autumn term – it's not fair, especially when I know not all staff are being called for cover.	Can I ask if there is a system in place to ensure fair cover usage across all departments?
My room has been used again for teaching at the last minute and I never get told. It makes it impossible for me to work or mark during my PPA time.	When my room is used for teaching, could I be provided with a place to work? I understand that these things happen last minute, but my books are all in my room and I need access to mark them on a regular basis after teaching hours are finished for the day.

In discussions, objective rebellion is your finest tool for moving towards solutions. Ask questions about how something will work, or why it will work in that way.

- I have 120 mock papers to mark for the deadline in ten days, but only have two lessons of gained time from year 11 leaving. That currently gives me one minute per paper to mark to a good standard, so is it possible to be covered for my two year 7 classes this week, as they will be independently writing and won't need to be taught content in those lessons?'
- I only work on a 0.8 contract, but have been allocated all directed time in line with a full-time member of staff. Could I ask which one of these duties I do not need to attend please?
- Is there an agenda for this meeting so I can plan for it on Friday before the weekend?
- I have my third timetable change of the year and it means I will need to attend every parents' evening as I have picked up a year 7 class and a year 8 class. Could I come in late for the following morning in both cases, to take the time back and not have an early start after such a late evening?'
- My break duty is on a day that I am at the other end of the school, teaching a challenging group where there are often children to speak to at the end to ensure there is a sense of restorative justice, and as a result, I am unable to be at my duty position on time. Can I swap with a member of the department, possibly Sam or Emily, who both have a PPA just before my break duty and might manage it better than my timetable allows?

'No' is not a dirty word

You're walking with your children through the town centre, and an RSPCA representative in his hi-vis waistcoat and pained smile approaches you, clipboard at the ready. 'Are you a dog lover?' He asks. Clever ploy. You can't say yes, because it will mean you are emotionally invested in now giving your soul in the form of a direct debit payment every month. You can't say no, because your children will be emotionally scarred for all eternity. Win-win for him. Several less effective schools are run in much the same way, reliant upon the emotional duty that we feel as teachers to do a good job.

One of the key messages that crops up in discussion with teachers is the attempt to use emotional leverage and extrinsic motivation to encourage staff to buy into less-than-favourable tasks or changes. 'Do it for the kids' is the emotional blackmail that whispers through the undercurrent of schools across the nation; it is the difference between goodwill and expectation, and it does not mitigate the latter – if anything, it discourages it. When you start to dwindle on goodwill, it is not because staff don't want to deliver; it is because they feel that they no longer have the energy or time to do so.

Yet in the short term, it works, which is why our less efficient schools continue to use it. It also builds resentment, exhaustion and ultimately, staff that leave, but we already know this as we stand here, the people that do it for the kids.

If we are going to do it for the kids in a way that is manageable, then we might need to consider the value to us as teachers too. If we continue to operate with the belief that our time and resources as teachers are infinite, then we won't last very long – and there is absolutely no shame in that, but it's an aspect of our profession that we need to start being honest about. It is as though we have forgotten that the week only contains a finite number of hours, and some of those are your entitlement rather than an optional privilege.

Lead with your objection; provide a solution. Leaders need to answer to the people they lead, but they are people themselves. Give reasonable deadlines; ask reasonable questions; request reasonable outcomes. Assume that people want to help.

It's for Ofsted

I have never seen or worked within an industry that treats their regulatory body with the same suspicion that we regard Ofsted. With a wary eye, far from the support network that I expected, senior leaders would refer to Ofsted as 'the big O', giving the organisation the same fearful wide berth that everyone except Harry Potter took with Voldemort. And interestingly, the section of the staff body that seem to fear them most are the staff that would be least involved in the inspection process. Where does this deep-seated terror stem from?

My earlier experiences with the idea of Ofsted are mixed as a result of the way in which messages were communicated around what Ofsted want: senior leaders shared their view that Ofsted were a support mechanism, a helpful arm of guidance to help schools to improve through careful monitoring and evaluation; in contrast, when visited by Ofsted in my NQT year, I was scared witless by the emails that circulated from senior leadership the day that we got 'the call'. We were summoned to an after-school briefing that essentially delivered the message, 'Stay until it's done. All of it.' I went back to my classroom and cried, overwhelmed and confused as to what 'it' was, and convinced that I would be solely responsible for our grading when my lessons were visited the next day. I dreamt that night that the head came to hand me my P45, with a smiling Ofsted inspector stood next to them.

I understand the gravity with which gradings can affect a school's success; there seems to be a certain level of embarrassment that comes with working for a school that either doesn't deliver on results or doesn't make the grade. Gradings can determine funding, admission figures, staff retention; in an area that poses something of an open marketplace, a poor grading following Ofsted can be the making or breaking of a school and can take years to come back from. Even if you are not a school to jump through hoops, there is a substantial amount to be gained and lost through Ofsted's verdict, and it can take years to demonstrate improvements to staff, stakeholders and the local community.

However, I do think that the vast majority of our fear comes from another source than the original beast, and by leading through fear and suspicion, it doesn't seem like the healthiest way to either consider strategy choices or collate information vital to our progress in schools. Senior leaders would do well to consider the language used with staff around Ofsted requirements, and instead of directing the agenda and to-do lists with the caveat of 'Ofsted says so', consider that hard, meaningful work is of merit, and confidence from a whole staff body comes from the merit of hard, meaningful work. It isn't deliberate for the most part: messages are delivered with good intentions and 'the big O' has developed from projections of the workload of others, but it does nothing but spiral staff into fear which ultimately has far from the desired effect. People do not operate well under severe, frequent bursts of inordinate levels of stress. As one teacher put it, 'I have always found that it is scaremongering by colleagues and SLT that has made an Ofsted inspection stressful, not Ofsted themselves.' School visits are so short that it is inevitable that there will be a level of intensity with the experience, even with the best of intentions to just show the work for the work. Not for Ofsted, but with Ofsted's consideration as an afterthought because the emphasis is on what is best for the school, the staff, the children.

And as with all feedback, the negative experiences spread faster and wilder and stick around for a far greater period of time than the positive; everyone knows someone with an Ofsted horror story to share. Most of these stories sift through schools like whispers, coming to strike fear into the heart of the yet-to-be jaded NQT, and with very little substance. What about the times that Ofsted actually acts as a positive experience for a school?

I spoke to Dr Emma Kell, speaker, writer and teacher, who unpacked the process of Ofsted through her experiences of inspections in school:

66 Ofsted get a terribly bad press, and sometimes with justification. I have no doubt that teachers have had some truly horrendous experiences with heartless and harsh inspectors. But, relatively speaking, how much contact have teachers actually had with inspectors in their careers compared to, say, their own line managers and colleagues?

The days of every teacher being observed and 'graded' by inspectors are long gone. I have to say that my last two Ofsted experiences (both within the last four years) have been fair and reasonable. One inspector asked me, as a middle leader, how I would judge the quality of students' work and got me to talk her through it – there's nothing unreasonable about this. For the second inspection, the pre-inspection briefing with SLT was short because the inspectors acknowledged that we were all busy and had work to do. Each of the inspectors was an experienced school leader themselves and clearly understood the reality of working in schools. On adjourning the meeting, the lead inspector made a beeline for the first students she saw: 'Are you proud of your school?' I heard her ask them. Again, a perfectly reasonable question. In both cases, the final reports were succinct, thoughtful and entirely fair.

What is so damaging about Ofsted, I believe, is the fear of it – the anticipation of it and the second-guessing of it, from frantically rewriting 'learning intentions' to creating documents about what 'a successful year 8 art student "looks like"' (I mean, come on...) – not for the good of the students but because Ofsted 'might want to see it'. Or the awful 'fur coat and no knickers' Ofsted 'rehearsals' that cause so much stress for teachers!

I would also add that I welcome Ofsted's emerging focus on teacher wellbeing. It is as yet a little vague, but to know this crucial issue is actually in the spotlight is most welcome!

I understand the purpose of Ofsted, and the way in which schools use reports to share their school narrative with pride for what their students and staff have achieved. I do stand by the belief that Ofsted play a key significant role within education, and I dismiss the notion that we could do without such an entity altogether. The regulatory body exists for us to have the opportunity to learn, grow, develop and showcase the incredible things going on in our schools. Nevertheless, when senior staff hold up Ofsted's guidelines as gospel, or as a way to indicate that things must be done (while they seem to hold little value to staff, student or even logic), then we've lost sight of our purpose. I suggest that instead of placing the emphasis upon Ofsted, predicting what may or may not happen when they arrive in the same manner (and with the same reliability of prognostication) that we would get from picking up a crystal ball, we do things for us. For teachers. For schools.

What can school leaders do to provide us with opportunities to apply such ideas? How can we create a series of schools that value objective rebellion and see it as a chance to get better?

Create structures to take the temperature of your school

Understand that staff will not always be honest with you. Not that they will deceive in a malicious way, but that they want to do a job well, and so may not always feel confident to share when things are not going well, especially to someone in management. There must be a variety of different ways for staff to voice concerns around both existing and new policy (as detailed below) but even when school is ticking over, find a way to gauge the short-, medium- and long-term climate of the school. One school took anonymous surveys at various pressure points, considering how these would impact responses, but also to help them create a 'You said; we did' at the start of the year, to demonstrate to staff that the senior team were listening.

Make spaces for people to provide solutions

The staff are your most important and accurate resource to check if there is a more efficient way of doing something. From what may seem smaller matters like movement at lunchtimes flow processes for behaviour policy or systems for parents' evenings, your staff are a brilliant point of contact to ascertain what is working and what isn't. Working parties are an ideal way to ensure that there is a place for staff voice at every level of decision-making within schools and demonstrate the value that staff voice has. Similarly, appraisal meetings are an ideal time to gain an insight from staff as to what has been successful or well received, but also to discuss the current challenges at hand. Craig Bonny-Meekings's idea to include a series of suggestion boxes also provides an anonymous method when the member of the staff in question either doesn't know who to go to with a suggestion or isn't quite confident to do so.

Don't rest on what's right; seek out what's wrong

Exposing difficulties and challenges within a school is a complex process, as there are so many elements working simultaneously and under the influence of each other that you must be an active participant and observe the more concerning features of what simply isn't working. The most effective leaders do not believe that their school plan has the capacity to be done or is the finished article – they overturn rocks and look into corners so they know exactly what the work to be done looks like. So, they can turn to staff and have the conviction to know that they have been honest about where their school flourishes, but also what is left to do. If you think you sit inside a perfect school, it merely raises a concern of what your definition of perfect is.

Finding your fit

'What you see and what you hear depends a great deal on where you are standing. It also depends on what sort of person you are.'

— C.S. Lewis, *The Magician's Nephew*

Identifying a school that aligns to your beliefs and values as a teacher is probably the most valuable thing you can do for your career. It has taken me several years (and schools) to realise the gravity of this and understand how fundamental it is to work in the right place for you. To truly feel invested in the community and school that you work within, you have to feel that you have freedom to teach in the way you teach, whatever that may be, but also that you are in a school where you legitimately have a voice. This can change as you develop and evolve professionally. Finding a school is like buying a house. Can you see yourself living in it? Does it have everything that you personally need? Does it feel as though it 'fits'?

Being in the right school empowers, asserts and develops you as a professional; finding your fit really is life changing. In the same breath, working in a school where things feel out of kilter, where your gut is telling you that the priorities or agenda or ethos of the school simply don't match your own can result in the very best teachers feeling demotivated and disengaged, and this can happen in an incredibly short amount of time.

Before visiting, view the advertisement and consider the language that has been used. Do these words resonate with how you approach teaching? If you imagine yourself as 'compassionate, strict and people-focused' and you find yourself looking at an advertisement for someone who is 'driven, dynamic and dedicated', it may not be quite the alignment that you hoped for. This will give you a bit of an initial insight as to what you may hope to expect from the school, or how you might sit in it as an employee.

Visiting a school before the interview is an ideal way to weigh up if a school is right for you. Here are a few things to consider that might give you an indication that the school looks after and values its staff:

Spaces
- Look at the surroundings and staff's reaction to them – do they notice what you notice? Does the space feel orderly and like it places a value upon the work that student and staff carry out?
- Is the space used effectively around the school? Is it well thought out?
- Are there spaces for staff to decompress, to be adults and have a specific area to work, or discuss with other adults? Do staff have quiet working spaces set apart from the staffroom?
- Is the building well cared for? By that, I don't mean new, but loved.
- Do classrooms feel clean and uncluttered?
- Do public displays give you an indication of the values of the school?
- Is there a staffroom? Is it used?

Space to learn
- Were you able to visit lessons?
- How did the students respond (if at all) to the member of staff with you? How did they respond to you?
- Do staff seem comfortable with visitors whilst teaching? Does it seem commonplace?
- What about your learning – is there evidence of CPD through a staff library, corner in the staffroom, CPD calendar up in a workroom?
- Is the school part of a large trust or alliance, with scope to benefit from the other schools?

Space to teach

- How does behaviour present itself in lessons – do you see behaviour managed effectively or use of the system in action?
- How do students respond to learning – do they seem connected with the content in the lesson? Does the lesson have a sense of order?
- With regards to secondary school visits: if you visit lessons for the department, are they well resourced? Do you see any evidence of resourcing in a way that suits your own style? Are there any routines/directives that seem to be whole-department or whole-school approaches that the children recognise?

It is important to temper this with the recognition that one classroom and one day does not make a school, but it should help you to draw together some musings to take home with you before applying for a role.

Interview days

We do things a little bit differently round here. Prior to teaching, I had been headhunted for every job except my first interview for the bank. Once asked for an interview, I would attend as one candidate and chat through my experience, perhaps complete a short task and be given the opportunity to ask questions, then go home to hear the outcome sometimes up to two weeks later.

We move at a different pace in teaching because the demands are poles apart from the world that I came from. To reward applicants for taking the time to apply to a school, we stage an interview day that can only be likened to the *Hunger Games*. Interview days are filled with a sense of urgency, and we have to be entirely transparent in our attendance in comparison to other sectors; my partner still finds it obscure that I would need to see my head as a matter of courtesy when I even apply for a role – I can't just book a day's holiday, after all!

The prospect of requesting a day for interview is incredibly stressful for staff: leave for interview attendance is not a statutory right, but a contractual agreement;[1] and I would recommend taking the time to have a discussion with your line manager or the head. The open dialogue is a professional, transparent way to present your reasons for applying, but beyond that, it means reference requests are not a surprise. I'm sympathetic to situations where this is not straightforward: I would recommend approaching your line manager to outline that you have applied for a position and your head had absolutely no idea. It's positive to share applications with senior leadership; it shows your desire to progress and the options that you have considered as part of your career map and could also prompt discussions for your plans within the school. I have applied for roles outside school and been invited for a conversation which has opened my eyes to opportunities for development in my current school that I may not have considered or been aware of.

- -

A few narratives that tell interesting tales of interview days:

❝ **Claire Nicholls, SENDCo:** My most recent experience was rigorous, to say the least. Teaching, student panel, data task, middle leader discussion and an interview which started with a presentation created on the day. The other candidates weren't happy; they thought it was too much. For me, it meant that I had the confidence to say 'yes' immediately when the job was offered. I liked the students, the staff and the ethos of the school. The day being so in depth meant I'd had the chance to find that all out and I was sure that I'd be happy there. I was right!

❝ **Haili Hughes, Teacher:** As a PGCE student, I applied for a job in quite a challenging school. I was starting to panic as it was April and I didn't have a job as I was waiting for the right one. I had taken a massive pay cut from being a national newspaper journalist to retrain and had a one-year-old so was under a lot of pressure to get a job. After reading the school's Ofsted report etc. and speaking to people who knew the school, I decided to withdraw. The next day, the head of department at the school I was at asked me why I wasn't at the interview and I told her. She replied with 'Oh,

---

1. For further guidance, refer to your own school policy or take advice from your local union representative.

that's probably for the best – I rang the head of department at that school and told them about your tattoos etc. and you wouldn't have been for them anyway.' I was appalled!

66 **Anonymous but hopeful:** Last summer term, I applied for a job via Tes. Received five weeks later: lesson details and arrival time. No further information was provided about the day, not even on arrival (although I was eventually given an itinerary as we were leaving with apologies). The headmaster had been in post for all of five days (I still don't know the true details). I taught a terrible lesson (technology failed me). I had two interviews: one very thorough and unexpected drilling from the deputy team; one lovely 'chat' with the headmaster. We had a tour and lunch. Six months later, I still hadn't heard, and they still hadn't appointed for the post advertised. They did say at the start of the day that it may be January before they could recruit, depending on numbers and agreement from owners!

There is such a vast amount of noise out there for newly qualified teachers and experienced ones alike when it comes to approaching an interview, it is a wonder their heads aren't spinning. Google searches throw up language like 'perform your best' and 'steps for success', but articles rarely mention the nature of the beast: namely, that teaching interviews are so utterly ludicrous, and incomparable to any other job on the planet.

You are given ambiguous details to a varying degree about your lesson requirements via email – sometimes with student details, sometimes not – and have to take along your equipment like a jack of all trades (resembling Dick Van Dyke and his one-man band ensemble), arms and legs flailing to keep a hold of four different worksheets, two whiteboard pens, name stickers, highlighters and a copy of your application form to nervously annotate whilst you wait. You may get a tour of the school; you may get sat in front of children who will interview you; you may mark work that you had absolutely no input in; you may teach for 20, 30, 60, 120 minutes; you may get shepherded into a side room and asked to leave; you may have lunch; you may meet the department staff with whom you will be working in close proximity should you get the job; you may decide you want to withdraw but not get the appropriate time to ask; you may want to leave as soon as you get there. You may have an interview; you may be called first; you may have to wait for the entire day; you may not have access to a drink; you may have a fancy drinks trolley sat in front of you with a contraption containing coffee, but you are too terrified to begin the type of task that only Ant and Dec would enforce in order to get yourself a hot beverage. If unpredictability is a key stressor, the levels of unpredictability that a teaching interview add to the interview process itself are extraordinary. Why have we made it so complicated?

How we can prepare ourselves to reduce the impact that interviewing can take by rewriting the narrative of interviews? Some ways to help with finding some clarity in what a pretty bonkers day can be:

Pre interview day scope

If you can, do the drive beforehand, preferably in the morning or rush hour. This may sound like a factor that should feature way down on your list, but I think you get a real feel for a school by visiting the community that it sits within. And as well as gaining an insight into the journey that you would make every day should you decide to take the role, it will help you to have an understanding of where that school features in the local area. Are the feeder schools nearby? Does it serve the community as a community centre, gym, library? Do most of the pupils walk to school? How might local school networks play logistically?

Only prepare for the controllable factors

We worry most about the factors that we cannot control, and so to ease this uncertainty, take care of the things that you can take ownership of. Plan the outfit; annotate the application; distil who you are and what you want to leave as key messages into three key points (*omne trium perfectum*: 'everything that comes in threes is perfect'). When our brains fail us, we remember in threes, and this simplification will help you remember what it is that you want to leave your interviewer knowing about you.

Ask. The. Questions

No one is going to think any less of you for wanting to be prepared. Anticipate the three aspects of the day that will cause the most unsettlement and email ahead so that you can equip yourself. Will there be equipment in the room? (Let's face it, the students should have pens and paper; penalising teachers for enabling learned helplessness would be pretty mean.) Should you be expected to be in school for the day? (This is particularly pertinent if you have childcare arrangements. I once finished my lesson before lunch in the first part of an interview, then wasn't called from the staffroom for the second part until 5 p.m.)

Make friends

I'm not even kidding. I met one of my closest friends on a teacher interview day. If you are going to be placed in a room with people all day, would it not be nice to get to know them? Not only is this just a nice, friendly way to pass the time (as opposed to staring down the other candidates with a rendition of the *Rocky* soundtrack accompanying your internal pep talk monologue), but it is the best way to calm your nerves. Avoid any questions that make it look like you're weighing them up: 'Which school are you currently at? In what role? How long have you been teaching?' – all these have the hallmarks of conducting your own interview within an interview. 'Did you have a good drive in? Any plans for the weekend? I love the display as you walk in!' Be nice. It will help with all the smiling, and you may end up meeting someone really interesting.

Don't be afraid to say no

There is a dusty manuscript somewhere that all senior leaders adhere to when it comes to interviews: they will ask at the end if you are a firm candidate for the role. It pays to have prepared for this because it is your opportunity to leave without judgement, or ask further questions that would help you to feel informed enough to answer the question. **All people do not fit all schools, and all schools do not fit all people.** And that's OK! It's very easy to get caught up in the intensity of an interview day, but remain methodical and as objective as you can be, as this is a key decision for you to make and it's vital that you feel as if you have all of the information to make it.

Primary headteacher and author Tracy Lawrence states that the more proactive the candidate is in equipping themselves in advance, the more she feels confident that they will be an ideal fit for her school. Here, she shares how candidates can demonstrate this without it becoming too strenuous:

❝ Lots of factors contribute to a successful interview. From my point of view, it is a bigger process than simply what you say on the day. By coming and looking at our school, you are showing me that you are interested in *our* school rather than *any* school. That commitment and drive is one of the main things. Wanting to support our children to achieve their potential in all areas whilst supporting them to feel secure and part of a family with an identity is paramount. Understanding our vision and communicating your approach is something that will also support this. The informal chat between two professionals whilst walking round the school should not be undervalued, and it is certainly one approach that I use to get to know an interview candidate and see whether I think that they will add value to the team. It also works both ways – I must stress that you need to feel that you will gain value from the team as well!

Ask questions if you have them. Don't force them if not. If the conversation flows, then that adds to the positive experience.

If preparing your answers, then think about your reasons for applying for the job. It really makes me think when someone's only reason for wanting to work at our school is because it's local. It certainly doesn't put me off if it's part of the reason, but it certainly does if that's the *only* reason. There are certainly more reasons at our school – our fantastic children, for one.

Finding and keeping the right staff in schools

The cost of recruitment is pretty burdensome on school budget in education, as schools with a recruitment concern know all too well. With costs of between £700 and £2000 for a national advertisement, and no guarantee that this will ensure quality or even a breadth of responses, this is a cost to schools before they even invest in the development of those staff once they're through the door. If only two people apply in response to an advertisement that cost an incredible amount to begin with, and the quality of these applicants doesn't align with the needs of the school or the expertise that you hoped for, what choice are school leaders left with: re-advertise with an additional implication of cost, or recruit and hope to develop the staff that apply?

There is a real sense of urgency when the recruitment window for the year opens and closes: those wanting to move schools must dedicate February to April to doing so, and the additional pressures of planning interview lessons and covering your existing classes create additional workload in itself. Several teachers report a feeling of dread when the window closes, as the closure brings the realisation that at least another term will be spent in their current school – and if you are unhappy in your current school, that term can feel like an incredibly long time.

There is also an implicit rating system with recruitment advertisements over the year, as roles are advertised in autumn terms due to existing staff shortages – you then have to do your homework in ascertaining the school messages, and why that gap may have appeared. Teachers start to recognise local patterns in recruitment, and when the same schools are repeatedly advertising for a multitude of roles, irrespective of the reason, it raises questions for prospective candidates.

Another solution to the crisis is the extension of the DfE-funded portal for teaching vacancies, which doubles up as the best-hidden vacancy service on the internet: tap 'teaching jobs' into a search engine and it doesn't feature in the top five. It has now been rolled out to other areas of the country, but as I write, from Northumberland to Buckinghamshire, the portal contains only 54 vacancies – some of which were for learning support and care assistants as opposed to teaching roles.

If the Department for Education are providing a free space to advertise, why are schools not using it? Frankly, because it isn't an accessible, renowned resource, and so it doesn't guarantee reaching the right people. The right people need to know about the right places; such is the trick of tricky recruitment. Alternatively, it is because the people aren't there to recruit in the first place. But keep the faith: they are there. 23% of all staff in the UK are currently 'actively job hunting' (a stronger measure than simply 'considering'); 73% of school leaders are experiencing difficulties in recruiting teachers, with 61% saying that the situation has gotten worse (42%) or much worse (19%) over the last year.[2]

- -

Matthew Evans is a headteacher in Oxfordshire and talks through how he approaches recruitment in a rural setting, using an innovative approach that he is confident means that he retains staff.

❝ We are a rural school in an expensive part of the South of England and attracting staff to apply for jobs continues to be a problem. For many teaching posts, we often get fewer than five applicants (that's if we get any at all). Aside from the national teacher shortages, a significant factor is that many people don't want to travel the distance required or to move into the area, given the house prices – particularly NQTs.

To compound this problem, the school has experienced significant financial difficulties. As a result, we can only appoint staff when someone leaves, and even then, we are under pressure to spend less and only appoint someone at exactly the hours we need. This means we frequently advertise late in the season, missing the pick of NQTs. The catch-22 situation is that many of our appointments are UPS teachers (often part-time working parents looking for a family-friendly employer) and our average teacher-cost has gradually crept up, making finances even tighter.

2. www.bit.ly/2EmdhOP

Fortunately, we have a very low staff turnover. This is because we work hard at being a great school to work at. Our students are eminently teachable, and we have cultivated a positive working environment. This means no audit culture, significant professional freedoms, flexible working arrangements and family-friendly leave arrangements. And we just try to be civil to each other!

Being a good employer has benefited our recruitment as well as retention of staff. Teachers talk, and over time word of mouth has ensured that we are known locally as a good place to work. We make a point of this in our recruitment pack by explaining how important it is to us that staff are happy to work at the school. We provide a list of 'Ten reasons to work here' which differentiate us from what other schools offer. We know this works as many of the teachers we end up appointing tell us that our reputation and values encouraged them to drive that little bit further. To be honest, we also draw in teachers who are disenchanted with teaching in their current schools, particularly with over-controlling senior teams. This is a sad state of affairs, but one that has meant I can continue to appoint great staff who deserve to be treated with a little more respect.

If we want to invest in people, we need to consider where those amazing candidates are, and what it is that they want. Why is this an urgent concern? Because the numbers aren't just startling: they're on the rise:

- The school system is retaining fewer teachers. In 2016–17, 9.9% of teachers left the workforce, compared to 9.2% of the workforce in 2010–11.
- Looking at secondary schools alone, the figures are even higher: 10.4% of secondary teachers left the workforce last year, compared to 9.4% in 2010–11. The overall average also masks variation by subject: NFER and DfE research shows leaving rates are higher still among maths, science and modern foreign languages teachers.[3]

3. www.bit.ly/36HNgFq

We are filling a leaky bucket: as the number of NQTs increases, the number of teachers leaving tries to compete – and is currently winning.

Looking at recruitment as a strategic retention method may be where we can start seeing demonstrative change in schools. Schools that don't suffer from a recruitment crisis are those in particularly accessible areas for staff and those that are renowned for the treatment of staff, financially or otherwise. People are leaving education, not just schools; so to start to tackle this epidemic, what can school leaders do to improve the quantity and quality of the staff that they recruit? How do we find and keep great teachers?

- **Make your school values transparent.** What are you offering staff, and what do you expect in return? Investigating schools before interview becomes like a work experience of what it must feel like to be part of the *Scooby-Doo* gang: asking around, taking people's opinions, and reading the subtext of the website copy are all ways that we try to fathom the type of school that we are considering applying for, when recruitment could be made more explicit and help to attract people to schools that 'fit'. How can school leaders ensure that teachers want to apply for roles within their school? More to the point, how can we ensure that the schools that we apply to are the right ones?
- **Are you clear in your advertising?** Do you want to work in a school where workload is considered in all that you do? Do you want to work in a school where behaviour is centralised to ensure that teachers can teach? Do you want to work in a school that celebrates your development as an individual? These opening questions can be really powerful in setting out your stall for what you would like your staff to value. If a teacher is looking for a school that supports their capacity to carry out further education alongside their role, then it may be that they look for a mention of flexibility. Be incredibly clear in the type of people

that you would like for a specific role – when recruiting, there really is no time for nuance.

- **There's no shame in branding.** In financial recruitment, we used a great deal of recruitment events and provided diverse, accessible ways for people to join the business. By providing opportunities to people and demonstrating what is on offer to those locally (as opposed to advertising using costly, national campaigns that may not reach those you would like), you are more likely to invest your time in conversations with those that will be invested in your school. Social media is also fantastic at building this idea of the school as a brand: education is sceptical of the negative connotations of schools as businesses, but that's what they are, and once you make your peace with that, it is worth researching how you can present your school in a certain way. One of the first things I do when exploring an advertisement for a school is find the head and any online presence they have. This may flag up previous roles, their key messages at conferences or their social media usage – we all talk about the mindfulness with our own social media being checked pre interview, but this works both ways. I want to see if the person that I would be working for leans towards similar goals and beliefs around education as my own. Podcasts, Twitter, conferences, partnerships with local universities – these are all ways of presenting your team as the face of your school.

- **Do you open your doors?** A school with a conglomerate approach in their local area or a keen nature to share the good practice that is going on inside their school with humility will open its doors to visitors so that they can exchange knowledge. Is there scope to visit the school and hear from key leaders about the work that they are doing? Can you visit lessons and see the everyday in action? Is the school open with its plan for improvement and how they have achieved it? In my experience, it is those schools that will be most interested in supporting your development. If schools struggle to accommodate for you to visit when an advert has run, it raises questions as to where the value lies if it isn't in sourcing incredible staff. Some of the most fantastic schools I have been to have only been in a position to provide 30 minutes at the most, but that was sufficient to form my perception of the school, and incredibly helpful when considering where I would fit into their system.

- **Do you have an innovative and proactive approach to sourcing staff?** In addition to the advertisements, does the school have a talent pool or local network that they are a part of? Many teachers have a particular focus on local schools that they would like to work at, even schools for different points of their career according to the direction that they wish to take. By opening up a talent pool for teachers to register an interest in a school, it really does widen the field for a school to demonstrate that they are interested in the right people, and not just the right people for right now; they clearly have a vested interest in building a team for sustainability. Recruitment has an entirely different face in education compared to various other sectors: we approach movement with some sense of negativity and some schools equate movement with disloyalty. I have known members of staff to be subjected to poor treatment from sharing a view to looking elsewhere, but it should instead raise questions in leaders: what can I do to develop people so that they could leave but don't want to? It is the answers to questions such as those that will shape longevity, but the facts discussed are a great starting point for staff that are seeking employment to be able to consider how a school could be a right fit for them.

On the day

As a school leader, how can you structure your interviews so that you find the right people for the right roles?

- **Open with key messages.** Most schools start their interview days with a short introduction from the head, and here is the time to set out a stall for prospective staff. I've heard, 'We are on interview: today is as much for you as it is for me,' but could we be more explicit in what exactly that means? A background of the school, the particular department history, successes – and challenges – to date and the direction or journey that the school is now heading along are all incredibly useful for saying 'This is us. Do you think you would fit in with this?' without leaving it to guesswork. Include staff of all levels and allow them to talk candidly about the school and their own experiences. Being left to follow breadcrumbs of clues over the course of the day is somewhat distracting from the core of an interview in itself, and it can be mentally quite an exhausting process to spread your energy between showing what you are all about and trying to figure out what the school is all about too.

- **Consider the purpose behind interview tasks.** Include tasks that endeavour to find out what it is that you want to see in a successful candidate. Avoid the inclusion of tasks for tasks' sake. Of course, it is helpful to see how candidates work under pressure, but it needs to be realistic pressure.

Great examples of tasks are the ones that springboard for meaningful conversations: data-related tasks are especially interesting in extracting information about candidates' approaches to strategy. When recruiting within finance, I would provide prospective sales managers with data figures for the relevant branches and ask them to form questions that they would ask of the in-house management to drive improvement. What was most interesting was that I seldom received the same answers from candidates, and it allowed for fantastic discussions around how to have supportive conversations with staff to develop a culture that worked towards positive change. As opposed to, 'Why is February conversion particularly low for that product?', we would share examples with recruits of 'What actions did you put into place as a result of reviewing February's data for conversion?' Tasks such as this in teaching interviews don't necessarily have to be set just for middle leadership: we encourage teachers to use data to inform their practice, when often the only interaction teachers have with data is inputting assessment, but why not set the tone of using it as a starting point for great discussions?

I once attended an interview where one task was for all candidates to participate in a group discussion around three key areas of education, and it was probably one of the most insightful activities I have experienced in my career to date. As we explored the topic of gender streaming, linear assessment and what it means to be an effective teacher, candidates were provided with the opportunity to showcase ideas, but also to demonstrate how to listen effectively, a quality that is so valued when working as part of a team. The dynamics moved towards a far more collaborative task where the outcome relied upon utilising others. Absolutely genius.

- **Consider the purpose of particular tasks.** The way in which student voice is executed during interviews in some settings is concerning to say the least. The NASUWT released a dossier in 2010 with over 200 examples of student voice abuse reported by their members, with the more shocking anecdotes making it to the front of newspapers: teachers referred to as 'Humpty Dumpty',[4] with the general sense that to include students in the process actually undermines the professional standing of teachers as a result.

I'm not disputing the value of student voice – the process of talking to students is valuable in understanding the way that a school functions for the candidate, and I think that there is a place to use student voice as a mechanism to gain feedback in relation to a classroom – but I would be hesitant to advocate the value of students interviewing a teacher, and how this contributes to the quality assurance of candidates on the whole. Student voice panels are often put together by teacher-selected students, at the higher end of the prior attainment spectrum, and this in itself presents an issue: these students are not an indicative picture of

---

4. www.bit.ly/2Re2bAB

the student body and they may find it difficult to answer questions with a frank and honest tone, if at all – I once asked a student panel if they knew where to go to within the English department for academic support, and was told by the supervising teacher, 'These students won't be able to help you with that.'

To have a really productive and enlightening conversation with young people as you tour a school can be so encouraging; I have met some of the most incredible, honest and thought-provoking students whilst being shown round schools. To sit opposite a desk in a setting that is unlike any other moment that will take place in my time as a teacher of those children is a little disconcerting, and unfulfilling. Questions such as, 'What's your favourite book?' and 'What kind of teacher are you?' don't feel demonstrative to show the school body who I am or what I can offer.

- **Give time for talking:** Meeting departmental staff has made my mind up on how I will fit – or not – within a school faster than any other method or tool used at interview. Next to meeting the head at the start of the day, it is key that people meet the people that they will be working closely with and consider for themselves how they will fit within the dynamics of the team. People make schools, not policies, and if you are not introducing staff to the relevant teams, it raises questions as to why. By stripping interviews to a picture of reality, as opposed to a curtain across the cracks (of which there are probably very few), it can provide candidates with the most reassuring, refreshing view of your school culture in action. If there is room to accommodate for a department gathering at lunch, or a middle leader meeting as part of the tour, this will cement how your teams work to support a whole-school vision through the very subtleties of the everyday, and can be really quite powerful. Rob Carpenter states that 'retention needs to be fed from teachers telling us how great the profession is',[5] and who better to promote your school than the people that work within it?

---

5.   Niall Allcock, We are in Beta interview, accessible here: www.bit.ly/36T5rbo

People before procedures
School systems

'It is not the strongest of the species that survive, nor the most intelligent, but the one most responsive to change.'   – Charles Darwin

'All we have to decide is what to do with the time that is given us.'
     – J.R.R. Tolkien, *The Fellowship of the Ring*

Who's leaving, and how do we stop them? Creating people-friendly schools

I often use the analogy of schools as a poor franchise: in contrast to striving to find a balance between consistent and contextually relevant, it feels like an apt metaphor to use as a preamble as we venture towards our conclusions. Stay with me on this one.

Store A has the highest staff retention in the entire region, with productivity of over 120% consistently for the last four years; staff value one another through staff social events, a hockey team, free transportation to work, healthcare and every member of staff working at store A has made their last dentist appointment for the last three years without having to reschedule or lie to say their car broke down. They offer the infamous Meatball Special on a Friday which means the queues are out the door – but that's OK, because they value the work. The work gives them a sense of satisfaction, which allows them to enjoy that feeling of a good job well done. Staff have pictures of their children on desks or up on the walls and find time to share stories of hobbies or holidays. If someone needs to leave early, the rest of the team move forward to close the gap that would be there, without question or criticism. If they want to try something new, they consider what must be given less attention so they can focus their efforts accordingly. Workload becomes a word that features less and less in the team's vocabulary, because the work doesn't feel as though it brings weight to their working day: it is a joy, because they are collectively working towards accomplishment together.

Store B paints a bit of a different picture. They operate longer opening hours to try to encourage new business – which doesn't leave time for any team-building initiatives, or sufficient training – but the sales figures imply that longer hours don't appear to be an effective strategy for productivity. Staff absence is high, because there is little expanse of time between one shift and the next, and as a result, there is a sense of disconnect between staff as they never really get to bond or build relationships over anything other than a mutual enjoyment of complaining about the work. The senior team have tried to bring in motivating initiatives, such as sports classes, a discounted membership for the local gym and goodie bags on a Friday, but it hasn't improved retention figures, or the productivity rate. Staff report that the work feels monotonous and relentless, with little reward because when they are busy, there seems to be a great deal of conflict around ambiguity of job roles, a lack of vision or ethos in what they are trying to achieve, and absence management. Staff salaries have been inflated to keep staff that have considered leaving; but again, this has shown little improvement to the morale and just made for a tighter budget overall.

Store A is a five-minute walk from store B, but the two franchises refuse to speak to one another, because the latter are too busy, and the former find the latter incredibly negative, adamant that any collaborations have a substantial impact upon their mental health. Whenever staff run into one another, store B dismisses their challenges by blaming store A for their woes, telling them they've got it easy because they have more custom, that they're on the bus route, that they've got that sports grant to get their hockey team started.

Anything here sound familiar?

The difference between the two establishments is so stark, and yet ever-present, and doesn't seem as though it is likely to change. How is it that, as a system, the educational sector lacks such consistency? How do we have schools getting it right for their staff, and yet five minutes down the road, a school that cannot seem to look at staff wellbeing in a strategic manner, throwing money at ideas that do not have any substance to them whatsoever. Furthermore, do we have any agency over this – or more importantly, can we have any impact to start changing the landscape so that we all work like store A? Is that really too optimistic of me?

As mentioned in previous chapters, the concept of martyrdom is something that we have grown rather attached to within schools, at all levels, and are reluctant to have our hands prised away from it. Workload becomes burdensome when it doesn't directly relate to the work that we set out to do, but instead of looking for solutions, school leaders direct their staff to state that the indirect work, the unnecessary work is, well, necessary, when that simply is not the case. As a result, we chase after and coordinate strategies in school that are needlessly complex, do not contribute to a job well done, but above all, take previous time away from the work that matters. They do not value the staff voice, or the staff themselves. As the non-teaching voices of society argue that we have an easy life, and the reality of our day-to-day experiences provides an entirely different picture, it is the argument of hard work that we cling to as justification and a pragmatic argument that those voices have got it so very, very wrong. We're not in it for the holidays.

It is this very argument that is the barrier to our development and evolution as a profession; we argue that we work too hard, and for too long, and as a foundation for debate, it means that we then have to hold ourselves accountable for this – by working too hard and for too long, as opposed to working effectively and within the constraints that we are human beings, not robots. When teachers discuss the prospect of working smart, those that have used the argument of hard work and those watching from the outside that argued for harder work both look on with scepticism. 'Smart' has a pretty poor reception now and is typically met with eye rolls over head nods.

There is nothing to be gained from working the very resource that we depend upon into the ground; and to view their complaints that the work is no longer hard in a rewarding sense, but actually just hard, isn't good enough. Teachers are the most important resource of the school; name one other tool that we can operate without? Knock the walls of your school down, remove the screens, and teachers remain. Teachers and their connections with students. And so, it is with this belief and value that we need to take a stark, objective look at the reality of the rationale that we are dealing with as a profession: what will schools look like a decade from now? What will the experience or expertise of the average teacher amount to? Because with the greatest will in the world, you can only be better if you have the possibility of betterment. We cannot build and continue to provide a service that values people if we avoid the creation of the structures that enable us to do so. Put simply, talk and research is just not enough: will we have brilliant teachers in schools five years from now? How confidently can we even answer that question?

People-friendly workplaces sit in abundance within a number of sectors and the aim of this section is for us to consider the practical implementation of what we have explored: how do we support people to teach? To teach as they enter the profession, to teach as they make the journey through their professional life, to teach whilst they have relationships, find connections in friendships, explore interests, value family, explore the world. How do we support teachers with compassion as they suffer loss or health concerns, encounter and manage grief, and as their lives follow a course that is fluid and ever-changing, ensure that the workload adjusts so they can meet life's ebbs and flows with strength and empowerment, not fear and anxiety.

How does this aid wellbeing?

People are at the heart of schools; whist I don't deny that paper and pens help the work, they are not the work. We are the work. Let us speak urgently: people are leaving. People are leaving at all levels, at all career points, for all reasons – but patterns do emerge, and statistical evidence provides us a multi-faceted picture to pinpoint the groups that are choosing to leave. Reluctantly so.

Why are they leaving? Accountability and workload are the first two responses,[1] usually. In order to make a concerted effort to keep teachers in teaching, we need to understand who is leaving. As of June 2018, there were 451,900 full-time-equivalent teachers in state-funded schools in the UK. In June 2017, this figure was just over 498,000. Who were those 46,000 teachers? At what point in their career, that we know takes a huge financial and personal commitment to train for, do they decide that it just couldn't be done anymore?

- 22% of newly qualified entrants to the sector in 2015 were not recorded as working in the state sector two years later.
- The five-year out-of-service rate for 2012 entrants was 33%,
- The ten-year rate for 2008 entrants was 40%.[2]

Whilst the report states that the determination of working out who is leaving and the specific factors are incredibly and understandably complex, the intake of newly qualified teachers also acts as a disparaging concern here, because if this cannot offset the leaving rate, that presents its own problem – but these patterns emerge from the data:

---

1. www.bit.ly/36UfQTZ
2. www.bit.ly/36TRuKj

- **Teachers with permanent contracts have higher retention rates, both in school and in the system.** (Yes, we love job security. For mortgages and stuff.)
- **Retention rates increase with age and experience, are higher outside London and in schools rated 'good' or 'outstanding' by Ofsted.** (Sadly, the banners still appear to matter – or is it that on the whole, these schools have better systems for recruitment and retention? Both, I would think.)
- **The deprivation of a school's area does not seem to be a major driver of in-system retention once other characteristics are controlled, but it is likely to feed in through the relationship between deprivation and other predictive factors.** (By that, it doesn't matter about school grading, but the in-house systems are good.)
- **Full-time teachers are less likely to leave the system than part-time teachers, but more likely to move schools.** (Because it's easier to find roles as a full-time member of staff? Because if you are part time, the role can feel more difficult? More on this later.)
- **Holding a more senior post in a school is associated with higher in-system retention.** (This is really interesting. We don't shy away from responsibility or duty then. The work that we associate with being a classroom teacher is the most influential in driving teachers away from teaching. The less responsibility, the harder the work? Or are we now asking more of classroom teachers than we should be?)

What conclusions can we draw from this?

That perhaps we should reward teachers with permanent contracts, because it is just and right if we want to fill long-term recruitment gaps, particularly for subject shortages that are an urgent concern. That professionals who have invested time and money into their education to provide a service should not have such accomplishments diluted down to that of a temporary contract. That people should be in a position to request job security so that they know they will be in a position to pay their mortgage for more than beyond the next year. That perhaps 'good' and 'outstanding' do not assist in providing a measurement for the needs of staff and are not an indication to prospective employees when considering whether a school is a good fit for them. That perhaps the cohesion of a staff body may play a far larger factor here and informs how we go about conveying the type of school when we advertise, or how we interview prospective candidates. That perhaps teachers are, on the whole, keen to work full time if the job will allow them to do so, because it's actually incredibly challenging to work part time as a teacher. That perhaps the more senior a position, the easier it becomes to stay in teaching, which would also aid the assumption that it is not the work that teachers struggle with, but the way in which the work is executed; the more autonomy in executing effective systems, and the less they are impacted by poor ones, the less likely they are to leave. In addition, the report outlined that 'Returners are also less likely to work full-time', which could indicate that those with existing knowledge of what shape teacher workload will take already understand the beast and so return with the knowledge of what they will find manageable and what lengths they are prepared to work to before they say, 'This is my line.'

How likely is it that those that are currently teaching will still be teaching in the next three, five, ten years? Teacher Tapp,[3] the innovative survey app created by Laura McInerney and Professor Becky Allen, asked this question, and what was insightful to note was that the more senior the role, the more likely a teacher was to consider remaining in teaching. Does this mean that the less time you're in a classroom, the more likely you will stay in teaching? This implies so. Perhaps we need to consider the different pulls and challenges that come at different levels of teaching.

---

3. For more information, visit www.teachertapp.co.uk and download the app. There are wonderful prizes waiting for you in the form of virtual badges that become more important to you than your own children.

To return to the two primary factors for leaving, it is indisputable that accountability and workload directly impact upon the classroom teacher, and it is here that I want to focus. We know that demand for teachers will rise as student figures rise, and the education sector will be called to address the problem, without the financial support needed from the government to do it effectively. We know that keeping teachers beyond a certain age is proving difficult, and as teachers, we can draw our own assumptions that I do not believe would be too far away from the truth: teaching is a physically demanding job, and it requires a level of stamina that means you need to comparably fit. That's harder as you get older; I do not have the energy I had at 25. End of story.

Shall we be slightly more optimistic? Those teachers that show a desire to leave don't always leave. Those teachers that do leave are generally reluctant to do so but feel that they didn't have an alternative. Those teachers that do leave aren't leaving for a higher salary. In some cases, they're taking a pay cut to change careers:[4] this could indicate that the career change is one that is driven by moral purpose, or that their moral purpose has been somewhat compromised to the extent that they look for it elsewhere. I would add that this should present us with hope rather than hindrance: teachers are not motivated by money; they're motivated by a sense of what it means to have true satisfaction that aligns to personal and professional core values. It is what Sir John Jones (and huge thanks to Emma Turner for signposting this) calls our moral imperative:

Stage 1: Where do we want to go? (The future as we want it to be/the values we champion)
Stage 2: Where are we now? (Remaining hopeful while facing the 'brutal facts')
Stage 3: How do we get there? (Turning vision into reality)[5]

---

4. www.bit.ly/2FQ6lL6
5. www.bit.ly/2ss6u34

If we reflect back to where we have come in this journey, I asked you to read 'my *why*' as a starting point because if we are to make change – great, instrumental change – it has to come from a starting point that chimes with our own moral imperative. *Why* do I want to leave, or think about leaving? *Why* now? *Why* is this happening, even though I love to teach?

People friendly isn't mother friendly, or parent friendly, or nearing-to-retirement-ready friendly: it is simply supporting people to have a sense of fulfilment outside of work as well as at it. That is what we need to provide *to people* so that this can be a profession not only to remain in, but to come to because it offers a true, deep sense of belief in the work that we undertake?

The essence of people-friendly schools is the mindset to support all, and not just the few. Not just parents, but grandparents, aunties, uncles, godparents, dog owners, kitten buyers, runners, artists, entrepreneurs, writers, readers, volunteers, learners, teachers. All people have the freedom to feel as though they have the physical and mental capacity to explore their interests and what is most important to them. In a vocation like teaching, where you give so much of yourselves, we need to recognise the importance of giving back to ourselves as well. Happy people create happy schools, but it is far more embedded than that: when people are placed at the centre of systems, productivity is better, role satisfaction is better, the realisation of individual aspirations is more likely. If we say there's no time for us to waste on considering what people do outside of work because of the work, we are simply looking at the retention crisis with blinkered vision. To consider how we place people at the centre of our systems, it is essential to think about the needs of different groups within that vast leaving teacher statistic, with the hope that we know those people may not be quite ready to leave just yet, and are receptive to being convinced not to.

Buckle up, because I'm talking to you.

What do people-friendly schools look like and where can we draw from to create them?

But we have to admit that the current picture is a bit of a bleak one, to say the least. I don't believe that teachers aren't valued: it isn't that simple (or this would be chapter 1). We battle an overarching theme throughout this section: **this is the way it has always been done**. And so, whilst other areas of the book intend to support you as the teacher, and equip you with expertise to help you navigate your way through making an impact on workload, this section aims to do something a little different: to equip you with a portfolio of evidence. To empower you to take case studies to senior leaders, to spark discussions through evidence to line managers, to challenge that mantra over and again, at various levels, so that we can start a whisper, a revolution that means our work – the work that we want so very much to carry out – is not at the mercy of others, but our own to conduct. If you are one of the people that responded under their breath with, 'Yes, yes that is me – I wanted to leave this year', then I hope to help you, should you need it.

Our sector shies away from the unpredictable but thinking differently about workload and our profession can open up great opportunities and possibilities.

- 'Virgin has never done business as usual, because we believe that the tried and tested route is not always the best path to success. Choice empowers people to make great decisions. Flexible working gives our staff choice. Through initiatives like working from home, unlimited leave, integrated technology, and wellbeing in the workplace – we treat our employees like the capable adults they are. If standard work hours no longer apply, then why should standard working conventions? Flexible working encourages our staff to find a better balance between their work and private lives, and through this balance they become happier and more productive.' *Richard Branson, founder of Virgin Group*[6]

---

6. www.bit.ly/2FR6P2q

- **AmeriCorps** employs an 80/20 rule, stating that 'up to 20 percent of AmeriCorps members' time should be spent on personal and professional development'. They're particularly well known for their VISTA program, which connects members with organizations working to alleviate poverty.[7]
- Insurance company **Aviva** has announced that all employees will receive 26 weeks' leave on full basic pay following the arrival of a child, regardless of their gender, sexual orientation or how they became a parent. Mark Wilson, the company's group chief executive, said: 'I want to live in a world where the only criteria for success is someone's talent, not their gender.'[8]

These companies have worked hard to keep the development and liberation of people at their core; by liberation, I do not mean an uprising, but a level of trust and freedom to live as well as work. Through strategic planning for high retention rates, they provide a roadmap of solutions to the issues that we face within education. They have examined how professional pressures can bleed into other aspects of a person's life, and then set about the task of trying to overcome this, to avoid it happening. They have considered what they could achieve if they remove limits on people and handed over autonomy instead. They have handed over a sense of trust and ownership and instead of outlining, 'This is the extent to which we will support you', they've switched that narrative to, 'We'll give you unlimited support, and feel free to take what you need.' It is a realisation that actually, by flipping the system, people will give more – and the productivity figures speak volumes as a result.

These are just three leading examples of how companies are listening to their workforce and trying to respond accordingly, and in a way that makes staff feel valued. Whilst we know that there are several elements here that we do not have autonomy over – Richard Branson's profit margin gives us a little bit of a run for our money – it is with a receptive, responsive approach that we can look to provide working, educationally relevant examples of what can be achieved at

7.   www.bit.ly/2t7XLDB
8.   www.bit.ly/30m84Qg

a local level, and how systems can be created to support staff at all points of their working life. Nationally, this can be the template that we start to use, so that in our best schools, we are making change by starting at ground level, supporting classroom teachers.

What is important to note is that people are being looked after, in a way that will truly impact upon their lives, and as a result of that care, productivity and profits increase for these businesses, and many similar-minded organisations worldwide. This leads us to believe that not only can we take something from this to use in our own contexts, but that there are viable, pragmatic ways of changing the structure of organisations so that they are realigned in such a way that they have a deep commitment to staff care. Still unconvinced that there is room for staff-centred schools? I want to offer a range of ways that we can look to create a profession that is not only desirable because it is, without a doubt, one of the most rewarding jobs in the world, but also enviable to those that don't teach, because the people that work within it are nurtured, supported and cared for as the most valued asset of the profession.

Who are these people?

The English department at Teachingville School, part of the Edutastic Multi-Academy Trust, is one that should be cohesive in terms of collective purpose, but the reality is quite different. The people, school and MAT aren't real, but we can recognise their circumstances, experiences, and reluctance to leave teaching as our own.

Lois

Lois's team are demotivated, tired and lacking in moral imperative when it comes to teaching. What they signed up for and what they actually do on a day-to-day, term-to-term, year-to-year basis are poles apart, and they are struggling to see an alternative solution. Lois isn't what we would deem a toxic leader: she is fair and encouraging of her staff and wants to utilise them in a way that leaves them feeling empowered rather than overstretched. However, staff morale has resulted in her asking less and less of them, for fear of adding to their task list, as she feels it would be unfair to request anything over and above the minimum operation levels because of the feedback she constantly receives. It isn't that the department members are not forthcoming; the department absence levels are concerning to both Lois and the school senior leadership team, and parents share concerns around the quality of teaching when any teacher sickness period spans beyond a two-week duration.

Lois has been thinking about starting a family soon, but knows that she will not be able to progress or even maintain her current role as a middle leader because these are positions that require a full-time presence in school; she has never known senior positions to be available on a part-time basis, and as a middle leader for a core subject, it is implied that this is also the case for her current role. As a result, Lois feels trapped: she wants to know that she did a good job as a department head before being in a position that she has to step down to start her family; and yet every results day, she leaves school to spend the last week of her holidays worried that she should have done more, and with the guilt that there is such a disconnect between the experience and expertise in her department, and the outcomes for students. Ultimately, Lois feels as though she applied for her current role to inspire staff and students, but ends up feeling torn between the pull of onerous data-driven tasks and monitoring that takes up so much of her time and wishing that instead, she could spend time investing in building the morale of her team and developing good practice. She doesn't feel she can build morale when she is lacking it herself.

The motherhood penalty and gender pay gap
Lois is one of thousands of women concerned that having children could bring their career to a standstill. Teaching appears to no longer be the ideal profession for starting a family, as figures indicate that of the 35,000 teachers that left the profession in 2014 (48,000

if we include those that retired), 6000 were women aged 30–39.[9] Removing our retirement figure from the equation, that's 17% of leaving teachers. The author of that report, Jonathan Simons, leads us to the conclusion that we can assume that the figure is maternity related, and I would be inclined to agree. For almost one-fifth of those that choose to leave teaching, it is because the role does not seem to fit around the new (or existing) role of becoming a parent. This seems unfathomable for the non-teacher crowd: how could this role not be the perfect fit? To teach children around your own children? Working 8.30–3.30, taking the holidays and weekends to spend endless time with your own child? Sadly, this is where it becomes evident that the role of teaching is warped by both media misinformation and common misconception. However, over half of teachers are parents, and so whilst we know it's challenging, we continue to try to juggle the two roles all the same. So do the figures indicate that teaching is a profession that we can sustain alongside parenthood, or that those parents came to the profession hopeful to do so, only to discover quite the opposite?

When Justine Greening announced that she would like transparency in pay, particularly those of men and women, schools presented a picture that I don't feel is hugely surprising, and in this respect, highlights the only way that we might compare teaching to a 'normal' job:

> The average annual pay for all women teachers in all state-funded schools including academies is £2,900 less than for their male counterparts (£37,700 compared to £40,660). The main reason for this is the far greater likelihood of a male teacher securing promotion, especially to headships. In all state-funded primary and nursery schools, 14% of all teachers are men, but 27% of headteachers are men.[10]

9.   www.bit.ly/2Rel72o
10. www.bit.ly/2FUHN25. The Office for National Statistics is also an ideal starting point for

Furthermore, of the 100 companies with the largest gender pay gaps reported last year, over half were schools or multi-academy trusts.[11] As a mother, you are inadvertently forced into making a choice between aspiration and parenthood, whether you are conscious of the choice or not.

- -

Sarah Seleznyov, Director of the London South Teaching School Alliance shares how they have supported women to drive school leadership in schools, irrespective of commitment to full-time working:

66 London South Teaching School Alliance works with the MTPT project, sponsoring a London-based cohort to take part in their accreditation scheme. We have chosen to support the project in this way in recognition of strong demand from our member schools for further professional development opportunities for teachers and school leaders on or returning from parental leave, particularly women teachers. Such opportunities are vital to ensure equal professional advancement for all teachers, regardless of their family commitments, and that the makeup of school leadership teams reflect this. We have supported this cause ourselves over the last three years with our own fully funded women's leadership programmes.

- -

I cannot change the world. But I urge you to keep having the conversations that make this a historical event and not a current one. If we are to hold valuable staff in high regard as a profession, we need to reconsider how we approach that definition of valuable. Are they valuable if they are in school on a full-time basis – is time in school how we measure that value – or can we start to explicitly value staff by taking the measurement of value in different ways – like the work? Or what skills they offer the school as a whole? Can we start to view staff not by the hours they are present, but by the advantage of having them as part of the formation of a strong and consistent staff body?

investigation into gender pay gaps across all sectors, should you have an afternoon to kill.

11.   Why do schools have a massive pay gap?, Branwen Jeffreys, March 2018, accessed at www.bbc.in/2FNlHP0

Kate Allely is an assistant headteacher and wellbeing lead for a specialist resource provision in Manchester. She shares her experience of requesting a flexible working arrangement as a senior leader, realigning values to lead by example, and the impact of such actions.

" I am the wellbeing lead at school, which is ironic because I have probably neglected my own wellbeing way more than I should. I'm an assistant head and run our specialist provision for children with SEMH. I also have two children: a teenager and a younger child who is autistic and had comorbid learning difficulties. Following my mum's death two years ago, I thought the best possible thing to do was to stay so busy that I wouldn't have time to think and I decided to begin a master's in psychology. One year on from beginning the course I realised that I had to do something for my own wellbeing. I had witnessed first-hand the cruelty of a person losing their own mind and was terrified of this. I approached my head and explained that I was struggling and needed to reduce my hours for my own wellbeing. My head was amazing and asked me to put it in writing to the governors. Thankfully they approved my request and I now have every Thursday afternoon off work. This meant that I had time to complete my master's, be a parent and look after my own wellbeing, all of which made me a better parent, teacher, leader and person.

Exploring a variety of flexible working arrangements can have a profound and demonstrative impact upon a staff body, which we will explore in further detail; but in Lois's position, is the exploration of a flexible approach alongside responsibility really so far from feasible?

What could this look like in school for Lois?

By examining the team that Lois leads, it may present a series of investable, successful solutions as a result.

Violet

Violet is in her tenth year of teaching, after a period in the role of assistant subject lead. She is now part time, working three days a week and teaching a range of classes shared between her and the other members of the department. She chose to relinquish her TLR at the same time as reducing to a part-time contract, after finding it increasingly difficult to juggle being a parent to a toddler and meeting the requirements of managing a key stage, and she felt incredibly jaded by the transition from full-time to part-time working in school.

Dropping her hours to 0.6, Violet was shocked to find that her TLR payment was also pro rated. As a result, she feels despondent and relatively resentful at the prospect of putting her career on hold so that she can parent her child, and feels financially penalised for this; but when she approached the governors to raise her concerns, it was stated that pro rata TLRs were usual practice. She feels as though she is not utilised to her full potential, and as an experienced member of staff, she feels frustrated and significantly out of the loop within the department. Surprised at how quickly she has felt a disconnect, Violet is now reluctant to run enrichment or take on additional projects and operates with an 'in at 8; leave at 3' mantra, completing her planning and marking judiciously but avoiding anything that stretches above and beyond her job description. As Violet is one of the most knowledgeable and experienced members of staff, Lois knows that she could utilise her to a far greater degree for the benefit of the department as a whole but doesn't know how to incentivise Violet so that she would even entertain involvement in additional projects.

Violet is one of many, many women that feel that they are put into this position when it comes to the matter of navigating part-time working in school. Not only owing to parenthood, part-time staff are, in many cases, not catered for at all within a school setting. In contrast to a supportive policy or strategic consideration, staff that request flexible working are usually put in the position to accommodate and compensate for not being physically present in the building five days a week. In a school where emails can fluctuate to 50+ a day, just two days of being out of the workplace can put you at an incredible disadvantage and some staff end up doing more work to make up for it, or work at home on their day off. Hence the discomfort of throwaway comments like 'part-timing it' and 'Friday off, eh? Alright for some'; there's a reasonably good chance that days off are spent planning, marking and playing catch-up.

Abigail Vincent, second in English and KS3 coordinator at a school in Northamptonshire, knows the deceit of a 'day off' all too well:

66 After the birth of my daughter, I dropped my days from five to three. These days were blocked together (at my request) so I had Thursdays and Fridays off. Initially this was brilliant: long weekends, and it didn't feel like I was completely abandoning my baby! However, after the first couple of months it became apparent that this was not ideal – the email chains I needed to catch up with on a Sunday evening were epic, assumptions were made that I should be aware of anything that had occurred on my days off. I started checking my emails on my days off just to try and save my Sunday nights which pretty quickly developed into working through my daughter's naptime. I was so stressed at missing so much information (that I was expected to know) that I asked to move up to four days a week the following year. I have stayed at four days a week since (return to work was 2013) and find this much more manageable, even after the birth of my second daughter in 2018.

Concerningly, when asked what they would do with a free day off in the week, 20% of teachers voted for 'work stuff',[12] opting to catch up on work so that they would be in a position to spend the weekend as weekends should be spent: with family, and friends, or books. What a strange profession we have become to have such a circumstance that when presented with extra time, a significant number of teachers want to work for free just to get the job done. It demonstrates how much we care, but also that the care has breached the boundaries a little.

Violet's situation presents two further issues: one, that TLR payments are not regulated or protected by policy in any way, so can be adjusted in line with a 0.8 contract- in essence, a school can

---

12.   Twitter poll: www.bit.ly/2QSJ0NY

pay an employee 4/5 of a TLR payment, without reducing the duties expected – without the duties associated with the TLR amended; and two, that this process is entirely inconsistent across the board. In some schools, we're getting it right; but often, TLR duties are put upon part-time staff without modification and yet the pay doesn't reflect that: In a recent Twitter poll that asked part-time teachers about their pay, 60% responded that they received a pro rata payment..[13] When this happens, without an amendment to duties, I struggle to find the justification for such a choice, outside budget pressures, which is simply not good enough.

A principal of a school in the Midlands stated:

> *The TLR is for a whole role, not a part of a role. It's not shared: it's a whole role. You're not doing half a job. You're doing a whole job. Like, you know, a whole one, wholly. So why would it be pro rata? Whereas if you're flex/part time then you are in fact sharing a role with* someone – hence you're paid for the proportion of the role you do. Yes? *But unless the TLR is officially job-shared then you're doing the whole role. And believe it or not, you can actually do a whole TLR role whilst working flex/ part time because it doesn't make you half a person or half as competent.*

If you are being asked to carry out a role and believe that a reduction of the duties of that role would mean that outcomes are compromised, it is very much worth having that discussion. In many schools, the process of pro rata payment is simply the habitual approach. In schools, we have staff like Violet who feel hindered by the limitations placed upon them by a part-time role, and this will have a profound impact upon their sense of purpose and the extent to which they have the automation to manage a workload when just the additional burden of being in school part time is difficult. How

13.   Twitter poll: www.bit.ly/2QV9wX6

can we support part-time staff to feel connected and not like part time is actually more onerous than full time?

66 Lyndsey Bawden, a head of department in Lincolnshire: 'I was part time for nine years; this role is my first full-time job since I had my children, but I was also a head of department on four days a week. I support part-time staff by not emailing them when they're not in work, so they don't come back to a mountain of work and messages to read. I also ask how I can support their working patterns. Wherever possible, I try to give them their own classroom! Being nomadic can often feel like you're not valued.

66 Clara, a head of department in Kent: 'My second in department worked two days a week. I made sure she never worked beyond her directed time and ensured that she didn't work parents' evenings on her days off as standard. I gave her very specific roles that could be done in the time she had. She was able to get done in two days more than most manage in a week, and she was a consummate professional. When she asked for two days, I moved heaven and earth to make it happen, because she was a complete team player.'

66 David, a part-time head of department: 'All of my department staff have an out-of-office set that states their working days, and there is no expectation to pick up these emails until they come back into work. I cannot control the inbound count of the school, but any department-specific emails I send, I mark the nature of the email in the subject line. For example, 'resource' or 'meeting' or 'due Tuesday' so that they can just shift to the relevant folder quickly and prioritise the time that they are in school.'

66 Alex, a part time Lead Practitioner in Birmingham: 'My head of department ensures all meetings are held on the days that I am at work, so I don't feel disconnected. Deadlines might be set on a Wednesday for 'three working days'; or if they're for 'next Monday', it is taken into account that I don't work on Thursdays and Fridays, and I am provided with the additional time so that it may be that my deadline is Wednesday. He understands how absurd it would be to set a task for me to complete when I'm not in school!'

Making the decision to reduce your working hours has not only a financial implication, but also necessitates the understanding that it may be more challenging to keep on top of the various ways in which communications are sent out or updates cascaded to particular teams. By providing a sense of acknowledgement for part-time workers, accommodating their needs and ensuring they feel part of the collective, it makes all the difference to their professional fulfilment overall.

Progress for part-timers: figuring out flexible working

- **Early requests:** Request as early in the year as possible for provision to be put in place, particularly with regards to timetabling; avoid split classes wherever possible to ensure that staff time in school is spent purposefully, and not spent chasing others to find out the content that needs to be taught next. Time is your most valued commodity and this is supercharged when you work part time – you do not want to spend all of the time you are not in work figuring out how you will track teachers down as soon as you get back into work. Further, to fuel timetabling that works, explore the capacity for 'double up' timetables at secondary (if you are a curriculum leader, this is a powerful way to not only develop staff but keep workload down): a timetable that avoids giving teachers every year group, and instead, they teach two groups of year 8, two groups of year 10. Not only does this reduce planning tasking, but also means that members of the department can work in clusters to improve subject knowledge. If classes do need to be split, liaise with that member of staff to outline how content can be taught without a constant back-and-forth approach to cover units.

- **Bolster up the benefits:** Outline exactly why you will be a tenacious addition to the team as a part-time employee. Sing up your increased productivity, the time you will have to read research or distil notes from listening to podcasts and share these findings with your colleagues, and the fact that you will use the time to explore interests, developing yourself both personally and professionally. Don't be tempted to scatter your application with an apologetic tone of, 'I can use the day to catch up' or 'even though I'll be part time'. This is a positive adjustment; make sure that the recipient of your letter can recognise that with language like 'driven by the balance' or 'motivated to explore' or 'galvanised by other interests'.

- **Assume a yes:** Structure your application so that it is not assumptive of agreement by anticipating objections. That the days selected will support the school's operation, that there will be minimal readjustment required and that those amendments that will take place will ultimately improve the standards within the department or school. That this will have a positive impact on school budget. That you are proud to work for a school that takes such a proactive, flexible approach to supporting their staff to maintain a balance between work and life.

- **A no is a question:** If your application is declined, view it as an opportunity to provide a solution. Work with your employer, not against them, to work out a scenario that could meet the needs of both of you. Consider where there is flexibility, but also where there is not – don't agree to something that leaves you feeling as though you've negotiated a solution for the school but not for you. For instance, could a late start or early finish work as opposed to having a particular day off? Is there a day where you could come in late and take up after-school duties or intervention sessions instead? Take the time to return to the table to discuss options, and remember that it usually isn't personal, but due to the requirements of the school at an operational level.

Part-time staff are an untapped resource in many schools; but with the right support, they can be the strongest members of any departmental team as the balance that they seek is fulfilled – and as a result, they can sometimes be the most productive, most positive forces within a department, and incredibly supportive of full-time staff where the challenges are different.

- -

- Value part-time staff equally and include them in all decisions and discussions to avoid disconnection.
- Challenge TLR reductions and clarify the rationale behind them.
- View flexible working as an assumptive improvement for both you and the school.

- -

Michael

Michael is five years away from retirement and is now at a stage of his life where he wants to start making plans for the next part of his journey. He has thoroughly enjoyed a 30-year career in the classroom, taking on a range of TLRs, but developed himself as a teacher first and foremost, mentoring several trainees and NQT staff as they embark upon their careers, and choosing to stay in the classroom himself as a result of a love for his subject. Sadly, Michael's elderly mother has a terminal illness and he acts as her primary carer around his full-time role at work. He isn't ashamed to admit that he finds it incredibly tiring to teach 22 hours a week, and whilst Lois tends to give him a range of key stage 4 and 5 classes as a result of his incredible knowledge base, this comes with its own demands and challenges, including the increased pressure of marking at particular points of the year, and increased scrutiny, particularly because the department's Progress 8 has been relatively poor for the last two years. Michael is one of the most reliable, trustworthy, professional human beings that Lois has ever worked with, but she has started to notice that the position is taking its toll on him. Teaching is a physical endurance test in itself, and Michael's demands from both the professional and personal aspects of his life have resulted in little more than sleeping, working and spending valuable time with his mother.

Keeping good teachers in the classroom

Michael is one of a dying breed: a teacher over the age of 50 in teaching. The Department for Education's report into the early retirement of teachers outlines that 'Among the full population of teachers working in 2014 (491,482 teachers), a small minority (2.2%) were aged over 60, with less than 1% 65 or over. The average age for all teachers was 39.'[14]

This was true of all levels of teaching, classroom teacher to leadership level, but it is very interesting to note the number of individuals that do retire earlier as a result of ill health. Teachers that took ill health retirement were more common in schools that had a high level of student absence, or a high level of students eligible for FSM. Top three reasons for early retirement? Cancer, mental health and illnesses affecting the nervous system – such as multiple sclerosis (MS), Alzheimer's disease, Parkinson's disease, epilepsy, shingles or stroke. Whilst grand sweeping statements from what is an incredibly intricate look at the patterns of teacher retirement are possible, it is safe to consider that the findings imply that retirement is more likely to be taken early if a teacher is still in the classroom, and still working on a full-time contract (although for transparency, the report admits not to have obtained knowledge of how long those part-time participants had been part time at the time of survey). In addition, as our life span is longer, you are now most likely to be a carer of someone aged 80 or over if you are aged between 45–64.[15] Subsequently, this means if you are caring for someone, you're relatively likely not to have retired yet yourself, and therefore still in employment, whether than be full or part time.

Taking the factor of workload out of the equation for a moment, Michael's day-to-day life is significantly pressured and yet still offers reward in terms of sense of purpose. The role of a carer is incredibly stressful, particularly in consideration of the shift in dynamics of that relationship if you are caring for a parent. The mental impact of these two separate roles will inevitably take its toll, and Michael

14. Department for Education: Teachers and ill-health retirement Annex F: Analysis for the Teachers Working Longer Review Research report November 2018 Nick Coleman
15. Redfoot D , Feinberg L , Houser A . *The aging of the baby boom and the growing care gap: a look at future declines in the availability of family caregivers* [Internet]. Washington (DC) : AARP Public Policy Institute ; 2013 Aug [cited 2014 Feb 28]. (Insight on the Issues No. 85). Available from: www.bit.ly/2Rgi35P

will be in a position where he has to choose between investing his energy into caring for his mother or attempting to continue to work full time at what is a physically demanding job for a period of time.

Compassion into action

Lois has the flexibility within her department to retain Michael's expertise and not lose a really knowledgeable member of the team. Through a rational and pragmatic approach, staff can be supported so that they can maintain a priority of care and continue to feel a sense of accomplishment in the workplace.

Yamina Bibi, a lead practitioner in South East London, shares her story of being a teacher-carer:

66 When my dad was diagnosed with bowel cancer, it was absolutely devastating. I could not have asked for a better school to be working in at the time. The moment I told my head of department and headteacher, I received the best support, the kindest of words and a hug. In an instant, my siblings and I became carers. I had to take my dad to hospital for chemo, regular appointments and all the other things that come with looking after an ill parent.

My school could not have been more supportive. I was regularly checked in on by my colleagues, including my headteacher; my lessons were covered by my colleagues without making me feel guilty and my students were the epitome of kindness. My headteacher recommended I see the staff counsellor, which was free and incredibly helpful. The kindness that was shown by the school was above and beyond anything I had seen and I know that without their support, my mental health would have deteriorated rapidly. I struggled quite a bit outside of school but knowing I had my friends and colleagues to support me kept me going.

Then the year after, when my mum was diagnosed with terminal leukaemia, they showed that support once again. I felt the unfailing support from each and every person and I could not be more thankful and grateful.

Michael could opt out of particular meeting times to accommodate for an earlier finish, without reconfigurations of directed time.

Alternatively, the school could increase his PPA time by an hour or two a week to avoid the impact and strain of full teaching days, instead giving over to creating schemes or assessment planning. Beyond that, Michael could work remotely for a period of his working week and contribute towards developing tools for the department that utilize his subject knowledge as a collaborative tool.

Remote working, you say? Don't be ridiculous, Kat. We are teachers; our work is in school; our job is to teach children in schools. Working from home or anywhere but in the building simply isn't feasible. If we allow remote working, everyone would want it. Right?

An assistant head in the South West shares her experience of moving to remote working:

66 I have always worked full-time. When I returned from maternity leave, I was told that I couldn't go part time and retain my role as head of English, so I just accepted it and arranged childcare accordingly. We were spending more each month on childcare than on the mortgage. I'm in a new school now, and once again I requested part-time working. I wanted two afternoons off for school pick-up. My head agreed to two afternoons off, and to my surprise, I was granted full-time flexible working, rather than having to take a reduction in hours and pay. She told me that I would be selling myself short to go part-time and had no doubt that I would continue to manage my role and responsibilities around these school pick-ups. This trust and investment in me as a professional has been invigorating. It made me realise that it is possible to support teachers in flexible working. It just takes careful thought and a willingness to be creative with timetables and staffing.

Flexible working isn't just for child juggling

As we move towards faster, busier lives – lives that don't have mini-downtimes or space for thinking unless we find it – the pull of a full-time week becomes more difficult to manage. As human beings, we fill our lives more than ever before; we give ourselves very little downtime, and teachers are particularly guilty of this. Term time for teachers, particularly at the beginning of new terms or the start of an academic year, is often accompanied by the idea that our lives should be placed on hold, as we assume our teacher armour and get to work.

However, we are people first and teachers second. In every single one of our working examples, teachers are working with school systems to find a mutually beneficial agreement, one that allows them to be people first and teachers second – which is how it should be, after all. Beyond that, teachers should be supported to follow routes that don't take a linear, narrow view to people progression; we, as professionals, have interests, outlets, hobbies, pursuits, and education that we wish to explore to consequently develop ourselves and enrich our lives. It will make us better people, but also better teachers. Flexible working isn't just for parents, but for those within the profession to feel that they can live and work, rather than one being exchanged for the other.

'This isn't an option in schools, though, is it?' I often hear this argument: the limitations of a timetable don't allow us to, and that is the end of that. However, flexible working is becoming much more visible in schools, and whilst the approval process may be inconsistent from one school to the next, it is becoming a more widely accepted feature within schools, which is really pleasing to see. With the recent release from the Department for Education of a collection of resources for flexible working in schools,[16] I am more optimistic and hopeful that people will start to view school staffing budgets and arrangements from a more receptive standpoint.

From stories of 80% of the workforce on 0.8 contracts, to job shares at senior leadership level, flexible working can be monumental in driving the profession in a direction to reclaim life before work, and people before processes. However, there is still so much work to be done and many objections to overcome on a more localised level. Particularly in core subjects, or middle management, where individuals are responsible for leading a team on a day to day basis, flexible working is seen as simply impossible. 'You can't be part time: you're English,' as though the pull of four lessons a week

16.   www.bit.ly/2tnt9xV

for year 11 is enough to be accommodating for staff. As if the second in charge of the department cannot be given the ownership to lead the department one day a week. As if there will be some form of mutiny if someone has a 10 a.m. start in comparison to the rest of us. If we think back to Michael, I'd like to think we wouldn't all go at him with pitchforks if he came in later on after an early morning washing, dressing and caring for his mum.

The data indicates to us that this isn't about the financial impact, and more about finding a sense of balance, as around one in six secondary school teachers would like to reduce their hours and could afford to do so.[17] As well as having a positive impact on staff, the benefits to schools are incredible: improved retention figures, decrease in absence and healthier budgets, as part-time workers on the books make it more straightforward to allocate the teaching hours required as opposed to not having any staff at all – which is what will eventually happen. Additionally, middle management is more than possible without having a physical presence 24/7 and builds autonomy in staff. If you still need some convincing, here are some starting points.

Germany are working fewer hours a week and are 25% more productive than us here in the UK. Effectively, they have achieved by Thursday what we aim to do in the entire week![18] Several corporate companies have already shifted towards a four-day week, lured by the productivity levels and decrease in sickness figures. One marketing company reduced all staff to a four-day contract but retained-full time salaries, and productivity increased by over 30%. [19] Whilst the voices averse to change may tell us it cannot be done, I've sourced a range of examples from senior leaders that say otherwise.

17. Report Part-time Teaching and Flexible Working in Secondary Schools National Foundation for Educational Research (NFER) Part-time Teaching and Flexible Working in Secondary Schools Caroline Sharp Robert Smith Jack Worth Jens Van den Brande Published in June 2019, accessed at www.bit.ly/2tbvImK
18. www.bit.ly/30mSx2R
19. Science Focus, Four-day week: could the UK be more productive by working less? Some workplaces around the world are trying to increase productivity by shortening working hours without changing pay. By Sara Rigby. 1st February, 2019, accessed at www.bit.ly/2Tsyxu3.

Dismissing flexibility as a way to support staff in schools with the statement that we have rigid timetables is just not going to ensure sustainability in schools.

- -

John Tomsett, headteacher at Huntington School in York, values staff as his most treasured resource:

❝ Who would you prefer your child to be taught by: a pedestrian full-time teacher or two sparklingly good part-time teachers on a job share? At Huntington School we openly encourage part-time working because we want to retain our best teachers. We have 112 teachers and over 50% of them are part-timers. Since 2007, every single flexible working request has been granted. We have part-time colleagues on the SLT, and we have both male and female part-time teachers. We have embraced flexible working; school staff are looking for a better work-home balance and we have accepted that workplace norms are changing. Ultimately, at Huntington we know that a highly trained, expert, happy, healthy, motivated staff is the best thing for our students. And we have no evidence whatsoever that split classes have any negative impact at all upon students' outcomes. So, we put staff first – the more contented part-timers, the better!

- -

To preach to the probably converted, it is often not about how feasible the concept is, but how receptive management are in what some describe as 'opening the floodgates'. Indeed, when I have discussed flexible working with senior leaders in the past, the key concern is that if they support members of staff in flexible working, it will then pave the way for all staff to be expectant of the same or similar benefits. This is quite simply untrue: staff have different needs at different points of their lives or careers. The flexibility that might support a member of staff looking to bridge the next few years to retirement is not the same, by any stretch, as that which would suit the woman in her thirties, looking to pursue a career in stained glass craftsmanship (true story). The truth is if we want to support and hold teachers in the highest of regard, we have to consider the long-term value of enabling people to be people. People who want to take sabbatical time out of their school role to teach abroad in a developing country, pick their children up from school on a day that they have a PPA at the end of the day, come in later one morning a week so they can train for a charity marathon, work from home one day a week to avoid the crippling cost of childcare, reduce contact time and utilise staff in other ways, or enable them to train in other areas of school life so that they can feel a sense of progression, or share a job role within school so that they can collaboratively implement strategy and learn from one another along the way. Not people that demand the grand moments in life, but people who want to ensure that they make time for the small moments with people and experiences that they hold dear. Not only is it supporting people through exploration of further education, interests and development, but it is beneficial for the school as a business and fulfils business needs.

- -

Drew Thompson, a deputy headteacher in a school in North London, outlines his approach to accommodating flexible working:

66 Our school introduces flexibility through our timetabling. Over a third of our 100 teachers are not in school full-time and whilst in many cases this is for childcare reasons or external work or course commitments, we aim to introduce opportunities through other means. We have teachers who spend part of their week at our prep school, teaching, for example, two days there and three days at the senior school. A partnership with another local school in this way allows those interested teachers a more varied teaching diet and can help fulfil curricular needs. We also have a 'protected time' slot that teachers can allocate in their timetable. This is deliberately built into our timetabling process and has been used in the past to give space for personal development at a time that suits the teacher. In some cases, we can give them an afternoon off to support their own pursuits. It provides interested teachers with an avenue to explore something entirely new.

- -

To help a little, here are some common objections to flexible working remotely, and some suggestions for how to address them:

If you're working from home, how will we know what you're doing?
It isn't about what I do, but what I produce. Stanford University actually carried out a study which found that those working from home were not only happier in their jobs, but had an increased productivity rate of 13.5%.[20] Not only can remote and flexible working free up classroom space as teachers can share rooms, but it also helps to work at home when doing strategic or solo work such as extensive resourcing, or data analysis to share with teams, or documentation that needs work like the department improvement plan, or staff handbooks, because schools are actually really distracting places to work, due to the nature of the 'just a minute' conversations. I feel the quality of the work I intend to do at home will be far improved as a result of doing so.

It's too expensive for schools and current funding constraints
It will keep me in teaching, which is a massive money saver in the long term. It means I will have a career that allows me to explore my own hobbies, or pick up my children from school, or simply improve my job satisfaction overall. I can suggest the hours in a way that works for both of us and it'll mean I'm loyal as a result. Happier staff means staff that stay put. 76% of employers saw staff retention improve when they offered flexible working[21] and it is really quite common practice in lots of schools now as an incentive to keep great staff in schools.

If we do it for you, we'll have to do it for everyone
In my case, I am asking for flexible working to fit around my children as they grow. For others, it will be different, and I think that every case will have someone with their own needs and requests. I don't feel that you would be under an obligation to give it to everyone,

20. Nicholas Bloom & James Liang & John Roberts & Zhichun Jenny Ying, 2015. 'Does Working from Home Work? Evidence from a Chinese Experiment,' The Quarterly Journal of Economics, Oxford University Press, vol. 130(1), pages 165-218
21. EMPLOYEE EMPLOYEE Outlook Report, CIPD, April 2016 VIEWS ON WORKING LIFE Commuting and flexible working, accessed at www.bit.ly/2u4uLwE

as it wouldn't fit the needs of the school, but not everyone would want it. 30% of the UK's working population (8.7 million people) wants flexible working but don't yet have it,[22] and it would be a true testament to this school to champion that, and so encouraging to both new teachers joining teaching but also new staff joining the school.

It's too difficult to manage on a timetable within schools

I would say that it is far easier to manage flexible workers if you know in advance, and this is why I wanted to put in a request before Easter, with plenty of notice for next year's timetable. I aim to be flexible to help us find a way to make it work. Perhaps I could resource a series of writing lessons for the one lesson a week that my classes would have without me? Or if I share a tutor group, I can ensure that I take registration on the days that I am working in school.

You're a senior/middle manager: we need to have you here on a full-time basis

Having a flexible working arrangement or job share can actually lead to a far more effective way of management; it means that staff have more than one point of contact, and my second in department/ designated deputy/co-worker in the job share and I can really develop our communication skills to manage people well and consistently. This will ultimately make the department/school a satisfying place to manage, because staff retention typically improves with good management and results in further staff retention. Several studies into remote working and flexible working demonstrate that 46% of companies that use remote working[23] report reduced HR issues; 95% of employers say it has a high impact on employee retention. There are a number of schools making it work to the extent that – dare I say it – management is an improved process because of the collaborative way in which they are approaching leadership.

---

22. Flexible Future for Britain, 2016, accessed at www.bit.ly/2uOMLv7
23. Global workplace analytics meta-analysis, available at www.bit.ly/386ReaN

You'll be less productive if you're not in school

A global survey of 20,000 businesses found that 72% of them reported increased productivity as a direct result of flexible working.[24] As a teacher, I am incredibly driven and used to working flexibly around my children and so you have absolutely no need to be concerned about my productivity. I ate breakfast, got through my emails this morning, all whilst having the remnants of toast crusts thrown at my head.

You have a core timetable and we need you here for set lessons

We can agree core hours when I'd be here, and my PPA time could accommodate for other times, if it is feasible. It would mean that I can pick up and drop off my children some days, which would mean the world to me. I'm happy to put together a series of suggestions that would mean I am making a solid contribution to the department, but that would also work for the school and my requirements. I would be keen to support with key stage 4 intervention, for example, and in addition to my GCSE classes, I would be happy to take intervention within my timetable which could work more flexibly and lift the pressure on staff for revision sessions later on and over the holiday periods. In addition, the administration that I could complete for the department would elevate masses of workload pressures on staff: I could complete mock paper marking once moderation is complete or create standardisation documents and any other strategies that would improve our consistency as a team. There are many ways that I could contribute to the teaching taking place in addition to the time that I teach in school.

We would need to see working examples of this in action to understand what it could look like

Brilliant! Great to hear you are open to paving the way for teachers to find a sense of balance in their lives. I have heaps of examples in this book I read...

24. www.bit.ly/36W1Ucj

Claire Mitchell, a part-time head in Leicestershire, shares her experience of flexible leadership:

  66 I have been a part-time headteacher for nearly a decade and count myself incredibly fortunate to have fantastic colleagues and a supportive governing body who champion flexible and part-time working. I have utilised flexible working in both the best and the worst of times and believe that it has not only allowed me to continue in leadership, but it has also made me a better leader too.

My first daughter was an easy baby and while I adored my time with her, I also valued being able to go back to the leadership role I loved and worked so hard for. Working three (and later four) days a week allowed me to balance family life with a career wonderfully well. I enjoyed having regular days at home and the days when I could be something other than 'Mum'. Working three days I could be flexible with my time, occasionally swapping round days or half days to either meet the school's needs (important meetings and events, Ofsted, helping out a colleague) or meet my family's needs (medical appointments, poorly baby, nursery nativity, family celebrations).

My second baby was less straightforward, having experienced an anaphylactic reaction to cow's milk at six months old when I was due to return to work from maternity leave. She was too little for an adrenaline auto-injector, so the weaning process was strictly controlled, and every new food felt like a game of Russian roulette. Our chair of governors offered an extension to my maternity leave or reduction in my hours until things were more certain, but financially and organisationally it seemed easier to return as planned. I rather foolishly soldiered on and said I would be fine.

I wasn't. Things got worse. My darling gran became ill and passed away the same day my dad went into intensive care for pneumonia. Filled with grief and worry, I couldn't think straight or do my job effectively. Work was piling up, I was making excuses, delaying deadlines, constantly firefighting and too exhausted to see a way through.

The chair gently said she had noticed things weren't being done as well as usual and that I needed support. This time I took her advice. We talked through various options: compassionate leave, working from home, reducing hours, split shifts, or working flexible rather than fixed days. Through this conversation

I realised that life could be manageable; it just had to be done differently. Importantly, the chair assured me that governors did not doubt my ability or commitment, but recognised I was going through a difficult period and required practical help until it passed.

I began to spread my three-day workload over five days so I could work around medical appointments and lengthy nursery handovers, and reduce time wasted sitting in traffic. Detailed planning with SLT colleagues made work manageable. Through this, I saw where I could pay back the favour – suggesting they timetable work-from-home days to avoid wasted hours commuting and to pick their own kids up one day a week from school, after a more productive day at home with none of the inevitable interruptions of daily school life.

Happily, my dad made a full recovery and my youngest was given the all-clear by the time she was three. I am back to working a more regular three-day pattern, but still enjoy the benefits of working flexible hours when either the school or family life requires it.

These personal experiences made me realise more sharply how important flexible working opportunities and wellbeing support for staff are. By receiving this support as a school leader, I have greater empathy for when colleagues may need similar. Flexible working requires teamwork and generosity; it requires detailed planning and careful, considered management; but flexibility also undoubtedly secures high levels of commitment – and most importantly supports a healthy, happy staff.

But these are all the people that work in great schools or are great leaders, Kat! What about all the examples I need to show of teachers in the classroom and making it work? Here you are:

----

66 **@Mumsyme:** I know an artist, an illustrator, a gardening volunteer, a few caring for elderly relatives, a couple of entrepreneurs, a couple phasing into retirement, someone who just wants to only work 4 days just because.

66 **@SallyJMcDonald:** I went down to 0.6 to do an EdD. I generally spend one of my days off doing schoolwork but my evenings and weekends are my own now.

66 **@Mathsteacher68:** I do 0.8 as my husband is older than me and retired so we have a retirement day and do pensioner stuff!

66 **Sarah Mullin:** I'm part-time deputy head from today. No other way I could manage raising three children and completing my EdD School has retained someone who loves their job, is passionate about driving social change and who will go above and beyond to make it work.

66 **@bookmiscellany:** I worked in a drama department with a part time HOD and she was brilliant. Took every care to catch up with me on her days in school and would texl me to ask me if I needed anything when I was an anxious NQT. She has a good balance between home and work: an excellent role model for me!

66 **Sophie Halford:** Having felt overwhelmed and extremely unhappy (which in itself stemmed from stress and fatigue) frequently when working full-time, I decided to request flexible working in the form of four days a week. Despite my anxieties that my request wouldn't be taken seriously as a childless woman in my twenties, my school granted my request and I now look towards the new academic year with a feeling of optimism and not the dread I had been feeling. I believe this change will help not only my mental health to improve, but my teaching too.

66 **@Ballard1000:** My first head of department was part time – an absolute inspiration. Highly efficient, motivational, defended her department fiercely and was excellent in the classroom. All that while bringing up three children: amazing.

66 **@Lara 2of4:** Last year our HOD was part time – and did an exceptional job. Highly organised and kept tabs on everything but trusted the department to run without a problem on her day off. Care deeply about the department and made it work well. Our second in department was key to this as well

66 **@Drjessm:** I think a school leader choosing to work part time shows that they can prioritise life/home over work. In my experience, that means they are more likely to allow those they lead to also have commitments outside of work.

66 **@Miss_BBates:** My HOD was part time. She was always ten paces ahead of everyone else, anticipating in advance what was required, highly efficient and just as dedicated as full time staff. When you're part time,

you often learn to use your time much more efficiently and she was very self-disciplined.

- Accommodate for staff, particularly where the demands of the job are competing with their personal demands.
- Recognise the benefits of flexibility for all teachers.
- Consider the other ways that teaching staff can contribute to the school operation outside of the classroom.

Imogen

Imogen is in her NQT year. After one year, on a marginally reduced timetable but being used for cover as a result of the high absenteeism within the department, she is already feeling pretty jaded about the teaching profession. Enduring a year of late-night working, weekends spent marking and putting her energies into unfamiliar specifications and the moderation of assessments to refine her expertise, Imogen feels as though she is old before her time as she battles significant bouts of anxiety in trying to deal with behaviour in her lessons so she is able to teach effectively. Her department are supportive, but she feels as though she is the only one that cannot cope, and so tries to deal with it individually – and as a result, is struggling.

She's lost any semblance of a social life. When she has booked in plans to see friends and family over the holiday periods, she feels despondent and disconnected from her non-teaching friends, struggling to know what to talk about. They earn considerably more than her, talk about dates they've been on and hobbies they've kept up, while she's lucky to have a meal that hasn't fallen out of the microwave, and she can't remember the last time she went on a run. She feels old beyond her years from the torrent of terse exchanges with teenagers, and she envies the corporate life that her friends seem to have, with adult conversation, company cars and private healthcare. She can't really see how anyone progresses in teaching whilst maintaining the outlandish workload at the same time.

Imogen loves the prospect of teaching, but just feel restricted by the hours and the current lack of challenge, autonomy beyond the classroom and social life. Teaching 22 hours a week is exhausting and with every year group on her timetable, Imogen is feeling such a strain, she cannot envisage how this is maintainable long term.

Teacher shelf life

A worrying proportion of teachers leave in those first five years, and within the multitude of reasons, the disconnect between the way in which we present teaching to the world and the reality of what the role actually entails tends to feature. Teachers' decisions to leave the profession were generally driven by the accumulation of a number of factors over a sustained period of time:[25] put simply, this is the result of several nudges as opposed to one large crisis point. Studies show that 'new teachers are extremely vulnerable and more likely to leave the profession', states Professor Jonathan Glazzard at Leeds Beckett University;[26] and a recent survey from Educational Partnership Support highlights that of the NQTs asked, two in five had experienced mental health problems in the last year.[27]

This is a concern that early-career teacher leaver rate is on the increase (the NFER report states that trainee figures are dropping and continue to do so)[28] and it is important that schools work to understand why people leave in order to put strategies into place to aid retention. The two most insightful factors of the report, in my opinion, are that almost half of leaving teachers are choosing to take up employment within the education sector; and that, on the whole, the wages of teachers that left for another job were 10% lower than those that stayed in teaching. Teachers are not leaving for more

---

25. Department for Education, Factors affecting teacher retention: qualitative investigation Research report March 2018 Cooper Gibson Research, accessed at www.bit.ly/35Wd7Ik
26. The Mental Health of Newly Qualified Teachers by Professor Jonathan Glazzard October 2018, accessed at www.bit.ly/2TuoLaX
27. www.bit.ly/2RhhzME
28. Should I Stay or Should I Go? NFER Analysis of Teachers Joining and Leaving the Profession Jack Worth Susan Bamford Ben Durbin Published in November 2015, accessed at www.bit.ly/2QWpro0

money, even though when in teaching, money can be an indicative factor as to whether they remain in that role or not.

What can we draw from that? Certainly that money does not make the world go round for teachers: the monetary influence of a role is not important; but there is significance in the extent to which the individual is being rewarded for the hours that they contribute. Not in terms of money, but rewarding their self worth as a professional. However, schools are transferring the pinch of funding onto staff by making it increasingly difficult for classroom teachers to progress through the pay structure simply for a job well done.

Cat shares her experience of an 'RQT M1 up' programme that was run by her school:

❝ After my first year teaching, we as RQTs were gathered to a meeting to be told that SLT would support us by assigning us coaches who were random members of staff across the school. SLT had a lot of ideas about how they wanted it to run – but it didn't go that smoothly. Different colleagues had different experiences and outcomes depending on who their coach was. For example, finding the time to meet with my coach was the biggest struggle because they hadn't factored in time to carry out meetings, or even considered that we didn't have any free time at the same time of day. So when I did finally meet with my coach, it had to be a 20-minute meeting at lunchtime, only for me to ask, 'What's the idea behind it?' and for her to reply, 'I'm not sure.' But because she could never observe me, it wasn't possible for her to be able to give the right level of coaching. Other colleagues involved said they received directed tasks, so it was massively inconsistent. Above all, it was bizarre that a programme was run so sporadically and didn't have any connection to our performance management targets, and so wasn't a reliable source of evidence. It didn't make any sense whatsoever!

Whilst Imogen appears not to be jumping through corporate hoops just yet, it can be incredibly demotivating to be taken through programmes and initiatives that bear little resemblance to our own professional needs within the classroom. Where are these educational roles for Imogen outside teaching?

International schools could be the alternative that entice those teachers in their twenties within the first five years. And you can understand the pull; the narrative around international teaching is tempting to say the least.

Freya O'Dell was director of English in a school in the UK, before making the decision to move to Italy in an attempt to find a balance. She says: 66 International teaching has been a great option for me because it has enabled me to regain my work-life balance. A great number of PPAs and smaller class sizes has meant I can get most of my work done in school, leaving evenings and weekends free. In addition, the lack of high-stakes accountability has been liberating. We are trusted as professionals and encouraged to teach in a way that suits us to help get the very best from pupils. I love it!

Hannah Crowe tells a similar story from her classroom in the Cayman Islands. After spending her time teaching in Spain, Vietnam and Hong Kong, returning to a teaching position in the UK each time always felt frustrating because of the restrictions placed upon her autonomy to teach: 66 International teaching jobs are appealing to many as there is a (usually correct) perception that teachers are more respected and valued by parents and students. In many countries, pay is higher and people get to do the job they love whilst living somewhere exciting. In many international settings, behaviour is better in the classroom, which allows teachers to feel they can actually teach, rather than coping with behaviour issues.

Let us not ship Imogen off. It is pleasing to know that most teachers leaving are reluctant to do so, or seek out other ways to remain in education, but it seems to be a response to the systems that they work within. Teachers want to continue to teach, and so what is it that determines that decision to leave? Of course, we can only speculate here to a degree, as data indicates such a variety of reasons for individuals, but 'engagement underpins retention.

Protective factors associated with retention include job satisfaction, having adequate resources, reward and recognition, and being well supported by management.'[29] If we can engage Imogen with the UK education system, then she might not feel inclined to jump on a plane just yet. Would our international teachers ever be tempted to return? Freya toys with the question: 'Positive moves have been made in England with the new framework, and I'm excited to see where this goes. I'm also delighted more and more SLT teams are discussing staff wellbeing. England has fantastically dedicated practitioners and the better we can support and nurture these practitioners, the greater the retention will be back home.'

Multi-academy trusts such as Burgess have the advantage of determining their own structure, and could utilise Imogen's tenacity by providing opportunities through alternative roles to the traditional structure. Perhaps Imogen demonstrates a thorough understanding of the transition process and could work across the primaries within the trust; or alternatively, she could be set to develop a project that drives school performance such as enrichment, or parent/school relationships. The recognition of your enthusiasm to progress, tempered with a mindful approach to workload, is almost as important as the number on the payslip at the end of the month. It's knowing that someone has recognised your worth and shows a genuine interest in developing the individual. It also opens up the opportunity to discuss that person's individual plans for the future far more explicitly. What direction would they like to take? What support do they need to get there? We can then start opening up dialogue between leadership and their staff away from the cold documentation of appraisals, and begin to look at people in a more human way, instead of simply assuming that we are all on a teacher-to-head track, with very little traction for taking the route off the beaten path. Creating opportunities for staff as a response to their

---

29. NFER: Engaging Teachers: NFER Analysis of Teacher Retention, Sarah Lynch, Jack Worth, Karen Wespieser, Susan Bamford, 09 September 2016 accessed at www.bit. ly/2FOtHQ2

strengths and potential is really effective management, but also keeps good people in schools.

The induction for trainee teachers in schools is in serious need of further evaluation and refinement; we use the word 'mentor', but is this what trainees need in the early stages of their career? It is useful to note that developing as a teacher relies heavily upon our own self-realisation and understanding of how to apply the expertise of teaching; but this process – mentoring – encourages trainees to eagerly look for someone to just tell them how to do it. Instead, perhaps we need to reform the mentoring programme as a coaching process, and start to have reflective conversations with teachers to help them to contextualise teaching for themselves, understand the structure of teaching and make a start – this is a long-term evolution, after all – to consider their own place within that (the chapter called 'A note on scoping out schools' starts to unpack this a little further). How are schools supporting those teachers coming into the profession, and how has this helped us to keep them engaged with the idea of staying?

I asked teachers how schools supported them most effectively in the early years of their teaching career:

66 John Sutton, Essa Academy, Greater Manchester: I've received targeted support on how to assess students and give feedback to them. Well-articulated and concise marking advice helped me manage my workload effectively and ensure students make progress. This allowed me to concentrate extra effort into cementing strong relationships with my classes and helped me get to know the young people I am responsible for.

66 Laura Bacon, Danemill Primary, Leicestershire: I was warmly welcomed by all staff, which was a lovely friendly start, instantly making me feel a part of the Danemill family. Continued professional development was prioritised. Most importantly, there were kind words of encouragement, a sense of trust and the understanding that if I ever needed help, I just needed to ask. I couldn't have asked for a better start!

66 Kristian Roebuck, Toot Hill School, Nottinghamshire: I'm a career changer.

Prior to teaching I was a project and business manager in the world of rail construction. My school has been super supportive this year in a number of ways. I was given the opportunity to teach physics alongside maths – an arrangement which has allowed me to earn a little extra money in my NQT year. I have been given my own classroom where all of my lessons are timetabled – it's a huge relief to have a base to teach from. Finally, my school offer great teaching and learning support. I have NQT training on a weekly basis and a subject mentor to help guide me through the year. I have also been allotted a weekly slot with the head of science and director of maths to help fast track my lesson planning and delivery in a busy first year – this has been invaluable.

Where are we educating our early career teachers about the profession itself? Do they know enough about the school system that they can make informed choices about their career path? If schools can start to consider how they equip teachers in these first few years with a comprehensive guide to the system itself, then perhaps they could spend that initial stretch of their first five years really getting a solid grasp of where they fit within this profession, and how it can accommodate what they want or what they set out to achieve.

The other valuable commodity we can offer early career teachers like Imogen is time. Where directed time is used like the treat box we keep in the kitchen cupboard, if schools stop to consider the impact that giving NQTs a further reduction to timetables would have, teachers starting their careers could spend the necessary time honing their craft, watching others teach with a specific focus (can I recommend questioning and modelling as ideal starting points – it was a very long time into my training before I saw well-exemplified modelling in action!) and taking that back to emulate in their own style within the classroom.

- Provide opportunities for ownership and challenge.
- Demonstrate a stable provision of support for early career teachers.
- Give focused, specific use of time to hone and refine new skills.

Stephen

Stephen has handed in his notice to leave teaching at the end of the year. He hasn't felt valued as a member of staff over the last year especially; but more than that, he doesn't feel as though teaching excites him anymore. With a degree in classics and currently completing a master's in philosophy, Stephen feels as though he has spread himself too thinly for the last year and wants to do more of what makes him happy. He did approach the head at the start of his master's degree to discuss possibly compressing his hours or reducing them so that he had time to complete the course, but his request was refused as flexible working 'is only really for parents' and 'the business needs mean we simply cannot accommodate', which Stephen interpreted as referring to the fact that sickness figures were high across the department and staff were needed for cover requirements. He feels penalised by the action of other staff and feels guilty for admitting it to himself. When Stephen chose to leave teaching altogether (as a consequence of feeling overworked and exploited for being the one member of staff that doesn't take sickness regularly), the senior leadership team didn't ask to see him to discuss his reasons for leaving or possibly even explore avenues with him in an attempt to get him to stay. He feels utterly undervalued.

Stephen has come to resent signing up for the master's in the first place, as the work he has produced for his thesis has been rushed as a result of some pretty hefty sleep deprivation. Reducing his hours would not have caused a significant drop in salary, and it would have made such a difference to Stephan's quality of living. His disappointment means that he now refuses to go over and above when asked to contribute towards work across the department, and he is usually seen rushing for the door as soon as the bell goes, or tapping the table at 4.32 p.m. as department meetings come to a close.

Stephen is an example of what happens when people feel that humanity is a little lost along the way in schools. I can guarantee to you that as a teacher, you know someone (maybe it's you yourself) that has had a similar experience within a school, where policy has formed conversations for limitations, instead of guidance for senior staff to use as a general benchmark. It becomes a discussion of what cannot be done, as opposed to how it might be, and this is where retention becomes one of our most underused and yet most powerful tools within teaching. What is being done to ensure that those that wish to are able to pursue interests that fulfil them as individuals so that they can operate as more productive individuals in the workplace? But also, what steps are being taken to gain an insight into why people are going to leave?

Learning from leavers

In some circumstances, the relationship between members of staff and their immediate line managers may have broken down to be in a position to discuss reasons for leaving in an open, honest forum, or middle leaders such as Lois may feel that they don't have the freedom within their role to make commitments to staff to accommodate their requests. Sometimes, the school is just simply not the right fit for the teacher. And now with retention being a key feature of Ofsted's work around recruitment, how can we gain a true insight into why teachers leave schools, as opposed to education as a whole?

The Department for Education's recent outline for recruitment and retention provides a clear set of actions for how to retain teachers within teaching through workload reduction, and furthermore how to attract the right people suited to teaching in the first place, with transparency and availability of information to Teach First and ITT applicants. However, I feel it falls short of identifying the reasons behind low levels of retention in particular schools or particular areas. The strategy document quite rightly states that 'teachers typically enter the profession with energy and a strong sense of collective purpose',[30] and there is a great deal that schools can learn and work to improve on from listening to those staff that leave.

---

30. The Department of Education Teacher Recruitment and Retention strategy, 2019, accessed at www.bit.ly/38cWYjA

The exit interview is a standard measuring stick for HR departments as a way to gather key information that can be used to inform future retention. Of 2269 teachers asked, 62% stated that they had not been offered an exit interview when leaving their last teaching role, and 18% did not know what an exit interview was.[31] We know that evaluation is the cornerstone to improve schools, and so why would the simple act of listening to leavers not be an intrinsic part of that process? The responses to the poll would indicate that either information is being collated, but in a limited fashion, or leavers aren't being provided with an appropriate method to share feedback because they are concerned about the way that the data will be used. Individuals shared that they were worried that the reference provided to their new employer would be influenced by their feedback. In addition, many leavers reported that they in fact offered to participate and the offer was politely declined, whilst others stated they were sent an online survey or provided with a feedback form and the whole process felt very impersonal because apparently they weren't deserving of a face-to-face conversation.

The difficulty comes with the way in which we handle leavers in schools: perhaps the relationships between leavers and colleagues has broken down, or it is apparent why the teacher is leaving and further enquiry doesn't feel necessary. Nevertheless, the fact that it appears we are not interested in collecting this data is a massive oversight; doing so could be very helpful in improving our school settings. By evaluating the reasons that people are leaving, we can not only gain an insight into how to improve the climate or culture of a school, but also have that dialogue to provide a sense of closure to their time within a school.

Within financial management, exit interviews were part of policy process so that the business could analyse the reasons that people left and identify patterns within regions but also on a national level when rethinking recruitment strategy. To encourage change within schools, we already know that context is key and that the

31.   Twitter poll, accessed at www.bit.ly/38ah6mk

elements for success and improvement vary greatly according to this context. What will determine a strong rate of retention in one school will be entirely different to the next; it is too complex a matter to just say, 'Pay people more money' or 'Provide healthcare.' Implementing an exit strategy really helps schools to rethink not only the day-to-day aspects that impact upon staff, but also the more developmental, strategic aspects such as professional development policy, staff restructuring, or even how to utilise staff in accordance with both their needs and the needs of the school in future. Of course, some findings will be bespoke to that particular employee, but a well-worded exit interview with the right member of staff can be really positively informative for change.

A few ways to ensure that the exit interview can reap rewards:

- **A two-phase process:** give staff an opportunity to talk to a senior member of staff to ascertain the reason they want to leave, but also to establish any unresolved concerns that the member of staff may have. No one wants to feel as though they are leaving under a cloud, and we have to acknowledge that not all schools are a best fit for all people. This process should be accompanied with a confidential survey that staff can complete either when leaving or after they have left (due to the nature of teaching, it may be beneficial for this to be completed each academic year to avoid identification of staff in the process). The survey gives staff the opportunity to share experiences in a safe environment and also to provide an honest review that may not be possible through discussion alone.
- **Use it as an opportunity to review conditions for staff.** Consider reviewing the entire school induction process, at both departmental and whole-school level; as a leader, what might seem like a straightforward process may actually have a significant impact upon staff's ability to carry out their day-to-day work: one teacher shared, 'The school moved briefings to a day that I wasn't in work, along with a great deal of part-time

staff, and moved registration to just before the second period of the day. It made it really difficult to set up for the day or provide cover when you might only be ten minutes late as a result of a last-minute appointment and it was really stressful to manage as a result. My form group room was on the third floor at the other end of the building from my classroom, so I was always late to registration and then late again to period 2. I felt that I lost a connection with my form group because I just became that teacher that turned up late all the time.'

- **The interview with staff should also be a moment to thank staff for their contribution.** Feeling a sense of completion and resolution as you leave a workplace is really important as that employee begins a new chapter of their lives and it will make such an incredible difference when a teacher thinks back on their time at a school, even years later.

- **Consider the significance of confidentiality.** The person chosen to hold the meeting will determine the information gathered as a result; it must be stressed to staff that any feedback they do provide will be confidential. Wherever possible, I would recommend that this person not be a line manager of the individual, but possibly a governor of the school, where qualified and appropriate.

- **Optional and not compulsory:** several responders to the poll mentioned previously shared that they had asked for an exit interview without response, or would have welcomed one, had it been offered; but the decision should ultimately lie with the individual, as with any data collection.

Areas of comment for exit interviews could include:

- **The induction process;** the experience of training and continuing professional development, both the content and the timing of particular sessions

- **Conditions of employment, including the opportunity for flexible working, if applicable;** were conditions set out to encourage a good standard of physical and mental health?

- **Workload;** how were relevant policies such as feedback, assessment or administration supportive or detrimental to overall working conditions? Was meeting time used effectively in school and directed in a way that enabled staff to commit to development?
- **Staff benefits;** this may be in regard to staffroom provision, end-of-term food, provision for staff workings late in the evenings such as well-lit areas, food, drink, breaks, space.
- **Opportunities for staff career development, and professional development overall;** was it straightforward for staff to understand and see their potential within a school system? Were staff supported in appraisal discussions to consider a career map that was suited to them and their professional growth?
- **Relationships;** what were the employee's experiences of departmental dynamics, management or parent/student communications and how could this be adapted or refined?
- **Overall experience;** could the employee give a personal assessment of their time at the school, but particularly in relation to how the staff's work-related stress is minimised or could be combated?

If you do leave a school, you are entitled to request an exit interview to provide an insight into the school as a whole, and give your opinion as to what improvements could be made. This data will be powerful for schools in driving change, and also when carried out with the correct format, it will create a brilliant working relationship as that employee moves to the next stage in their career.

Heads of schools – the best heads – thrive because they understand that their primary role is to care for their staff – particularly during the times that staff are not caring for themselves as well as they should. When emails are sent asking staff to finish early after a late night, and yet monitors are still lit up in classrooms late into the evening; when senior staff circulate local events to aid wellbeing but staff insist on doing the work in their living rooms in front of the telly instead. These are the signals to us to do something differently with our most valuable resource in the building.

Emma Sheppard - mother to two wonderful children, lead practitioner in English and founder of The MTPT Project - discovered a way that maternity leave enabled her to transform her maternity leave from a career break into an opportunity for positive impact.

Here, she talks through how we can aim to create people-friendly schools for all teachers, the current barriers in place and what we can do to work to overcome them so that teaching becomes an enviable career, not an avoidable one.

What do you think are the key barriers to teachers achieving true work-life balance, particularly families?

This is a really complicated issue and, as of yet, can only be discussed in anecdotal terms. Instead of a main set of barriers, there appears to be a range of factors that create a perfect storm for teachers when they become parents, sometimes resulting in them leaving the profession altogether as their personal priorities take precedence.

Some of these barriers include but are not limited to the following:

- **School policies:** Sensible marking and feedback, behaviour and planning policies can make a huge difference to parents' work-life balance, and the simple existence of one policy that requires teachers to work hard, rather than smart, can make life unachievable for many. Teachers required to complete large volumes of marking in English, humanities or primary subjects, for example, can be faced with an impossible task when they simply cannot take this marking home because they have a different job to do after school caring for children. The same limitations apply to those who have other caring responsibilities – for elderly or sick relatives or friends and family who are emotionally dependent on them.

  Equally, unsupportive behaviour policies that create conflictual, time-consuming and emotionally draining working days force teachers to question why they are spending so much time being verbally (and sometimes physically!) abused by other people's children at the sacrifice of time spent with their own. Many parent teachers who find themselves too emotionally exhausted to be present with their children become disillusioned with the systems in which they are working. Of course, this doesn't just apply to parent teachers – any teacher routinely submitted to inefficient working practices will eventually burn out.

- **School culture**: Even where sensible policies are in place, the human touch necessary to create positive or toxic working cultures can be essential to support parent teachers' wellbeing. Schools, like any other workplace, are rife with discriminatory atmospheres, which target pregnant teachers and working mothers more than expectant or current fathers. Comments questioning teachers' professional commitment, diminishing their capabilities or limiting their careers can have a huge impact on teachers' ability to find perspective for their work-life balance: they work harder and longer hours to compensate, or prove a point, or feel guilty for being a 'bad parent' and a 'bad teacher' when lifestyle demands mean they can't meet the mounting external expectations from colleagues and their family.

- **Childcare logistics**: A more specific to the parent-teacher community is the wider issue of childcare logistics. There are a multitude of ways to organise childcare with some preferring to involve family members, work with childminders, nurseries, nannies or arrange childcare as parents using flexible working arrangements. Nurseries, childminders and wraparound care are incredibly expensive. It can be financially unviable for teachers to return to work following maternity leave, especially when they have a small age gap between children or are not the main breadwinner in the household. The most popular nursery hours are 8.00 a.m. to 6.00 p.m. Those that run from 7.00 a.m. to 7.00 p.m. do exist but are the exception rather than the rule. These timings simply do not match either the teaching day or an average baby or toddler routine (if such a thing exists!). There is also the fact that nurseries run all-year-round contracts, so teachers are paying for childcare during the school holidays. When children get to primary school, teachers are expected either to be both at their children's school gates and welcoming/dismissing their own students at exactly the same time of day, or to invest in wraparound childcare. This could come in the form of highly competitive breakfast club places, or by continuing to pay for a nanny or childminder to do the drop-off and pick-up.

Some teachers benefit from flexible working arrangements or family support that enable them to do this; but for some, the transition to primary school can present even more challenging logistical barriers than early childcare. As teachers, we know how important it is for parents to communicate with, understand and support their children's school, and yet many teachers can only physically meet their own children's teachers at parents' evenings – as long as they don't fall on the same date as evening commitments at their workplace.

- **Lack of flexible working opportunities:** Discussion around flexible working is gaining much traction and is endorsed by the DfE (and any sane organisation working within the education sector). There are schools that are working fantastically well with their staff to create sustainable, flexible cultures that benefit all staff, not just parents.

  Flexible working still seems to be the domain of mothers – an outdated and prejudiced perception that is as limiting for women as it is for men, not to mention exclusive of non-parents and those with other interests and commitments in life outside their working hours. If schools are unwilling to budge on flexible working requests, then they risk losing experienced staff by driving them into the ground (when an open dialogue could reveal that all that is required is an additional hour in the morning, or an evaluation of workload-related policies, or a job-sharing arrangement that benefits whole-school retention and succession planning).

- **Individual mindsets:** By far the trickiest barriers to teachers with families are individual mindsets. Despite the points mentioned above, there are teachers across the UK who seem to be achieving inspirational and incredible things in all areas of their lives. They are simultaneously great practitioners, leaders, parents and spouses, and this is often entirely down to their own internal dialogue and self-empowerment rather than judgement.

  These teachers roll their eyes at the rhetoric of 'guilty working mother' or 'emasculated part-time father' so prevalent in society and the media.

They focus on – and delight in – a career that allows them to nurture others; act as a role model of education and learning for their own children; transfer skills between home and school for everyone's benefit; retain an individual professional identity as well as the innate emotional purpose of parenthood; and benefit from 13 weeks' paid holiday a year whilst 'making a difference' to colleagues and students.

These teachers often have significant support systems, either through partners, family and communities, or by pragmatically outsourcing things like childcare, housework and accessing professional coaching or mental health support services. Whilst none of these teachers would argue that parenting and teaching is easy, they tend to approach the barriers mentioned as exciting logistical puzzles to be solved.

Is it as straightforward as workload? From your research and experience, are other agencies at play here?

Even with the best workload-reducing policies in the world, teaching is an open-ended task with a bottomless to-do list. As well as concrete strategies like flexible working arrangements and childcare better tailored to teachers' routines, teachers need to be trained from the get-go to work sustainably and around other hobbies, personal relationships and outside interests. Cultures and narratives need to shift from treating teaching as an all-encompassing 'hard' job, to treating it as a joyful career full of variety and flexibility. Teachers need to be given the very clear message that there is a stopping point, and that they are in control of this stopping point – whether this means leaving at 3.00 p.m. to do the school pick-up and making up the working hours after the children are in bed, or completing a standard 8.00 a.m. to 4.30 p.m. day with no evening or weekend work. Coaching, support and a shared narrative are needed to normalise a reasonable way of working as the right way of working.

As a school leader, what could be prioritised to ensure that staff feel that they have a realistic chance of maintaining a balance between work and life outside of school?

Policies on marking, planning and behaviour that are effectively supported and implemented

Open and explicit dialogue around the desire to reduce workload and be 'life friendly'

- Reducing obligatory evening commitments and completely eliminating any expectation to teach revision lessons on weekends or in the holidays
- Modelling from the top by openly demonstrating how they balance leadership and personal lives without suggesting that they are in some way superhuman

Could you draw upon some practical examples?

When I returned from my second maternity leave, I began using a visualiser for my year 11 lessons in particular. Not only did this benefit my group – who needed explicit, direct instruction and crystal-clear modelling – but it also cut down a significant amount of my planning. We plan as a department, but it can sometimes be more difficult and time-consuming to follow someone else's PowerPoint than to simply achieve the given outcome for the lesson or explore a text or an extract or teach strategies and skills for a writing task. I would simply turn up to the lesson with little prior planning, other than the extract, and the final exam-style question or task. A mixture of effective questioning and knowing the group really well meant that this is all I needed to secure great progress for them. My head of department observed this on a learning walk, and instead of remonstrating me for not adhering to agreed school and departmental planning and delivery policies, she asked me to talk her through my thinking – and then ordered visualisers for anyone else in the department who needed them!

In the latter stages of my second pregnancy, I was emotionally and physically exhausted working full time and running after an 18-month-old. It took breaking down on more than one occasion at my desk for me to open up to my line manager and safeguarding lead and explain that I was struggling and accessing CBT to manage perinatal depression and anxiety. Even sharing this with them was a huge relief, and I used my own support system to identify practical strategies that the school could use to help. I asked to come in late two mornings a week in the last six weeks of my pregnancy, which my leadership team agreed to. This flexibility made a huge difference to my wellbeing.

We use a zonal marking policy at school, which requires us to mark two extended pieces of work a half term in detail, boxing this piece of work out with a pink box. Whilst this is still fairly traditional in comparison to some schools who have done away with written feedback altogether, it is a huge step from the 'red pen on every page' policy that crippled me during my first pregnancy and would have been completely unachievable as a new parent. I'm part of the teaching and learning team, and the assistant principal in charge of T&L and principal are open to evolutions to make our practices even better. They share best practice at marking nights, carve out time within our directed time specifically for marking, and have reduced the number of marking cycles needed at key stage 3 during year 11 and year 10 mocks. We've now even moved to two data drops rather than three, and so will have reduced our marking load across years 7–10 for the next academic year. As an English teacher, still on a high timetable, this makes a significant difference to my workload, and therefore the hours I need to be physically present in school.

I lead on the school's ITT provision, a role that has grown year on year over the five years that I have held it. Observing trainees, managing mentors, planning and leading CPD sessions, attending obligatory School meetings and general reporting and administration – it all takes up a significant amount of time. Whilst my timetable is equivalent to a head of department, I still teach a lot! To make up for this, I have been paired with a School Direct trainee for the last three years who takes on an increasing number of my teaching hours. My skills as a mentor and experienced practitioner are put to better use supporting a new teacher to take full responsibility for year 7 from September (and sharing my key stage 4 marking load) than teaching that year 7 group myself. My energy and expertise are saved for key stage 4, coaching, mentoring and developing other members of staff across the school, rather than monopolised by constantly being at the chalk face, and the logic of this is really rewarding. The promotion of other staff members into 'trainee' lead practitioner roles, and the upskilling of heads of departments to develop their observation and feedback skills also means that less of my time is spent observing individual trainees, and more time is spent leading a group of mentors, middle leaders and new lead practitioners, developing the necessary skills to effectively support trainees.

In your opinion, what is the blue sky vision to schools being family, or person friendly?

This is a massive question, Kat! Currently unpublished research demonstrates that there are, thankfully, more schools getting it right and providing life-friendly conditions to work in than not. The reality is therefore comforting: the issue is that teachers don't know how to find those family-friendly schools and actually, when you are interviewing, you don't always know if a school fits your values or is a family-friendly place to work.

The MTPT Project is currently exploring ways to recognise the fantastic practice that makes teaching such a family-friendly career and how particular schools have made positive shifts in cultures so that their schools are great places to work. This will empower parents to make effective choices when seeking new roles, take more autonomy over their career paths or make informed decisions when they are choosing somewhere to work. We want to provide working examples to other schools (who may not be working with such family-friendly practices) of the fact that small changes can make big differences: small attitudinal, logistical and practical improvements can increase their popularity, improve their reputation and consequently, make it easier for them to hire and retain good staff. This is a rigorous standard to work towards, because declaring that your school is family friendly needs to be an authentic statement; in the same vein, schools could also use this approach to identify key areas of their development. Actions might be making parental leave options more explicit to staff, part-time options for training opportunities, or providing a working party for those teachers. Ultimately, family-friendly schools should be about teachers who happen to be parents having good experiences in schools.

REFLECT

- What features of your current day-to-day are there to support you as an individual? Take this week to speak to staff at your school: how does the school take steps to support staff to find a balance between life and work?
- What would you like to incorporate into your working week that you currently struggle to manage? This may be a twice-weekly run, creative writing, playing on a football team, meeting friends, or even not taking work home so you can sit in front of the telly.
- What are the current barriers stopping you from doing so?
- Now, separate this list into reasons that are within your control, and those that you feel are outside your authority.
- Now, consider one reason that you allocated to 'outside my authority'. What conversations can you have that could actually shift this to an aspect of your day-to-day life that becomes something that you now regain control over?
- Look back at the list. Which reason feels the most achievable to change or eradicate? Why?
- This Reflect is a little different, because it aims to find discomfort. Can you work out the reason as to why that task feels the most difficult? What is the rationale behind that aspect of your workload or working day? It might be simple logistics of timetabling requirements, or the number of meetings that put you in rush hour for your journey home.

Crisis indicators

'In times of crisis, we must all decide again and again whom we love.'
— Frank O'Hara, *Meditations in an Emergency*

Holding hands and sitting it out
Through the immortality of all the seconds,
Until the blunting of time.
— U.A. Fanthorpe, 'The Unprofessionals'

Crisis indicators are the chimes before the alarm bells; the ways that you are being told by the universe that something needs to change or improve in order for you to continue. Your body or your brain is poking at your instinct to say that something isn't quite right, and you are better off listening to it.

Why have I written this section? Because people feel broken as a result of schools. People dread going to work every day, or tackling particular aspects of their role, or teaching classes they teach, or seeing people they work with. People speak of panic attacks, of crying in classrooms, of the frustrations and anxieties they endure every day. Their mental health is taking a relentless battering over and over again. Is it all down to the education system allowing this to happen or is it down to particular school leaders as a result of their own pressures? Whatever the reason or cause, it remains true that people are leaving, reluctantly, knowing they cannot do it anymore. I find that really saddening, but I also know how quickly that feeling can arise. When support mechanisms aren't in place, or we suffer from crises in our personal lives, the everyday becomes somewhat exigent. Furthermore, when you feel completely unsupported, and things start to unravel, it becomes more difficult to find a sense of order and regroup. I think we also ignore signals in the run-up to reaching crisis point – I know I have – and it's too tempting to 'power through' tiredness, or just spend another 30 minutes at the laptop at night. However, by doing so, we put ourselves in second spot to the jobs list.

At its least offensive, a mild crisis indicator could be struggling to operate as well as usual because you're tired, or, for whatever reason, you've worked more hours than usual. You may have had late meetings, several deadlines, or little non-contact time and it is that point in the term where things are pretty overwhelming – *are*, not *seem*. At its strongest, you will lose your temper easily, or feel what seems like an irrational sense of frustration at what are normally manageable tasks or feel tearful and not be able to pinpoint why. Crisis indicators are usually a product of accumulative issues that have yet to be dealt with. Equally, they can be matters we have dealt with, but they have consumed a substantial amount of energy. However, there are immediate things you can do to realign yourself, put yourself in a position of focus to understand what long-term change needs to take place. Without this, you can become a victim of a repeating pattern or cycle, resulting in being constantly overwhelmed or overloaded. To cope with crisis, we must understand it a little better.

Explored in the 1940s by Erich Lindemann as a result of his examination into how we cope with grief,[1] and later expanded on by his colleague Gerald Caplan,[2] crisis intervention looks at the acute measures that can be put in place immediately following a crisis to deal with the short-term impact and effectiveness. James and Gilliland define a crisis as 'a perception or experience of an event or

---

1.   Erich Lindemann, Symptomatology and Management of Acute Grief, *American Journal of Psychiatry* 1944 101:2, 141-148
2.   James, R.K. (2008) *Crisis Intervention Strategies*. Brooks/Cole: Belmont, CA.

situation as an intolerable difficulty that exceeds the person's current resources and coping mechanisms'.[3] Whilst being at crisis point can be daunting or sometimes frightening, it is at these stages of our lives that we are actually most receptive to the idea of change and solutions; we are willing to consider strategies to improve our mental health, because crisis has brought us to a point that it is unbearable.

> *There is no decision that we can make that doesn't come*
> *with some sort of balance or sacrifice.* – Simon Sinek

Here are some practical ways to deal with the immediate impact of a crisis, if you are at work or home and experience an overwhelming sense of anxiety:

RIGHT NOW

- **Count the room.** If you feel panicked, internally count things around the room that you are in. It helps to re-centre your thoughts and stops the racing sensation that you might be experiencing. You do not need to do this with your outside voice for it to work.
- **Make a list of three things to do.** The rest can wait. Three things that you need to address or deal with or that will help you feel more purposeful and reach a sense of resolution in your current context. If you make this list and they still seem unmanageable, then dissect them further – it will mean that the jobs are too big in their current form. 'Re-plan assessment model' is not a thing. 'Arrange a visit to a school whose assessment model looks promising and applicable to your own setting'? That's a thing. 'Ring the plumber'? That's a thing.
- **Do *not* compete with others.** Several teachers share their despair with me and often. They feel a complete lack of control because of repeated negative experiences as a result of poor working

---

3.   James, R. K., & Gilliland, B. E. *Crisis intervention strategies* (4th ed.). Belmont, CA, US: Thomson Brooks/Cole Publishing Co, 2001.

relationships. If you are caught in a cycle of cruelty or one-upmanship, walk away. If it is a battle of wills, smile and bow out.

- **Call a non-teaching friend.** Ask about their day. Listen. Eventually they will ask about yours. You may crumble. That's OK. Perhaps the fact you've just listened to them offload their own grumbles – their children, the fact that their partner didn't buy the right bin bags, the fact they've got to try to go to Tesco on the way home – may give you that breathing moment you need to re-centre before talking to them about how you're feeling. Ask them just to listen. It's tempting for them to interject and try to fix the problems with advice but you may be able to reflect to a greater extent just by talking until you run out of things to say.

- **Limit your interaction with social media.** It gives you a warped perspective of what is actually going on. We've been sold the internet as either a gift or a curse, but this is contingent on so many of your own contributing factors – and ultimately, it is both. On the internet, people are working 24 hours a day, at high capacity. Living their best life. This is not real. You're real.

- **Marginal gains work not just for getting stuff done, but for resetting your brain.** As some who functions at a high capacity for 96% of her day, I know I'm not alone here in the teaching community. To counter this, I switch off for 15 minutes when I can feel that I'm just not getting things done very efficiently due to tiredness, or the fact there is just too much going on. 15 minutes of music (without giving into the temptation of checking my phone at the same time), reading, playing the piano or playing with my kids means that I can be present, and it doesn't necessarily need to be for a long time to feel the impact of that.

- **Ring Education Support on 08000 562 561.** Talk about what you had for lunch if you're not sure where to start. Even if you haven't had any lunch yet. Do not be isolated in how you are feeling or fall into the trap of self-deprecating that the way you are feeling is something to view as a failure or fault.

- **Go on a phoneless walk.** 'Walking is the best medicine,' said Hippocrates over 2000 years ago, and I stand by that. A study of over 88,000 people found that a weekly walk can avoid earlier death.[4] It doesn't need to be for long (remember my 15-minute slot rule), but you need to be present. Consider the percentage of your day that you have been in real life as opposed to in your phone.
- **Don't get caught in the trap of thinking that it's all or nothing.** It's a whole pile of books, or failure. It's all of the to-do list, or failure. *The world's greatest achievers are two things: failures, repeatedly, and those who apply marginal gains to their everyday practice.* It took me a long while to realise that. As I sit in Starbucks on a 60-minute deadline before getting back to the boy circus of my home I can assure you that this whole book is built upon a collection of failure and marginal gains – trust me!
- **Put yourself in a place where you can take a moment.** Schools are intrusive places when you need a moment alone, and the publicity of having to keep things together can be a big ask at times. I once worked in a school with windows everywhere and it was impossible to find a quiet spot. Don't feel that you need to explain why; sometimes, the added pressure of being in front of a class is overwhelming enough when you are not feeling your best. Your car, the toilet, even the top end of the school field if that is what it takes.

LATER ON

- **Reflect on the moment of your crisis point.** What drove you to tears, or anger, or simply the feeling that you could not continue doing what you were doing? Using the self-reflection part at the end of this section will help you to dissect that moment so you can understand it a little better.
- **Be mindful of projection.** When I'm at a sticking point, it becomes all too easy to blame the entire world as opposed to looking at what I'm doing. Be gracious. Surround yourself with

---

4.   *The Guardian,* January 2015,

the right people, personally and professionally. Find an outlet that means you can maintain professional integrity; often, those at home will give you the compassion to understand that you are not what you say, and that it is just a reactionary response at the time. Colleagues that know you less well may not translate your curt email or making yourself unavailable in the same way. If you know you are projecting, use the realisation as a good excuse to distance yourself until you have more clarity.

- **Work to anticipate your high energy points, and recharge.** If you recognise that this comes up a certain point every year, ramp up both your time outside during your working day (remember, we're aiming for 15 minutes, no biggie), and go to bed at 8 p.m. one night a week. That, my friends, is an absolute game changer for your energy levels. When was the last time you slept like you were eight years old? One of the most important lessons I have learned in the last decade is how impossible it is to work at a sufficient level of production without sleep. Hormone regulation, appetite, brain function and memory are all governed by sleep and you simply cannot operate at the level you would like without a decent amount of sleep. If it comes to a decision between marking and planning or sleep, always pick sleep. Unmarked books won't impact upon you. Less sleep will always impact upon you.

- **Seek professional help.** If you are finding that your crisis points can't really be traced to a certain situation as a result of anything in particular and aren't improving, please do seek help. There is no shame in taking care of your mental health, and mine is of equal value to my physical health. I cannot be the teacher, partner or mother that I wish to be if I don't take the time to look after myself. Patrick Ottley-O'Connor, motivational speaker and headteacher, describes this with an analogy about oxygen masks, and it could not be truer. If we are to look after others, we must look after ourselves first of all. In addition, we need to our look after our mental health like we need to breathe. Those who attach stigma to mental health fluctuations in a different regard to physical health are not being entirely honest with people, or themselves.

- **There's no quick fix, but it's about making a start.** Above all, remember that crisis points are often cumulative and deep-rooted. They arise from a range of factors that you will need to address in order to avoid finding yourself in the centre of repeated incidents that have become more frequent in nature. There isn't a quick fix. Taking time to sleep, breathe, or be outdoors are all temporary remedies to what may be a much more complex situation. Hence, we need to stop talking about wellbeing and start addressing all of the things that we can control that ultimately contribute to our wellbeing.

Things that I use when it gets a bit brain-busy:

- **I sleep with a Spacemask.** An eye mask that insists that you get a decent night's sleep, these are wonderful. Since my first son was born, I have never slept well. I think it is that fear that you get as a parent – completely rational, of course – that you may lie in one day and wake to find a *Night Garden* mural on your kitchen wall whilst the curtains burn in a blaze of arson-originated fury. When I am tired, I am easily upset, easily angered and cannot make good judgement calls; I'm pretty useless. If, like me, you also are horrendous at detaching yourself from your phone, these are an absolute godsend. These really are incredible for making your brain switch off and giving you the physical and mental rest that is essential to finding some clarity.

- **I spend time with people that don't care about teaching.** It can become a struggle to stop and leave it alone, so I use time to detach myself from teaching. I make train sets with my children. I go on holiday with my friends or I'll visit my mum, who gets bored by teacher talk after approximately 4.8 seconds. Teaching can be so all-encompassing that we need this. Ironically, taking time away from teaching is necessary to being able to teach well.

- **I ask for help.** I have tried to leave teaching twice, and each time, I have been lucky enough to be surrounded by the most incredible support networks on the planet. And it's not just for major crisis points. A strong team of people will reach out and support you at any point when you need it. I call upon so many different people for advice and wisdom. From resources, to leadership, curriculum planning to baby woes; the different circles of support I have in the MTPT Project, the Litdrive team, the #teacher5aday community and all of the people that I have gotten to know in eight years all repeatedly and generously give their time, words or help whenever I need it. If you are feeling isolated, reach out to someone who may be able to help. Always.

A note on hidden illness

Suicide is the most common cause of death for men between 20 and 49 in England and Wales.[5] In 2015, 75% of all UK suicides were male, and male mental health is an aspect of managing staff that we have a moral obligation to consider, not just in schools, but as individuals. The NFER report stated that in addition to the analysis around female or early-career teachers leaving, experienced male teachers have a heightened risk of leaving.[6] Is this perhaps because of the status attached to progression in its traditional sense? Perhaps, and Jamie, a teacher of 13 years within the classroom, commented on this:

> " We meet up with teaching friends in the holidays, and I am the only one that hasn't yet secured a head of department role. It shouldn't matter, and I'm not sure if that is the route I want to take, but when I meet up with old school friends, I am the lowest wage earner by a long shot. A friend makes double what I make in a year in his career in banking. I feel a sense of inferiority in comparison, both financially and in terms of where my career is going.

---

5.   www.bit.ly/2Rg5J6S
6.   NFER: Engaging Teachers: NFER Analysis of Teacher Retention, Sarah Lynch, Jack Worth, Karen Wespieser, Susan Bamford 09 September 2016, accessible at www.bit.ly/2FOtHQ2

Amongst the contributing factors outlined by the CALM (Campaign against Living Miserably) masculinity audit is the fact that 'men are not only less likely than women to open up to friends about being depressed, they're also more likely to exhibit risk-taking behaviour and feel more frustrated at life's challenges'.[7] The male suicide rate in the UK is dropping,[8] but as I am sure we can unanimously agree, this is not a time to be complacent. What can schools do to ensure that there is provision for those that aren't as forthcoming to discuss their mental health in times of crisis? Do we provide outlets for all staff to hold their hands up without be interpreted as a sign of weakness, or lessening self-worth?

Many teachers are concerned with being able to explain employment gaps, or how it would be received if they were honest about their current or previous mental health history; they worry about whether this admittance would actually hold them back from progression, based upon the idea that they wouldn't be able to manage any additional pressures to their workload. A teacher in a school in the UK outlines that managing mental health in the workplace presents its own challenges, dependent upon the amount of information you want to share:

> 66 My main issue is that my medication greatly reduces my ability to empathise without it being a conscious process. This can make social interaction and managing children tricky at times as I can misjudge my responses. I also go through periods of feeling completely inhuman and I have to spend massive amounts of energy on interacting as 'normally' as possible with others. This causes me to burn out quickly. I'm pretty private about my struggles with the medication's side effects for two reasons: firstly, I don't want to have to explain why the side effects are better than being unmedicated; and secondly, I don't want people knowing that I struggle to care about other people at times.

7.   CALM Impact Audit 2017/2018, accessed at www.bit.ly/2TuyOg6
8.   Office for National Statistics. Suicides in the UK: 2017 registrations. www.bit.ly/2Tt5qHj. Updated 2018.

The Educational Support Partnership provide a structured programme for schools to utilise in line with local policy.

The Education Support Staff Wellbeing Programme gives effective response across a whole range of issues that can trigger stress, threaten mental wellbeing and lead to crisis. People reach out for help with managing anxiety, dealing with conflict, bereavement, family breakdown, financial issues, caring responsibilities and difficult situations at work and home. Over 60,000 education workers are signed up to the programme through their schools, colleges and organisations. Through the programme employees can access confidential, instant, wide-ranging help.

Education Support understand that teachers, like everyone, are not superhuman. There will be times in your life when your wellbeing is challenged, and you need support. You bring your whole self to work and so the support the programme speaks to an individual's personal and professional life. Asking for help in times of difficulty is a simple but effective solution. Education Support believes that everyone should have somewhere to call where they can speak to professionals in their field (be it for counselling support, legal information or financial support or for other topics).

The organisation helps callers see their strengths, find solutions to difficult situations, find a more positive outlook and seek further help where required. You do not have to be in crisis to use their service. Their counsellors often say they wish callers would seek help sooner before their situations become unbearable. You can take proactive action.

Many tell Education Support that using the service and speaking to them kept them in the profession; some even tell them that the service has literally been a lifesaver. Education Support find that the majority of those who engage with the counselling service see a marked improvement in wellbeing scores (as measured by the outcome rating scale) from the start of counselling to completion.

By investing in the programme, schools demonstrate to their staff that they care about their wellbeing.

Education Support urge you to take notice, pause and reflect on your own wellbeing and that of your colleagues.

We have to understand that whilst there is a stigma in place, we must rely upon open dialogue and an understanding that all illness is illness. There is also the requirement for people to be able to have full control and privacy of an entity that may be privately very difficult for them, and that they have the freedom to share to whatever extent they choose on their terms. What is key is that support mechanisms are in place so that the individual feels that they can disclose or reach out for support, should they choose to do so; but in addition, intervention and help is provided in an entirely non-judgemental way.

Some great resources for keeping your mental health tip top:

- www.bit.ly/2thXY7j – The NHS is a great starting point to establish or reassure any nagging feelings that you have about moods that repeatedly present themselves or won't shift.
- www.bit.ly/2NBtnsd – The Education Support Partnership have trained counsellors on hand, 24/7.
- www.headspace.com – Headspace is a wonderful app that enables you to practice mindfulness through either a period of relaxation, or more structured courses of meditation. Andy Puddicombe, the co-founder of Headspace, has a Ted Talk that outlines the value of just ten minutes with the app. Whilst I have a sporadic relationship with mindfulness, I find that Andy's voice is just wonderful for getting me to sleep. Alternatively, www.calm.com is another fantastic tool and built as a long-term habit, or used for a particularly intense crisis point. The programmes are really powerful for practising present moment thinking when external factors can become really quite daunting.

What if it's not me?

Sometimes, we spot the signs of crisis in others before we do ourselves, and it's harder to find the balance between concern and intrusion if it is clear that our colleague or friend is going through a difficult series of events, and riding out the tensions of such events, and we don't know how to help. Whilst this is not an exhaustive list, here are some ways to identify crisis indicators in others and some ideas of what may help.

What do I look for?

- **Disregard:** a lack of motivation can be something that gets overlooked or doesn't seem important. Everyday tasks that usually feel quite manageable become monumental and unimportant. This could present itself as a lack of being 'put together', but may occur through a lack of enthusiasm for events, topics that would usually raise an interest. To pinpoint it further, it is an indifference to most things.
- **Distancing:** if you haven't seen a colleague for a one-to-one chat, or you feel that they are isolating themselves from others, this can also be another sign that they may need support. If we struggle, it becomes more challenging to hide it from others – particularly others that know us well. Of course, that doesn't mean hunting someone down to demand a chat but it can be a useful indicator to be mindful of the distance and frequency of that distancing.
- **Defence:** if someone feels overwhelmed by their circumstances, workload or external pressures, they will be quick to feel threatened or confronted – even when the language of a discussion is not intended to be as such. In the same vein, the individual may swing between vocally expressing their productivity in a rather combative way, trying to ensure that no one suggests for a second that they wouldn't be able to cope. They will refuse help and interpret such offers as implications that they are not able to manage.

What can I do?

This is really entirely down to the context of the situation, how long the individual has shown indications that they are reaching trigger points and the cause of such trigger points. If you can, and you have that existing relationship with them, offer help in a nonconfrontational way. Some people just need their workload to lighten in order to be able to tackle other pressures. Don't isolate that person with your help: share useful resources with several people, them included, or highlight a particular method of working to them: it is slightly less critical to say 'A few staff have been marking in this way and it's helped me not feel as overloaded!' rather than 'You seem to be struggling, have you tried this?' If you have a middle or senior leader that you feel would be a supportive person for finding solutions (as opposed to associating crisis indicators as weaknesses), talk to them. It really does come down to how you gauge the situation: notice and make choices that give them the necessary space and time to move through whatever it is that they are trying to manage at that moment.

Leave this book in their pigeonhole. With chocolate. Always with chocolate.

REFLECT

Consider your trigger points: time of the day/week/year? Could you start to predict the pattern? How does this help you to understand the underlying cause of them and what you could do to anticipate them?

Let's take this one stage further – if you could predict your next crisis point, when do you think it will be? What will cause it? How do you feel in the run up – is there anything that you, or your surrounding personal or professional network, could put in place?

Let's consider your personal network. What do you reach out to them for? For example, if one of the things you reach out to them for is 'to talk problems over with them', do you do that effectively? Do you have people within this network with whom you have a positive experience of resolving challenges or obstacles that present themselves to you? Or do these conversations lack a resolution? Perhaps this network of people could be useful to you in a different way, if that is the case.

Now let's consider your professional network (and because teachers are awesome people, you may find that the two groups coincide). Who is your official point of support? Prepare a two-tier solution: a short-term fix that will alleviate the pressure, but a workable long-term solution that improves conditions on a more permanent basis. Sometimes, someone who is in a position of management may not know what it feels like to carry your workload, or when your stress points may occur. Here are some examples of how you might seek support in a two-tier approach:

You have urgent marking to complete for mock exams.
- **Now:** Ask for in-house cover for two key stage 3 lessons to complete urgent marking for mocks, which will make you feel more on track
- **Long term:** Request to change your break duty to another day, because it currently takes place on your only full teaching day, in addition to when you have a whole-school meeting in the morning and another meeting after school. You find the entire day incredibly stressful, and simply moving your break duty would enable you to have a little breathing room.

You have data entry deadlines to meet tomorrow, but your daughter is ill and you need to leave work as soon as possible.

- **Now:** Request an extension, explaining the situation and that you do not have the time allocation between now and the deadline to input the information required.

- **Long term:** You work Monday to Wednesday, and data announcements and reminders get communicated to staff on a Friday, which means you always feel like you are playing catch-up. If a data reminder could be mentioned in staff briefing earlier in the week, it would enable you to prepare the information by your final working day.

It may be that you don't need a plan for both 'now' and 'long term', but compiling possible solutions in advance will help to shape a resourceful discussion and will also help you to feel as though you are taking control. For example, I speak to a great deal of teachers who, having signed up for this career where we are lucky enough to be able to take holidays four times a year, haven't given themselves any sort of life break for a considerable amount of time. Remember, if you were in a non-teaching job and felt pretty run down, you would just book a day's holiday to recuperate. Our odd days off are replaced with the gift of a structured term/holiday system, and so it is vital that we use the holidays to realign and go back refreshed. I know, I know: it's easier said than done when deadlines come in from line managers on the final day of term or mock marking deadlines are set just after Easter holidays. Read the objective rebellion section next so we can start thinking about how to deal with that. Your holidays are your holidays.

Sometimes, I find that it isn't the task that is causing my stress or frustration, but my approach to dealing with things I know I will find difficult. For every task that you are putting off, there's a five-minute job that you will reach for instead because you either find it easier on your time constraints or find it easier on your skillset. Think about the tasks you avoid and what's making you avoid them.

What has the biggest stress impact upon your day-to-day life? Imagine the barriers are not an issue; what would improve this situation so that this does not have a detrimental effect moving forward? Write a wish list and share with a colleague or friend; how can you turn that list into something pragmatic to request from your line management?

What can you tolerate right now, what will you be able to tolerate once you feel in a better position, and what shouldn't you tolerate at all?

A manifesto for workload
The future of wellbeing

'Never doubt that a small group of thoughtful, committed, citizens can change the world. Indeed, it is the only thing that ever has.' – Margaret Mead

There is an undercurrent from sceptics that potential strategy around wellbeing and workload reduction is unrealistic, and that teaching is just teaching: this broken nature of the profession is simply a by-product of what it means to be a teacher. With the greatest of respect, I think that's ridiculous. Even if it were a valid claim, to continue to work people into the ground – to the point that they no longer recognise what it was that they set out to achieve – is the most outrageous way to keep teachers in schools. If we honestly think that it is acceptable to continue with such discrepancy across education as a whole, we are more than mistaken. Dismissing teacher dissatisfaction isn't merely irresponsible; it will ultimately determine the state of teaching in the future. Want to debate the rising mental health rate? Consider teachers. Want to look for a stable solution to the attainment gap that, as we stand, looks practically impossible to close in our lifetime?[1] Consider teachers. Want to examine any political premonitions you may have about the format and shape of education in the future? What we do now, at all levels, counts.

---

1. www.bit.ly/2R2OF3Z

We have a duty of care. We, the collective body, as an amalgamation of agencies: our regulators, the larger authoritative agencies and authoritative bodies, responsible for the poorly directed or poorly timed introduction of initiative and instruction; senior leaders, for driving change with 'the big O' as the underpinning whisper of such changes, muttering it at INSET as though they were not referring to trained professionals, but a Darth Vadar silhouette. ourselves, for carrying out practice that does not sit comfortably with our greater sense of purpose, or for saying yes when we mean no. We are all responsible for the current state of the profession as a consequence. The inescapable truth is that some schools are operating at a poor standard, or without enough qualified staff present to teach children. An even harder truth is that at some stage, an individual or group of people made poor decisions that led them to this current point. In consequence, we now find ourselves with several teachers that say they do not want to teach anymore, anywhere.

What would happen, then, if these leaders were so focused on driving change and providing a high standard for children that teachers got lost along the way? Have we mis-defined resilience as simply working too many hours? Our deep-rooted attachment to martyrdom means that some will look upon this book and shake their heads, content and almost in a love affair with the work, because the work makes their role measurable and gives a tangible quality to a role that is mostly about learning, something which we have historically struggled to measure (and continue to do so), which, I would suspect, is how we have ended up with some pretty outlandish policies in the first place. Some will read this book as something of an idealistic approach to workload reduction, and that with restricted budgets, challenging demographics and a confinement of time, the ideas are simply not feasible in our profession. Some will look over the strategy outlined in this book and think that it cannot apply to their school or to their staff because Ofsted's requirements place a particular infrastructure on our schools that is unavoidable. It is those people that I hope to speak to here, because more schools are getting it right, and more schools are open to making further improvements as we continue to evolve as an industry with longevity and a sustainable approach to our staff body.

Those groups of objectors are the minority, and that is comforting to know. This chapter is for them, and if you work within a school setting where you could only dream of such changes, please do take the opportunity to read through the following incredible practices implemented by school leaders throughout the country, photocopy the odd page and wave it like a flag of hope under the noses of your senior leaders.

Pivotal change is possible, but it isn't through talking about social clubs on a Friday, or staff speed dating sessions to make friends; it isn't through a kayaking INSET day or cutting a meeting short by ten minutes and letting the staff body know the extents of your generosity. There are schools getting it right, and their unapologetic and contagious approach to wellbeing through workload reduction is catching.

Far from the toxicity of school leadership, poor Ofsted experiences and overburdening process, these schools have developed and refined processes to ensure that the teacher is the most protected and regarded commodity in their school because they are quite simply more than a commodity. These schools view teachers as humans, of heart and head, turning the cogs of the school with purpose and perseverance. As a result, those schools are the ones that have staff singing from the rooftops. Those leaders are the ones that have staff cheering them on from the sidelines at Saturday conferences. Those schools have minimal retention concern: losing staff doesn't worry them because they have invested in the staff that they have, which means that staff are reluctant to leave. Those leaders have worked in schools with a poisonous air and know what it means to feel undervalued and demotivated; they have endured a disconnect between the work and the outcome and questioned the rationale behind policy without apparent reason. They've moved through school systems, usually with a determination to change things for the better; they seek to lead because they are filled with the same impetus that we all share as teachers – that common cause – but also because they have seen it done badly, and they find it concerning and want to do better.

It is in those leaders' schools that we will find leaders of the future, because those are the teachers that have been developed as experts, treated like human beings and trusted to have a voice of contemplation in moments of both small and great change. Those great leaders are the ones that recognise that a deep, thoughtful approach to maintaining teacher wellbeing has nothing to do with the one-day training course or how to write a great to-do list and everything to do with the removal of anything that obstructs the teacher purpose. These voices are the ones that we should look to when formulating a concrete plan in schools that will give admiration and regard to today's teachers, consequently refining the narrative for teachers of the future.

Who is doing it well?
Workload reduction

We are not at the mercy of others when we examine the issue of workload, but it is a collective process in which we must set the parameters of what is or is not achievable, in line with objective dialogue. It is not that teachers cannot cope; it is that as professional human beings, we need to permit ourselves the self-worth to draw a line at our own capacity for work. It is not unmanageable *for us*, but unmanageable *for anyone*. It is not that we choose not to work; it is that we choose to work to live – and without the option or ability to do both, we do ourselves an incredulous injustice.

I spoke with Jonny Uttley, CEO of The Education Alliance – a partnership of four secondaries, two primaries and a SCITT in Yorkshire – regarding his commitment to staff to ensure that there was absolutely no evidence of monitoring or over-scrutinising of the work that staff within the trust undertake.

Jonny worked with several colleagues across the trust to develop two key documents that outline the intentions of the school as a whole, and the leadership competencies and behaviours section gives all prospective and existing employees of the trust a concrete promise: this is our duty to you; this is how we will live our values so you know what to expect from us; this is what you can hold us to our responsibility to serve the staff of our schools.

❝ Over a period of 18 months, we worked with our union county representatives to develop a Workload Charter for staff across all our schools. The charter speaks for itself and is a live document that we review and seek to improve continually.

For me, the most significant part is the section we wrote on culture; an attempt to articulate how we want leaders to act and how we change our systems to reduce anxiety and stress in the organisation. After all, no amount of workload reduction will keep people in the profession if the culture in which they work is all about surveillance and low levels of professional trust.

By publishing this, we have committed ourselves as leaders to try to live up to the standards we have set, and this is further underpinned by our trust's ethical leadership qualities that all leaders are required to demonstrate.[2,3]

- -

My ideal? That all schools lay out their commitment to staff as a tangible way to share what it is that they intend to do to ensure that their teachers have the best possible starting point to carry out the work essential for children to succeed. Jonny's trust, Sam Strickland's Duston charter – these schools are combating any trace of a recruitment crisis by being proactive and unapologetic in communicating what it is that their schools do to value the work. Here's something to think about: if a teacher is looking to work in your town, county, region, what strategies have you implemented so that they can learn the narrative of your school? The days of perusing a school website, scavenging over the word choice of the principal's statement, or looking fruitlessly for clues in the school newsletter back catalogue should be long gone, and

2.   www.bit.ly/2R30s2f
3.   www.bit.ly/375cygO

replaced with a transparent guide to what a school is all about. In the same breath, if you aren't making this explicit to teachers, how can you be sure that a) you're getting the right people for your setting – people that are with you on the journey you have laid out before you as a school; and b) you won't just lose staff to the school down the road that takes the time to compile an intentioned document such as this?

Removing accountability

A positive uprising is necessary to change our schools from the ground up, but with visionary leaders like Jeremy Hannay, headteacher of Three Bridges Primary School in West London, passionate and motivated teaching staff will have the backing that they need to achieve this. We don't have a retention crisis: we have good people working in poorly designed schools. We don't need to strip schools of poor leaders: we must support those leaders to work in a more effective way, and to ultimately understand that leading through short-term fixes and plaster-sticking values just won't retain the people that can drive a school forward.

The disconnect between the ideals put forward in schools with the justification of Ofsted no longer washes with individuals, as Three Bridges's most recent report indicates.

Jeremy shares the key drivers behind his ethos, and hopes that others will share and take from his approach:

66 About four years ago, we really started to interrogate our values as a school. What we discovered was that our practices and our values were out of alignment. We believe in collaborative learning and development experiences for our children, but we tell our adults what to do. We believe in enquiry and mistake making as crucial to growth, but we had high-stakes observations and competitive structures for teachers. We believe in adventure but monitored compliance. So, we changed.

We invested heavily in collaborative research, working and development for our staff because we believe in allowing our teachers to flourish intellectually, socially and emotionally. As a school, we have regular learning and lesson study taking place in our own school or between partner schools. We lead research groups across schools and internally. We work collaboratively to support each other and bridge the gap in our wider community. When you're constantly refining practice, high-stakes observation becomes irrelevant.

We co-constructed our pedagogy and practice because we believe that consistency, quality and engagement come from ownership and study. Nothing is 'done to' our school. We read, trial, explore and attempt many things. We refine our programmes and understand that nothing is permanent. We collectively agree what best practice looks like and support each other in improving. When you collectively construct something, no one needs to monitor you to make sure you're doing it.

We embed trust because we believe trust is the cornerstone of personal and professional growth. There is no more 'proof' required. No marking for evidence of feedback; no planning pro formas for evidence of planning; no book scrutinies for evidence of work; no learning walks for evidence of compliance or consistency. We speak up when we're struggling and support when we're soaring. Nothing great has ever come from constraint.

We use professional capital as a metric because we believe that great schools and systems are aligned. We recruit people that are aligned with our values. They fit for us, but we also fit for them. We support and encourage further study; we facilitate professional learning communities and collaborative systems of working. We ensure that the professional teacher is developed and supported so they feel comfortable and confident making instructional decisions for their children and themselves.

The simple fact is that there is no pupil wellbeing without teacher wellbeing first. Having teachers that are happy, optimistic, positive, inspired, challenged and growing is crucial to leading an incredible school. This means reducing power relationships and creating more lateral, collaborative relationships between school leaders and teachers so they may do the same with our children. The conditions for our teachers must be nutrient rich – enriching their professional lives so they may enrich the lives of our children. We have no hope of creating the kind of schools we want if our adults are not happy collaborators.

Staff care

To truly dedicate thought and deliberate intention into developing a better standard of care for staff, we must eradicate accountability as a method of management, and build the architecture essential to voice and autonomy that results in professional trust. Only then can we turn our attention to looking after staff in a sincere and significant way that has meaning for teachers. If we are able to remove barriers to reduction of work, senior leaders can then acknowledge their duty of care to the people that work within their schools. At times, in our bid to carry out the work and feel a personal sense of pride in what we do, we can act in the throes of martyrdom, as we take on more than is physically possible or manageable. Subsequently, we need others who have the privilege to be able to take a strategic overview of staff's mental health. At times, we need others to intervene our workload where we have not intervened for our our mental wellbeing.

- -

Helen Raiston, head of the Rise School, Feltham, shares her whole-school approach to wellbeing in a formation of foundations, utilising this layered approach to ensure that the holistic aspects of teacher wellbeing are coupled with concrete, tangible strategies to ensure staff are considered and cared for:

The Rise School in Feltham, West London is a small SEND school for pupils aged between 4 and 18 with an EHCP with a primary diagnosis of autism. We have about 75 staff and we place significant leadership focus on crafting The Rise as a great place to work. Our fantastic middle leader Manaz Pimple wrote our wellbeing vision: 'The Rise School will be a school where all members of its community feel valued and flourish.' Our list of wellbeing initiatives includes:

- Discussing mental health, sharing the principles of positive psychology
- Staff-led cooking classes
- Secret buddy scheme
- Guided relaxation
- Knitting clubs
- Perkbox employee reward scheme
- A well-equipped gym

I'm very aware that the above could seem tokenistic; however, our wellbeing 'layer' is sincere and authentic because it sits on top of fundamental consideration about workload and culture. If we were just doing schemes like secret buddy in isolation, then it becomes vacuous and meaningless.

I asked the staff during an INSET to complete this sentence: 'At The Rise, the way we do things around here involves....' The answers were humbling and included, 'embracing imperfections' and 'lifting each other up'. How, as leaders, have we established this culture?

- We are approachable and 'open door' – staff can (and do!) come and speak to us about all sorts!
- We role-model gratitude, including the shout-outs in briefing, but beyond that: thank-you cards, notes, post-its, mini treats etc.
- We consult with staff authentically – we don't ask if a decision has already been made, but often invite opinions and ideas (e.g. do we want to move to a model of twilight INSETs?).
- We invest significantly in CPD and have a 'say yes' approach to it: a well-stocked staff library, sourcing of relevant online courses, self-directed CPD menus, high-quality external speakers and so on.
- We actively promote a culture of feedback, including providing structured and frequent opportunities to give it to one another. We revisit this idea of improvement and challenging existing systems on a termly basis in our teams.
- Our default PPA allocation is 17% (not the statutory 10%), which equates to 5/30 lessons (rather than 3/30) and is often greater than that.
- We moved from 12 data drops (beginning and end of each half-term) to 3 in a year (end of each term).
- We have reduced the amount of narrative/commentary expected in reports; we give out reports on parents' evenings to encourage the conversations to happen that way.
- We evaluate and stop certain activities if they impact workload
- Our whole-school calendar with every twilight, parents' evening, data drop and ISP deadline is shared a year in advance, allowing staff to anticipate work demands ahead.

My role is to consider these layers: to keep my eye firmly on the culture of our school and the workload we ask of staff, and also to provide and inform staff about a series of proactive ways to manage their mental wellness.

Now the true task: to set about finding these schools. Well, we can't, in the sense that we must forge them for ourselves where we can. To make a fundamental improvement to the landscape of the profession, we have a duty to ourselves – and an even more vital duty to the teachers of the future – to ameliorate standards for everyone, if we are to stand any chance of rewriting the narrative for early-career teachers. Instead of being warned off by horror stories and hearsay of the profession, those that take the time to consider teaching and dare to peek into the classrooms of our schools will be inspired by what they see, hear and read.

The key is remaining true to our values as teachers, says Hannah Wilson, head of secondary school teacher training at the University of Buckingham Faculty of Education, and keeping good teachers in the profession is viable, if we work to educate them at different levels of their career:

How do you think the landscape has changed for teachers since you entered the profession?

I can't remember when I started using the word 'wellbeing' when talking about teaching. It wasn't a word that was on my radar when I did my PGCE 18 years ago. And it's only really become a buzzword in the last four or five years.

Going back to the start of my career, in my NQT year, I worked for a school where I would go home early on a Thursday because I didn't teach Thursday afternoons; I was trusted to go home to do my marking. We all went to the pub for lunch on a Friday and I don't know who ran the school or who looked after the children! I could pop to the shop in a free lesson and there was just trust that we were professionals: we'd come and do our jobs, but we were allowed to do the life bit around it. I have not worked in a school since where you have either the time or the permission to get out of the building during the working day.

Skipping forward to my fifth year of teaching, I can remember every day sitting down with a cup of tea in a free period with my work friend. We all worked super hard and would put in the hours but we still had time to sit and have lunch and a cup of tea together every day – just for 20 minutes, nourishing the soul, making human connections. But that all got squeezed out in the six years that I was there. Since then, in the rest of my career, I honest to God cannot remember when I have sat down and had a cup of tea and a chat that wasn't about work or a meeting.

Since then, as a head, I was really conscious that I wanted to try and get some of that human connectivity through – just put some humanity back into school. Things like free lunches for staff were a no-brainer to me. I spent six years as a senior leader skipping lunch every day, or being in the car at 5.30 p.m. and being so hungry because I had not eaten since breakfast at 6 a.m. I think that's the bit that really worries me about the system: the frenetic nature of schools, the urgency of everything that needs to be done and be done now, the constant demands and impact of being pulled in all directions.

We talk a lot about being child centred; we don't talk about being people centred. And when I say 'people', I mean every single person working in that school community has a universal entitlement to be well and to be happy and to fulfil their potential. Even in school where we say, 'We look after our staff; our staff look after our children', we still fall short of it, even with that constant focus. I just feel like the system has changed so much, something's got to give, and at the moment it's the teachers that are giving, which is really quite saddening.

Do you think reclaiming that is possible, then? What are the key barriers that are keeping us from being people centred?
That's a really good question. I think half of it is the high stakes, the accountability and the constant inspections. However, I don't think it is always the external pressures, but how they manifest themselves and how the governing body, the MAT leaders and the SLT interpret that.

There have been additional pressures like increasing class sizes, reduction in budget, staffing structures becoming much more skeletal. I've worked in lots of schools where redundancies or staff turnover mean you're not filling teaching roles; many people are teaching out of their specialist subject.

You've got a lot of schools that are functioning on early-career teachers – and while I've met some brilliant NQT teachers in my time, I've seen schools where literally half the staff are in the first five years of their career, because the schools are trying to cut costs and save money. And yes, you might have young, aspirant professionals with high energy, but you're missing the essential wisdom and experience in the building.

I feel like there are many layers to unpick but people are voting with their feet. I advise and help so many people with career moves and I always try to keep them within the profession and say to them, 'Don't ever feel trapped in a job or department or school where you're not happy. There are more jobs in teaching than there are teachers right now, so don't be a martyr and stay; go and find a school with the right culture for you where your values are aligned.' I feel like sometimes we get emotionally blackmailed to stay in these jobs for the children. There are children in every single town in this country who need us and deserve a great teacher. Don't get pressured into just working in this one school because within six weeks of being at another school, you will be as established and have as good relationships with the next group of children too.

Thinking about taking control at a teacher level, one thing that crops up in the conversations that I have with teachers is that they don't feel in control and they feel that their options are limited. Is that a realistic, pragmatic solution? To just vote with your feet? Is voting with our feet going to help what is essentially a systemic problem?
There are several parts to this. There's finding voice and agency within your school, and being empowered enough to say, 'No, this isn't right for me; I'm going to find a different job,' as opposed to leaving the system which we know. We are haemorrhaging teachers. People are leaving the system. We're trying to make sure that they don't leave the system, and instead they leave that school and find a different school because not all schools are the same.

When it comes to career advice in general, I do think it's lacking for educators. What advice are we giving our beginner teachers, NQTs and RQTs about their career trajectories? I know I felt like a pawn on someone else's chess set at the start of my career and I got promoted every year for 16 years. I was so flattered to be recognised and promoted, but did I actually stop and think: is that the right role for me? Is that what I want? I do think sometimes we get taken down the wrong path on our journey and we need to stop and be true to ourselves.

With regards to empowerment in a school, I just feel like staff voice is really important and we need to make sure that staff voice isn't SLT voice – that we have that conduit to the SLT or the governing body. Sometimes we need to take stock of what we are doing: what's going well and what we like and how can we get through a neutral compromise. I think a lot of schools – particularly academies – are quite scared of teacher voice because of union activity, or rumours about losing staffrooms to break up the staff body. There was a great article recently about the need to bring staffrooms back to schools because the sense of community and the sense of belonging – our teacher identity – has gone. I do think having lots of separate team offices is great, but you can be quite dislocated from the rest of the school.

Externally, I think we (as a system) need to do a better job of just helping people unpick and navigate the landscape. I talk to trainees about being contextually literate: do you actually know the difference between a free school and an academy? Do you know what an SLE is versus an LLE or an ALE? There are so many acronyms and initialisms now and we recruit so many teachers from overseas. How do they know the difference between working for a free school academy and a maintained school?

I have a friend who is a banker and he was given career advice every year about where he was in his career and what his next steps were. He had a career coach that was completely objective to the business that was looking after him. Education in the UK has become so nepotistic: it's what is right for that one school and not what's right for the system. I have heard horror stories where headteachers are giving bad references or ringing up heads to say, 'Please don't interview my head of English; I haven't got anyone else who can be Head of English. Please, do me a favour as a fellow head,' and people blocking moves and promotions. Not all teachers are aware of how many deals are being done behind the scenes before we even get to interview. It isn't transparent and isn't fair to the rest of the staff body when that's done behind closed doors. I've knew a brilliant head of MFL who was ready for assistant head, and interviews kept coming through – but every time she got an interview, she was blocked and not allowed to go.

How can we advise leadership teams to value their staff?

Recruit on values: in school, we wanted teachers who were aligned with the vision and values of the school and we had a long list of people waiting to apply for jobs and looking to work for us because we were really transparent. We also didn't try to recruit with rose-tinted glasses or try to pretend that the school was perfect and flawless. I would have 120 people having coffee in our school on a Saturday morning, and I would say, 'These are the ten things that our school is not, and these are the reasons why you wouldn't want to work here; but these are all the reasons why you would want to work here and why our school is fabulous.' We would probably convert 120 into about 55 applications. By meeting the SLT and hearing about the school vision of values and hearing about the warts and all, the people who applied then knew why they were applying and had clarity about why they wanted to be a teacher – but a teacher in our school. I think that's really powerful.

We need to make sure that we're pragmatic or we don't make promises we can't meet, because I've gone to interviews where I've been promised the world which hasn't been the reality, and that straightaway creates disillusionment or disenfranchisement. I think the more transparent and honest we are, the better. That's really important.

Lastly, it's culture and ethos. When I'm running career workshops, I get them to think about their current job. I make a list of all your values and then look at your school website and make a list of all their values and tick off the ones you have in common, because the school you joined ten years ago might not be the school you're in now, and that might be why you're feeling dislocated. When you go to apply for your next job, do the same thing. If after doing that due diligence, that research on that job, you're not seeing yourself and your values reflected, you're not going to be happy, no matter what they tell you.

People take jobs for pay rises and commissions or because they're close to where they live or they're close to where their partner lives. I think it's rare that we really drill down to, 'Is this school the right fit for me? Am I the right fit for them?' I just think that we need to be really honest with ourselves about who we are, what we need, where we want to be and not wedge ourselves as square pegs into round holes.

What about the teachers that feel as though they don't have free choice of movement?

What about the teachers that are being systematically bullied, who have to follow policy, who can't muster up objective rebellion because the school culture just doesn't allow it; the ones who attend more meetings that they get to sit and eat hot dinners? The educated academics who repeatedly endure such treatment and bastardisation of their role as educators that all of their academic accomplishments just get distilled down to nothing more than tick-box tasks and the delivery of a substandard curriculum? Can we honestly say that we have paid homage to them over the last 300 pages?

They are the ones I write to the most because I know what it means to be one of those teachers, and I know how vital it is to feel like there is an allegiance between what you believe and what you have the freedom to practice every day. I know what it means to not be thanked for hard work, and to feel as though your hard work isn't sufficient, without support or nurture. I do believe that as a collective agency, we have the privilege and volume of teacher voice that will make possible what feels so incredibly impossible. So that instead of saying yes, we say why; or instead of opening the laptop at 10 p.m., we sleep; or instead of letting the ping of an email on a phone govern our anxiety, we remove that email app and replace it with Headspace, because that's a better use of five minutes. Because those people are the people that will stay in the right schools for them, and then go on to lead schools like absolute heroes by breaking these horrific, perpetual cycles created in toxic schools.

I want to propose my manifesto for you, because you are the ones that will cause the micro changes necessary to keep teachers in the building. If we are to place teacher care as the number one priority for education, so that teachers are in a position to make student care their number one priority, we need to close the chapter on burdensome workload, misdirected treatment of teachers, and afterthoughts of surface-level wellbeing initiatives. I want to encourage you to place your physical and mental health at the forefront of your workload, and consider for yourself: is what I am doing of value? Does this truly contribute towards a sense of professional fulfilment for me? Am I doing something on a daily basis that I have faith and a sense of belief in? Am I somewhere where we value the work and not the superficial? Do I feel utilised and empowered as part of the bigger journey?

A manifesto for schools: core demands

1. Place a priority upon the work.

The work is what should drive everything you do: teaching is what is central, and all else comes second. The best leaders will tell you that the priority is the lesson, because if the basics aren't right, there is no room for mastery. Your behaviour policy may be fantastic, revision sessions happening five days a week, Friday staff sports club up and running (empty, mind you); but if we do not place real value on the learning, then the school is an empty shell. If your team are reluctant to share their lacking confidence around particular knowledge, share your own experiences with them. Come from a place of honesty so that the focus can then be consistently on the work to be done. Share your plans; welcome help with them. Bring others on board and appreciate the moments that conversations are available to discuss the big questions, the big matters at hand. Make time for these in the busyness of schools, but don't overheat – because that will hinder the work. The work is what gives you true purpose.

2. Balance workload with fewer things in depth.

This is quite possibly the finest thing to do as an individual teacher, subject lead, or senior leader. Focus on the main thing and work slowly and purposefully to master it. Only move on when it is truly a thing to marvel; before then, choose the next thing to work towards with proficiency. We work quickly and intensely in schools, but we can only really move away from silver bullets and create a space for deep, powerful thinking about how to make change for ourselves if we do one thing at a time. If it doesn't serve a purpose, get rid of it. If it is only being done because that's the way it has always been done, get rid of it. If it's for Ofsted, get rid of it. If you're not sure if it serves a purpose, find a way to check, and then get rid of it. If the unit of work feels lacking, address it. If the marking isn't yielding results, speak to someone about it. For every new initiative you want to add, take something that isn't as effective away. Balance the books on workload time costing: if you want your team to mark exam papers within a specific timeframe, does that timeframe allow for it? What can you remove that is of less use to enable them to complete the task? View time as your second precious commodity to teachers and be sufficiently frugal, but splurge on the things that matter, and your staff will notice.

3. Eradicate hierarchy and give staff a voice.

Eradicate any semblance of hierarchy. If you lead people, support them. If they make mistakes, support them to learn from them. Lead with the mantra that no one sets out to do a bad job; probe for honesty and give honesty. Make it explicit that struggling with workload isn't a personal weakness: the workload is unacceptable, not the person's inability to complete the work. Avoid projection of your own workload onto those that are looking to you for support; and if you feel overwhelmed yourself, speak to those that are there to support you. Allocate spaces for staff to respond and be consulted. Breathe a culture that accepts that if we do not consider time objectively, the job can become larger than the job holder. Accept and welcome questions. Expect ideas to be challenged so they can evolve; and recognise this process as part of growth and evolution.

4. Ensure that humanity is central to schools.

Ask how people are. Ask how their children are. Ask where they were on holiday. Start every meeting with a personable conversation, because it's nice. Treat people as people before operatives; understand that work will always be secondary to their lives, as it should be. Make time for people – on your terms, but make time. Understand that sometimes life is hard, and people don't, on the whole, work to upset others on purpose. Reflect upon how much of your day is spent being a human, and not just a simulation of one, which can sometimes happen when you teach. Actively seek out opportunities to be more human. Consider where time can be used to find human connections with others. Work on the connections that seem the toughest. Realise that your desire to be human will not always be met with mutual humanity. Question and respond to lacking humanity with humanity itself.

5. Train staff in order to move them onwards.

Ensure that opportunities are both abundant and far-reaching to all corners of your staff body. Be responsive to their needs over the self-concocted needs of the school; by bringing staff along in their own personally professional journey, you are investing in the school. Find ways to utilise existing staff so that they can develop one another; be generous and transparent in your local area with the provision of training opportunities that you have; open your doors to neighbouring schools to build community cohesion and create a symbiotic training provision. Appreciate that as people grow, and the climate changes, training needs will naturally alter and be reactive to that.

6. Avoid fear.

'Big O' means nothing. As a profession, we refuse to use a regulatory body as a method of fear, spiralling and scapegoating staff into making poor decisions, or even simply decisions with Ofsted at the heart of them. View Ofsted as a support mechanism, not a method of constraint. Do not seek out 'what Ofsted wants'; instead, return to the narrative behind what you do: why do we value this aspect of our work? What makes it valuable? How can it be further refined? What do we still need to work on for our staff and our children to flourish? To plan for Ofsted is to show you care – but without the care itself. Be fearless in your thoughtful, meaningful work that you know is right for your context.

7. Master gratitude.

Say thank-you – and mean it – at every opportunity you get. If your thanks are genuine, they will never feel overdone. Ensure that you are saying thank-you for things after a direct experience that you have seen or felt so that it feels meaningful. Thank everyone, at all stages, for all work. Give thanks in a multitude of ways, and with a sense of observance: for those that run trips, to those that wash your mug up when you rushed out to duty. To those that covered lessons, to those that spent lunchtime tackling algebra with year 8 without even a notion of what algebra is. Give thanks in corridors, in front of children, in pigeonholes, in meetings. To demonstrate the power of collective purpose and hard work, and always as the first thing that is said. Before the data request, before the lesson feedback, before the quick reminders in the things that may be forgotten as you are seven weeks deep into a half term and people are tired. The first thing.

Over to you

Whilst we would benefit from the allegiance of school leaders taking an undiluted sense of duty to staff and their physical and mental health, ultimately, we have a personal responsibility for our own wellbeing, and that comes in the form of refusing to accept lesser standards, identifying the trite maxims that float around school as a false intention and calling them out as such – but before all else, taking the stance that it is us, the classroom teachers, who influence and control policy. Teachers are becoming something of a dying breed, and so rather than acceptance of poor practice, invalidating interactions with senior leaders, or merely the sense of defeat that you may undergo as a consequence of feeling as though you are just a minor cog in a rather cumbersome machine, remember that you are the masters of such change. This is a collection of my thoughts, my experiences, my perceptions of a complex institution; but collectively, any improvement relies upon your calling out that the current way is simply not good enough – for you, for the children you teach, for the preservation and development of our education system so that it will last the distance. I started to put words down onto paper because I wanted to write a book that I wish I had had as a petrified NQT, jumping through hoops but not really understanding why something had placed the hoop in front of me to begin with. Overworking, overproducing, overcommitting, overmarking, overcompensating, overpromising because I had so little clarity in what the deep-rooted values of my teaching practice were, and so I looked to others to tell me instead. Later on, I wanted to write a book that I wish I had had when I paused to contemplate leaving the profession, irrespective of money invested in my training, the sacrifice of time for myself or my family, the emotional investment that I had handed over willingly because this was what I wanted to do every day, and I couldn't quite fathom why it was so difficult when I was being so reasonable with my demands.

Change is possible – and it will happen, if we collectively commit to not just being invested in ourselves as human beings but being invested in our profession. Surface-level care is just not sufficient to run something as glorious and magnificent as teaching. For that reason and that reason alone, I implore you: stop talking about wellbeing.

REFLECT

- What are your key values? Why do you want to teach?
- To what extent does your current place or current school align to your key values? Try to be pragmatic here and consider both ends of the spectrum to get a balanced view.
- What is currently challenging your sense of purpose in your current setting? Try to name tangible components of your day-to-day work.
- What could you do to overcome these sets of challenges? Who could you talk to with an aim to improving your job satisfaction overall? What support do you need with this?

Now, put this into practice and compile a set of actions to make this a reality. You may want to use this structure to help give clarity to your plans. Be concise and make the actions as small and manageable as possible to make them achievable for you.

- What will you do now?
- What will you do in three months?
- What will you do next year?

For example:

I am trustworthy, knowledgeable, and I value family before all else. I have high expectations and believe that education is the sensible answer to most of our problems in society. I want to show children what they can do with knowledge and where it can take them.

I'm repeatedly struggling to keep on top of my marking against a policy that doesn't make sense to me. A frequency of every fortnight isn't achievable and isn't planned for in the units of work I teach, so I always run out of time before the assessment and we don't do anything worth marking to justify fortnightly marking. I just feel like it takes me away from spending time with my kids for an entire day every weekend, and I resent that. It gets in the way of my subject knowledge reading and any sort of cultural trips that I would love to take my own children on at the weekend, and for what? It's the most useless way of marking.

- **Now:** I will talk to my head of department about trialling whole-class feedback with my key stage 3 classes.
- **Three months:** I will collate and evaluate the data gathered; I will then request to deliver to the department. I will share this information with key members of staff in other departments, and if the data is positive, I will ask for a meeting with the teaching and learning lead to share this information. If needed, I will gather working examples of schools that have had Ofsted reports praising whole-class feedback. I will time-cost the existing marking policy to highlight the concerns I have that it is not possible to mark with the time that teachers have available.
- **Next year:** I will ask to be involved in being part of the working party that reviews the feedback policy.

- Lastly, what three personal intentions do you now have as a result of reading?
- What will you do to ensure that these don't get forgotten?
- When will you review these actions to be certain that they remain a priority to you?

I would love to hear your intentions or what you plan to do next as a result of reading. Please do share them with me via Twitter (you can find me @saysmiss), using the hashtag #StopTalkingAboutWellbeing. I would absolutely love to follow your journey.